# REGAINING COMPASSION

## FOR HUMANITY AND NATURE

# CHARLES BIRCH

## To David Paul

---

North American edition, 1993
©Copyright 1993 by Charles Birch

Originally published in Australia in 1993 by:
New South Wales University Press
P. O. Box 1
Kensington NSW 2033 Australia

Cover of the North American edition by Bob Watkins

10 9 8 7 6 5 4 3 2 1

**Library of Congress Cataloging-in-Publication Data**

Birch, Charles
    Regaining compassion for humanity and nature / by Charles Birch.
    Includes biobligraphical references.
    ISBN 0-8272-3214-4
    1. Caring.    2. Interpersonal relations—Moral and ethical aspects.
    3. Environmental ethics.    4. Religion.    I. Title.
    BJ1475.B47 1993              177              93-32180

Printed in the United States of America

# PREFACE

## TO THE NORTH AMERICAN EDITION

I wrote this book in Australia, which is my home country. Yet in many ways it reflects values and commitments I came to discover in the United States of America.

The religion I had embraced as a youth taught me the meaning of strong commitment to certain values of life. But it was attached to an interpretation that was narrow and cramping. It was evangelical and fundamentalist, and was totally unable to accommodate the world of science that I was entering. My conversion to a more open faith that took both science and religion into account came to me exclusively from the North American continent.

I was introduced to a more liberal Christianity through the sermons of Harry Emerson Fosdick of Riverside Church in New York City and then later through Paul Tillich of Union Theological Seminary. Tillich's distinction between secondary concerns and ultimate concern became critical in my thinking. The more philosophical side of my thinking, which had to embrace science, came from Alfred North Whitehead, whose books on science and philosophy were mostly written at Harvard University. It was then natural for me to gravitate to the thought of Charles Hartshorne, who was in the department of philosophy at the University of Chicago in the heady days of the chancellorship of Robert Maynard Hutchins. Hartshorne had earlier been an assistant to Whitehead. While I was a graduate student at the University of Chicago in the 1940s I came to discover the theological side of Whiteheadian thought, for the university's Divinity School had at that time probably the most distinguished faculty of Whiteheadian scholars ever assembled together anywhere in the world.

From the influence of Chicago it was natural that I should turn to Hartshorne's student John Cobb, Jr., at the Center for Process Studies in Claremont, California, and his colleague David Griffin. There, both process philosophy and process theology are integrated into postmodern thought.

I am neither a theologian nor a philosopher, but rather a scientist. Science by itself never showed me the meaning of purpose on a cosmic scale, nor the meaning of compassion for humanity and nature. I am indebted to the people I have mentioned—all of whom I came to know personally, with the exception of Whitehead—and others for showing me these connections. Specific ways they contributed to my life and thought are apparent in the chapters that follow.

Charles Birch
Sydney, Australia
July 1993

# CONTENTS

## A NEW CONSCIOUSNESS

## CHAPTER 6        203

## AT-ONE-MENT

## REFERENCES        238

## INDEX        246

People say that what we're all seeking is a meaning for life. I don't think that's what we're really seeking. I think that what we're seeking is an experience of being alive, so that our life experiences on the purely physical plane will have resonances within our innermost being and reality, so that we actually feel the rapture of being alive.

*Joseph Campbell (1988 p. 3)*

I use the word *compassion* to indicate what Christians do to actualize Love in time and space ... it is to give the cup of cold water to a stranger ... *compassion* is showing reverence to another being ... ecology, as it is now developing, provides us with new religious understanding of our being, of other beings, and of being ... from *compassion* we must defend the continued existence of our fellow animal, plant, insect and marine species, as well as the integrity of landscapes, seascapes and airscapes that are periled by human activity, whether or not these in any way affect human existence ... we must extend *compassion* to rattlesnakes and not just to koalas.

*Lynn White (1978)*

# ACKNOWLEDGMENTS

John B. Cobb Jr., David Paul and Peter Farleigh read early drafts of the complete manuscript. Paul Abrecht read Chapter 4. Basil Hetzel checked the section on the physiology of stress in Chapter 1. I greatly benefited from their criticisms and suggestions. Peter Farleigh is one of the few people I know in Australia who has studied and absorbed the works of A. N. Whitehead and other process thinkers, which are centrally important to my thinking. It has been helpful and supportive to me to have a fellow traveller on that road in my own land.

# INTRODUCTION

This book is about relating: relating to oneself, to others, to other living creatures, to the world and to God. Alongside Freud's will to pleasure, Nietzsche's will to power and Frankl's will to meaning is another more basic human striving and need, the will to relate. Only through relationships can we satisfy our will to pleasure, power and meaning. When we are blocked in our will to relate, alienation, loneliness and even sickness intervene.

Relating is about making connections. There are two sorts of connecting. When railway carriages are connected to each other, the only difference the connection makes is that one carriage pulls the other along. There is a second sort of connecting that transforms those that are connected. It is compassion. Two lovers relate in that sort of way. It is an internal relating as contrasted to the external relating of the railway carriages.

When we fail to make connections that are critical for our lives and the life of the world we become adrift like small rafts on the ocean. If we are successful in making appropriate connections we find fulfilment in life. A young surfer was interviewed on television as he waited for a wave in the ocean at Bondi Beach in Sydney. What are you thinking about all the hours you wait there? he was asked. He replied immediately: I am waiting for the ultimate wave. Some waves are so trivial that he can afford to let them pass him by. But not the ultimate wave. He waits all day for that one.

There are waves in our lives. Many of them pass us by, hardly disturbing even the surface of our lives. But there are other encounters of a more ultimate kind. A proposition of this book is that the most ultimate encounter is to experience a oneness with ourselves, with others, with the world, with the universe and with God. I call that at-one-ment. It is the opposite of being adrift and separate from the rest of existence.

Why should I, a scientist, write about this? I have two reasons. There is an ambiguity about science and technology. They have made it possible for us to relate to the world in all sorts of ways previously impossible. They have contributed greatly to the external relations of life that provide us with food, clothing, transport and communication. This should have freed us from preoccupation with the material things of life.

But for many, if not most people, science and technology have had the opposite effect. People have become preoccupied with the material things science and technology provide us with, to the neglect of that which matters most in our lives, our feelings, affection and love. We have lost compassion. There are many reasons for this. One important one is that we absorb from the age of science and technology the materialistic framework within which it was developed. Much of science and technology gives us a mechanical picture of ourselves, the world and the universe. That sort of picture has been called the modern worldview because much of our world is based on that image. It suggests that the universe is unintelligible, senseless and accidental and that humans are no more than a fortuitous concourse of atoms.

But there is another image of the world and ourselves that is more lifelike and compassionate. It too derives in part from a science that is developed within a less mechanical framework. So scientists such as Paul Davies write about 'the matter myth', meaning the myth of the mechanistic, materialistic universe (Davies & Gribbin 1991). They ask: is there something else going on out there? They respond that there is more to the world than cogs in a gigantic machine (Davies 1992). That warmer and more lifelike image has been called a postmodern worldview. Few of us as yet seem to have absorbed that image into our thinking about the world around us. That requires us to rethink the ways in which we might regain compassion in the world.

A second reason for writing this book comes from reactions to my previous book, *On Purpose*. In a sense this is a sequel. Non-scientists and the less philosophically minded found some of the central ideas difficult to grasp. On the other hand these readers seemed to want more, but in a less philosophical framework. A second group of readers of *On Purpose* I had hardly expected to reach. They were young people who had a strong fundamentalistic Christian faith. They had hardly considered any alternative to fundamentalist doctrines of religion. They had indeed some dissatisfactions with their faith, which had mostly to do with the problem of evil and suffering in a world presided over by a God of love. For a long time I have been convinced that fundamentalism has no solutions to offer to that problem. *On Purpose* suggested to some of these readers the possibility of an alternative more credible faith that was yet consistent with a Christian position. They wanted to know more, though they had their suspicions about where that might lead them.

There was yet another group of readers whom I had hoped to touch. They were people who had been brought up in a conservative Christian faith, who had rejected most, if not all of it, and who yet had a sense of being adrift on a huge ocean of nothingness. Some of these readers got in touch with me and asked for more. They wanted to explore further. Some of them were members of the Eremos Institute in Sydney, which is largely committed to that sort of exploration.

In a sense, each different group of respondents to *On Purpose* needs a separate book as a follow-up. Yet I have attempted to have all three groups in the back of my mind as I wrote this book. I also had in mind those who have not read *On Purpose* or anything like it.

I hope it is possible for any reader to start from scratch in this book. I would hope all might discover some of the liberation of life and thought which I have found in these ideas for myself.

At a meeting in Sydney at which John Shelby Spong, the Episcopal bishop of Newark in the US, spoke about his book *Saving the Bible from Fundamentalism,* an ex-fundamentalist and sceptical young man asked Bishop Spong this question. 'What special contribution does religion have to make to a world which now has access to so much information and understanding from science, philosophy and all the other disciplines?' The implication of the question was that we know immeasurably so much more now than ever in the past that ancient ideas of religion have become obsolete. The youth was implying that there was now no place for religion in the world. His question is an important one.

I do not recall what Bishop Spong had to say in response to this question. My own mind switched back to a proposition of Paul Tillich (1959) in his book on religion and culture: 'Religion is not a special function of man's spiritual life, but it is the dimension of depth in all of its functions' (p. 5). It is in this sense that I find a real place for religion in modern life. Let me explain.

Religion is not a special function of the human spirit. The history of religion is one in which it goes from one spiritual function to another to find a home either to be rejected or swallowed up by them. Religion came to the ethical function and is accepted so long as it helps to create good citizens and good soldiers. But as soon as it makes claims of its own, it is thrown out as dangerous or superfluous. Religion looks around and finds the intellectual function of the spiritual life as a special way of knowing. But religion soon finds itself being rejected by the new knowledge of science, as for example happened in the Darwinian controversy. But says Paul Tillich (1959):

> In this situation, without a home, without a place in which to dwell, religion suddenly realises that it does not need such a place, that it does not need to seek a home. It is at home everywhere, namely, in the depth of all functions of man's spiritual life. Religion is the dimension of depth in all of them. Religion is the aspect of depth in the totality of the human spirit. ( p. 7)

The dimension of depth means that the religious aspect points to that which is ultimate and of ultimate importance. In its most basic sense it is ultimate concern. That is why religion has a prominent place in my thinking.

There is a widespread loss of belief in religion, especially in intellectual circles. This is due in part to problems inherent in the traditional concepts of God and in part to problems inherent in the modern materialistic worldview. Attempts to make God and the modern worldview compatible have been unsuccessful (Griffin 1989).

A thesis of this book is that there is a credible alternative to the materialistic worldview and a credible alternative to the traditional concept of God. There are, in fact, parallel changes in recent years in the understanding of scientific and religious truth. Yet there is a failure of both wider communities to keep pace with these parallel changes. The emerging postmodern worldview allows for the recovery of belief in God while eliminating the fatal problems inherent in the traditional idea of God.

Things are happening that we should know about. Someone once said that the world is composed of four kinds of people: those who make things happen; those to whom things happen; those who watch things happen and those who do not even know that things are happening.

Things are happening around us of which many of us are largely unaware. Some of us get glimpses of these happenings but are afraid to let them happen to us. We feel inadequate to the call for a more ultimate concern about our lives. We make the mistake of supposing that we have to know the truth before we can act upon it, whereas we can only know the truth by doing it. There is a place for contemplation in solitude. There is also a place for action before we have sorted out our lives. So Vaclev Havel, the first president of post-Communist Czechoslovakia, wrote:

> When I find myself in extremely complex situations, I worry about whether I'll be able to sort them out. But I wouldn't want this to sound as though I'm just a bundle of panic and misery and lack of self-confidence. On the contrary, this constant self-doubt and the constant uncertainty are what drive me to work harder and try harder. So in fact it's a productive characteristic, in terms of its results. If I have accomplished anything good, then it's mainly because I've been driven by the need to know whether I can accomplish things I'm not sure I have the capacity for. (Havel 1991, p. 8)

William Sloane Coffin, a former pastor of the great Riverside Church in Manhattan was discussing a complex moral issue. In a sermon he said: 'We learn more if we don't try to understand too soon ... the journey from the head to the heart (and vice versa) is a long one'. The truth about life comes from opening ourselves to experiences of strength through anxiety, confidence through hesitation and self-rejection, inward power adequate for outward tension, the voice of a friend out of the fog when all direction is lost, a second chance when we discover that the end is the beginning. All great moments in life involve a step forward in faith, trusting in new possibilities for life. We don't create these possibilities. They create us.

The first chapter of this book introduces the idea of relationships that are transforming for life. The second chapter is about the consequences of that understanding for living in our relationships with others, including non-human life. The third chapter is about our relationships with the world at large and in particular with the environmental crisis we have created. This chapter is rather different from the others because I found it necessary to give some details of what is wrong with the way we deal with the environment and how that might be rectified. The process of rectification includes a new understanding of society, politics and economics which is largely the subject of the fourth chapter. But how do humans respond to the need for change? That is the subject of Chapter 5. The sixth chapter gathers together many of the strands of previous chapters to weave a synthesis within the framework of a postmodern religious vision.

I have dedicated this book to my young friend David Paul. His background has been very different from mine in many ways. That has been a challenge to my own life and thought. His life also has seen much more tragedy than I have ever experienced. Yet he has overcome those circumstances with a courage and faith that have inspired his friends. I keep on asking him how? I want him one day to write a book on how he discovered the power to see it through. He combines a commitment and openness which I find quite rare these days. His life has been a light on the path for many who have been fortunate enough to come to know him. Through knowing him I have asked questions I would not have otherwise asked and pursued issues I would not otherwise have explored.

In addition to the inspiration I have found in his life and thought, which I hope is reflected in these pages, he has read with great care early drafts of the manuscript of this book. I found in him a meticulous and thoughtful unofficial editor. When there were issues on which we had quite different perspectives, he was always tolerant and understanding and I always learned from him. It is with a sense of great gratitude that I dedicate this book to him.

# CHAPTER 1

# A NEW CONSCIOUS-NESS

I am a part of all that I have met;
Yet all experience is an arch wherethro'
Gleams the untravell'd world, whose margin fades
For ever and for ever when I move.

*Alfred Lord Tennyson, 'Ulysses'*

What is needed for a holistic sensibility to become a reality
in our time is a change of consciousness in the way we see
our world and ourselves in relation to the world.

*Sallie McFague (1987, p. 51)*

I will remove from you your heart of stone and give you
a heart of flesh.

*Ezekiel 36:26*

he important frontiers of the future are spiritual, psychological and social, not technical and industrial. Somehow or other we have to discover how to live supportively with one another on a crowded planet, fulfilling our lives instead of being pushed around like marbles by an inconsiderate society. Religion, politics and economics will have to come together in a single vision of the meaning of life. Whereas the 'modern worldview' based on mechanistic science, technology and the Industrial Revolution is primarily about the development of things, the postmodern worldview is primarily about the development of people (Birch 1990). It will enable people to break out of the spiritual and social limits which thwart real progress today, just as the modern worldview enabled them to break out of the constraints which limited technical capabilities two hundred years ago.

This book is therefore about relationships, more particularly those relationships that make for richness of experience. A central discovery of my life has been the recognition that 'I am a part of all that I have met'. And that is an arch through which gleams all the future yet to be experienced. I am my past and reach forth to my possible future. My inner relationships with the world make me what I am. Relationships are what matter.

In the wonderful phrase of A. N. Whitehead 'the present is the fringe of memory tinged with anticipation'. My past is ever present in all sorts of ways, but it looks through an arch to the next step in the future with anticipation. In a way this may sound obvious, perhaps even commonplace. Yet to accept this is to give the lie to a widely accepted view of human nature that most people accept implicitly, if not explicitly. It is the notion that each one of us is a separate individual, atomistic, particle-like, a skin encapsulated ego, with clear boundaries between us and all other selves. It is as though we are very much alone in the world, just occasionally lowering the barriers that separate us from others, though not for long.

A recent study of the lives of American men came to

the conclusion that friendship was largely absent. The study found that close friendship with a man or a woman is rarely experienced by American men (Levinson 1978). Novelist Patrick White said in a radio talk, shortly before his death, that most people are like folded umbrellas. He went on to say that we are a society obsessed by money, muscle and machinery. Our society is a materialist one. We model ourselves unconsciously on the view of the world derived from the so-called Newtonian universe. That universe consists of separate particles pushing each other around but never influencing each other within. In the society of humans we meet outwardly all the time, but we don't really meet inwardly.

The new consciousness is analogous to the new physics which denies there are any such entities as particles uninfluenced in their inner nature by other entities. It pictures the universe as one and indivisible. As McCusker (1983) says 'This is not to say that the idea of chemical atoms for instance, is completely false ... they are not fundamental building blocks. They are more like the eddies on the surface of a river. The universe is seamless but not featureless' (p. 150). In a similar vein physicists Paul Davies and John Gribbin tell us we do not live in a cosmic clockwork but in a cosmic network. They go on to say that the doctrine of mechanism which penetrated into all branches of human inquiry is now dead (Davies & Gribbin 1991, p. 6). The new physics recognises fields of influence such that an electron at one end of the universe is affected by an electron at the other end or any distance in between. Einstein referred to the effect as 'spooky action at a distance'. In the new consciousness, as we experience it today, there is a coming together of our understanding of the world around us and the world within us. That is a frontier of the future.

We are not like the billiard balls of the Newtonian universe, pushed around by outside forces with no inner life. Yet we tend to think and live as though it were otherwise. When, for example, did you last share in another person's life, with masks off, without pretence, without acting to be what you were not, simply finding one another and becoming in some sense a part of one another, not coalescing but remaining individuals?

Without coalescing is important because I am not referring to the state of 'falling in love' or 'being in love' in which boundaries seem to disappear and two become as one, at least for a time. One individual feels he or she cannot live without the other. This, like any obsession, is an irrational state. It has been called love 'sickness', even a form of madness. Francis Bacon said it was impossible to be in this state and at the same time be wise. Plato would have it that 'falling in love' is the mutual recognition on earth of souls which have been singled out for one another in a previous and celestial existence. To meet the beloved is to realise we loved before we were born.

C. S. Lewis said that those who are 'in love' are normally face to face, absorbed in each other; friends, side by side are absorbed in some common interest. Those who are 'in love' are always talking about their love. Friends hardly ever talk about their friendship (Lewis 1973, p. 58). The latter surely depends upon the level of friendship. A person may say he or she has many friends when what they have are acquaintances. But friendship can go to deeper levels that involve caring and affection. The friendship between David and Jonathan discussed in Chapter 2 was of that sort. They were more than friends, less than lovers. Perhaps we need a word for that kind of compassion which we all long for.

Dorothy Tennov (1979) gave the name 'limerence' to the state of being in love which she studied in some hundreds of people. She describes how the limerent person cannot rid the mind of the beloved for one moment. The person is unremittingly and uninterruptedly occupied with the image of the beloved. The experience is intense and quite often disturbing. The limerent person regards the object of love as embodying all earthly virtues and as the one person who can give meaning to life. They may see qualities in their beloved that are not really there. They may see what they want to see and hear what they want to hear, moulding their beloved in the image of what they wish their beloved to be.

This kind of intense experience was described brilliantly in the yearnings of Anna Karenina for Count Vronsky, in the fanaticism of the middle-aged man obsessed by attraction for a youth before his death in Venice and above all in the relationship between the French philosopher Peter Abelard and his pupil, later a famous nun, Heloise. Formidable obstacles to their love included Heloise's enraged uncle and guardian who saw to it that Abelard was castrated. Yet Heloise's limerence for Abelard continued with intensity while she was an abbess of the convent of the Paraclete. She would recall, even during the Mass, images of the times they were limerent together. Such is limerent love.

The further meanings of love are explored in Chapter 2. Suffice it to reiterate here that love which is chaotic self-surrender or self-imposition is not real love. Much romantic love has these characteristics. Real love, as distinct from limerence, does not destroy the freedom of the beloved. It does not violate the beloved's individual and social existence. Neither does it surrender the freedom of the one who loves.

Love does not desire to possess, but to be a continuing channel of grace. Each person 'takes account of' the other, which means each brings to the relationship an originality that belongs to each alone. This originality is not lost in love. It is shared. One of the categorical conditions of love is that there be a transforming relationship without destruction of individuality. We can still retain our individuality while at the same time being involved in others and being members one of another. As John Donne said in his 'Devotions': 'No man is an island, entire of itself. Any man's death diminishes me, because I am involved in Mankind'.

# COMPLETELY PRESENT

Australia's praying cartoonist Michael Leunig (1991) says it all:

> God let us be serious.
> Face to face.
> Heart to heart.
> Let us be fully present.
> Strongly present.
> Deeply serious.
> The closest we may come
> to innocence.

The word that speaks to authentic experience one of another is sympathy. A. N. Whitehead (1978) said 'sympathy is feeling the feeling in another' (p. 162). The root meaning of sympathy is being simultaneously affected with the same feeling (pathos). It is also called compassion (meaning feeling with). To love another person is to allow that person's feelings to affect oneself. To protect ourselves, we largely shut out the feelings of others from enriching our experience. A friend of mine, deeply bereaved from the death of his wife, had received great comfort and support from his women friends, but his male friends seemed embarrassed to meet him. They passed by with a perfunctory expression of sympathy. They didn't want to share his feelings of grief. A friend of mine suffers from almost constant pain. Most of his friends seem unable to accept that fact and prefer to ignore his pain than to let it concern them. To share another's pain, grief, joy, interest and understanding is to be enriched in our lives. To be able to respond means to be responsible. Jonah did not feel responsible to the inhabitants of Ninevah. Like Cain he could ask 'Am I my brother's keeper?' A loving person is also a responsive person.

Sympathy with another is not identification with. It is possible, by a certain distancing of ourselves, both from our own feelings and from those of the other, to enter into a relationship of feeling with another in which both maintain their own integrity in a larger whole that is enriched by their contrasts. In this way good counsellors are genuinely sensitive to the feelings of the client without losing themselves in them.

Nevertheless, the necessary condition of a genuine relationship is to be *completely* present, one to the other. How often can we say that of any relationship? When someone is talking to us we are only half listening and preparing what to say next. Martin Buber (1958) tells of a student who came to him for counsel. Buber listened to his story and gave him competent professional advice. The student went away and took his own life. Buber goes on to tell how he was searched to the core of his being as to whether, if he had been really completely present, really engaged, really in sympathy with the student, the outcome would have been different.

Those who knew Paul Tillich as a teacher say he was always awake to all the possibilities of any occasion and eager to comprehend the meaning contained in these possibilities. This is why he was such an extraordinarily effective teacher (Pauck 1965).

*A first principle* of being completely present is the realisation at every moment that life depends as much upon our response to events around us as upon the events themselves. Said a sympathetic friend 'Affliction does so colour life'. 'Yes' responded the young woman, helplessly crippled with paralysis in all her limbs. 'And I propose to choose the colour!'

It is possible to act creatively in *any* situation. In desperate situations, if there were not some new possibility there would only be despair. A Nazi concentration camp would seem to present one of the most despairing and negative situations imaginable. Yet pastor Dietrich Bonhoeffer was able to write in his last letter from Flossenberg concentration camp 'what is happiness and unhappiness? It depends so little on circumstances; it depends really on that which happens inside a person' (von Wedenmeyer-Weller 1967, p. 29).

*A second principle* of being completely present is the

recognition that each moment of life is an end in itself and not just a means to some future goal. It is now, each moment, that we miss the pearl of great price. The here and now matters. A friend speaking about a deep friendship said 'I just enjoy it one moment at a time'. It is savouring the richness of experience of the present and not a future projection of happiness. Why keep putting off until tomorrow the life we can live today? The depth of experience of the moment to which one is fully given is what matters. Whatever satisfaction we may achieve in life comes through the strength of our engagement with what is around us at each moment. Voltaire in *Candide* went so far as to say that to be engaged fully was the way to keep the three great evils of boredom, vice and need at bay. It was to 'cultivate our garden'.

Jesus had an extraordinary capacity for being fully present in sympathetic awareness. He was fantastically aware of every person who crossed his path, especially those no-one else noticed. In a crowd he became aware of the need of a woman who gently touched him. He knew the meaning of that touch. On another occasion while walking with a crowd he became aware of a man up a tree all by himself. He was a man of small stature and had climbed the tree so that he could see Jesus as he passed by. Nobody noticed him. Jesus did. 'Come down from the tree' he said to Zacchaeus, 'I want to stay in your house today'! Zacchaeus hurried down and welcomed Jesus into his home with great joy. As a result of the encounter we are told Zacchaeus became a changed man.

The loving glance is full of insight. From the slightest sign, a half word, a pained smile, it sees in a flash the most complex inner condition. It seeks a harmony of meaning, a unity of souls. Such loving comprehension creates a sense of oneness with the other.

Tolstoy, in his *Twenty-Three Tales*, devotes the final one to describing a king who is in search of an answer to each of three questions: How can I learn to do the right thing at the right time? Whose advice can I trust? What things are most important and require my first attention?

Disguised in simple clothes, the king visited a hermit deep in the wood and asked him his three questions. Getting no answer but finding the frail hermit on the verge of collapse, the king took over the hermit's spade and finished digging his garden. At sunset a bearded man staggered in with a badly bleeding stomach wound, dealt him by one of the king's bodyguard who were scattered through the forest to protect him. The king washed the wound, bandaged it with a towel and handkerchief, and kept changing the bandages until the flow of blood stopped and the man could be carried into the hut. The king slept the night on the threshold of the hut and when morning came, found the bearded man confessing that he had lain in wait for the king's return from the hermit's hut, having sworn to kill him for a judgment the king had once given against him. He begged the king's forgiveness and pledged to serve him. The king, promising to send his own physician to attend him, rose to go but again put his questions to the hermit, complaining that he had still received no answer to them.

The hermit insisted that the king twice received his answer on the previous day. For when the king appeared on the previous afternoon, the hermit in his weakness did not see how he could finish digging his garden, and the king had relieved him. This was the right thing to do at the right time and the most important thing to be done. Furthermore, had he returned through the wood at that time, his enemy would have killed him. Secondly, when the wounded man appeared, staunching the flow of his blood and relieving him was the right thing at the right time and made a friend of an enemy. 'Remember then' added the hermit 'there is only one time that is important. Now'. And further, 'The most necessary man is he with whom you are and the most important thing is to do him good, because for that purpose alone was man sent into this life'. The king was completely present, though the circumstances were quite unanticipated. Each moment of life is an end in itself and not just a means to some future goal.

A *third principle* of being completely present is willingness to be interrupted. What one calls the interruptions are precisely the real life. Jesus told the story of a man who was set upon by robbers on the road to Jericho. He lay there half dead and helpless. Others who had urgent business in Jericho passed on that busy road. One was a priest, another was a member of the aristocracy of that period, possibly both were returning from worshipping in the temple in Jerusalem. Both of them saw the wounded man but passed by on the other side. Then there came a layman who was also a foreigner. He renders first aid to the victim. He brings him to an inn where he can have shelter for the night. More than that, on the following day when he must continue his journey, he pays in advance for such further care as the impecunious stranger may need. Jesus told this story in answer to the question 'who is my neighbour?' But no definition of neighbour emerges from the parable, and for a very good reason. Love does not begin by defining its objects. It discovers them by being completely present wherever you happen to be, even when you have quite other busy plans for that moment. Love is willing to be interrupted, even when plans are already laid for a busy day.

## STARTING WITH TROUBLE AND ENDING WITH HOPE

'All that I have met' includes the bad as well as the good. Both can be transforming influences. The bad may transform us in bad ways as when dominating or unloving parents or childhood traumas leave what seems to be an indelible mark screwing up human lives. That can lead to despair, which literally means without hope, and even to self-destruction.

Yet we do not have to be screwed up forever. Nor do we have to live forever without hope. Not all negative experiences need become deep seated. There is the devastatingly negative experience of rejected love. The hope that yearned toward another is disappointed. The heart is empty and cut off from the world. Self-pitying depression comes when we think we must have something and that it is unbearable not to get it. Sad as such an experience may be, it is not a tragic event in life. The one who can endure the loneliness of disappointed love, without bitterness and rancour, and goes on to affirm the healing that time can bring, experiences the human predicament radically and creatively.

There is a cost to being a subject who feels the world. The gain of feeling is double-edged. Feeling lays us open to pain as well as pleasure. Its keen edge cuts both ways. Lust has its match in anguish, desire in fear, purpose is either attained or thwarted. The capacity for enjoying the one involves the capacity for suffering the other. Yet the feeling creature, human and non-human alike, strives to continue living.

Life is a mixture of uncertainties and ambiguities. It takes all sorts of circumstances for us to work through them. Life is largely an exploration into unknown territory. Many people live on the surface. For those who plunge into the depths, life can be both rewarding and traumatic. There is pain along the path of life that seeks more life. Pain protects life by warning against destructive forces. Yet at the same time it may drive life to despair, even to self-destruction. But pain can strengthen life and raise it to a higher level. So Wordsworth writes in 'Character of the Happy Warrior':

> Who, doomed to go in company with Pain,
> And Fear, and Bloodshed, miserable train!
> Turns his necessity to glorious gain;
> In face of these doth exercise a power
> Which is our human nature's highest dower;
> Controls them, and subdues, transmutes, bereaves
> Of their bad influence, and their good receives.

Harry Emerson Fosdick of Riverside Church in New York broke from his prepared sermon one Sunday to say:

> Here I am today, an older man talking to you about the secret of spiritual power in general, when all the time what I am really seeing in my imagination's eye is that young man

I was years ago, shot all to pieces, done in and shattered in a nervous breakdown, foolishly undertaking too much work and doing it unwisely, all my hopes in ashes and life towering over me and saying, You are finished; you cannot; you are done for. People ask me why in young manhood I wrote *The Meaning of Prayer*. That came out of young manhood's struggle. I desperately needed a second chance and reinforcement to carry on with it. (Fosdick 1958, p. 172)

That reinforcement and second chance came out of this youthful struggle.

There are many hurts in life. We may become concerned about the hurts of others. We do what we can to relieve their hurts, but we find we can be hurt badly ourselves in the process. That is when our concern for others becomes over-concern. We know when that happens because we feel ourselves hurt. We become gloomy and depressed. We are acting irrationally. What our friend wants from us, is not to be depressed and pained but that we pull him or her up to our level of cheerfulness and hope. I learned this lesson from a student who came to me in a tragic situation which seemed to me almost hopeless. As he left me I burst into tears. His response was to remonstrate with me for adding to the misery of the situation! What he needed was someone whose concern lifted him up to a higher level of confidence and ability to suffer and endure with hope. He told me as much. I never forgot.

Paul tells us that five times he received thirty-nine stripes, three times he was beaten with rods, once he was stoned. That was the beginning. Starting with trouble he ended with hope. In his letter to the Romans he wrote: 'Trouble produces endurance, endurance produces character, and character produces hope' (Romans 5:3–4). This contradicts the usual impression that hope is dependent on hopeful circumstances. Here we are told that at the very point where things look bad, the road to hope begins. We learn endurance, not amid easy situations but in adversity. Meeting adverse conditions with endurance, one builds the sort of character that enables us to confront with hope even the most desperate circumstances.

Such seems to have been the experience of at least some of the hostages who endured up to five years imprisoned in confined cells in Lebanon in our time. They repeat the experience of Pastor Niemoeller, imprisoned by the Nazis, who wrote from prison to his parish in Berlin: 'Let us thank God that he allows no spirit of despair to enter into Cell 448. In all ignorance of what is coming I am confident, and I hope to be ready when I am led along paths which I never would have sought for myself' (Fosdick 1954, p. 106).

Niemoeller learned by going where he had to go. So may I learn by going where I have to go. In so doing may I ask not for tasks equal to my strength but strength equal to the tasks.

Hope is not the superficial by-product of favourable circumstances; it springs from one's character, from what one is and cares about, and believes in. The seventeenth-century poet John Gay wrote 'While there is life there is hope'. A deeper truth emerges when this saying is reversed 'While there is hope there is life'.

Life is a passion play (the word passion literally means to suffer). So says philosopher Holmes Rolston. He suggests there is something divine about the power to suffer through to something higher. Life is advanced not only by thought and action, but by suffering, not only by logic but by pathos. Nature itself is cruciform in its struggle and suffering. The secret of life, he suggests, is to realise that it is a passion play (Rolston 1987, p. 144).

Did anyone in all history suffer alone as did Jesus; deserted by all friends and relatives, disowned by his followers, in agony in the garden of Gethsemane? His sweat was, as it were, great drops of blood falling to the ground. Yet he went on from Gethsemane to the cross. What happened there has been called the loneliest death in all history. Jesus' nation had rejected him as a traitor. His church had rejected him as a heretic. He was alone. The Roman soldiers spat upon him. Pilate had washed his hands of him. The crowd jeered at him. His friends, all of them, forsook him. He was alone. Then his heart broke in the most desolate of all cries: 'My God, my God, why hast thou forsaken me'.

The pain and suffering on the cross was not the end of it all. It became a transforming influence in the world. Here was a life, the potency of which gets at the heart of the world by caring enough about the world to die for it. We may not be able readily to explain the nature of a world in which tragedy and suffering are so manifest. But Jesus himself never said 'I have explained the world'. He did say 'I have overcome the world'.

In the seventeenth century the humanist scholar Muretus, a fugitive from France, fell ill in Lombardy. Looking like a vagabond in rags he asked aid of the doctors. The physicians discussed his case in Latin, not thinking that this bedraggled pauper could understand the learned tongue. '*Faciamus experimentum in anima vili*' they said ('Let us try an experiment with this worthless creature'). And to their amazement the 'worthless creature' spoke to them in Latin: '*Vilem animam appellas pro qua Christus non dedignatus est mori?*' — ('Will you call worthless one for whom Christ did not disdain to die?') Humanist though he was, Muretus had learned from the death of Jesus the intrinsic value of all human life.

Reflecting on the life of Jesus, Paul Tillich (1963) wrote:

> But we know in some moments of our lives, what life is. We know that it is great and holy, deep and abundant, ecstatic and sober, limited and distorted by time, fulfilled by eternity. And if the right words fail us ... we may look without words at the image of him in whom the Spirit and the Life are manifest without limits. (p. 76)

# THE FELT CONNECTION

'All that I have met' is all people whom I have met and discovered in all of life's circumstances. But it is more. Indeed, the new consciousness can be said to include the universe. But that is too large a step. Take it step by step to include, first, the ones we love, our family, our friends, our pets, the animals and plants in the wild that we appreciate and a sense of the wholeness of the universe. Some such understanding is basic to discovering our place in the society in which we live, in the world community of people and in the whole of the natural world and its ecology.

Science, for all its great achievements, has virtually nothing to say about this. If our awareness of ourselves and the world is informed by scientific models alone we are singularly bereft. I am referring to the levels of understanding in which we actually live our lives, our relationships, our aspirations, our hang-ups, our personal choices and our moral dilemmas. About all of these science has no precise answers and no complete descriptions. There are reasons for this.

Until quite recently science concerned itself exclusively with the outward aspect of things, either ignoring or excluding the inner aspect of things which in ourselves we recognise as our feelings. These are the felt connections we have with our world. There are similarities in this emphasis to transpersonal psychology (*trans* meaning beyond), to transpersonal ecology (Fox 1990), to certain forms of Buddhism and Hinduism and to non-dualistic interpretations of the Judeo-Christian religion. My own interpretation of felt connections is informed by process thought and process theology (Birch 1990).

The new consciousness refers to the inner nature of ourselves and of other individual entities in the universe. Existentialism sharply distinguishes human experience from everything else. Process thought sees it as a high-level exemplification of reality in general. Hence the understanding of human existence takes on an added depth of importance. When we discover the real nature of the relationships of one person to another we are gaining insight into the nature of nature itself at all levels, from protons to people. But first we need to explore further the nature of human experience itself.

What happens when I become a part of all that I have met? Science cannot tell us what happens. It can tell us something about hormones and nerve impulses recorded on a screen. But it tells us nothing about our felt connections.

We are not like sponges that absorb water from outside which can then be squeezed dry leaving the sponge unchanged. We are not like the ball which, receiving a strong kick, gets a dent that returns to its normal shape in due course. Neither the sponge nor the ball is changed in its nature by what happens to it.

But we are changed by all that we have met. Of course in this context the word met means something different from a kick or a soaking in the rain. Met in the sentence 'all that I have met' means to be changed. There are some sorts of knowledge we can only have by being changed in the process of knowing. It is not 'information about'. It is knowledge by acquaintance. The only relevant form of learning in that case is by initiation.

Creative transformation is involved in every authentic human experience. That is what makes us subjects and not mere objects. A subject has felt connections with the environment. And when something is felt the person is changed. A mind or soul stretched by a new experience, a new idea, a new friendship, never returns to its former shape. At times that stretching may be so transforming that we organise our whole lives around a new centre. That brings with it two results. It lifts personality up into greater significance. People now matter more. Secondly, we discover a sense of newness with which the world of objects is viewed, a sense of having discovered reality. It is a new feeling of possession of and participation in the world.

## RICHNESS OF EXPERIENCE

Life affirms itself in us. It reaches out to new life beyond what seem to be its present limits. Life longs for more life, for more abundant life, for greater richness of experience. When life ceases to grow and to strive for more life it becomes a distortion of life. This is true of all life as well as human life (see 'A gradation of intrinsic value and a diversity of rights' in Chapter 2). A human being cannot live in a condition of emptiness for long. If we are not growing toward something we do not merely stagnate, we can become despairing of life altogether. There are words to describe the opposite of a fulfilling life: estrangement, alienation, disenchantment, anomie, playing it cool.

There are four aspects of alienation or estrangement. We can be estranged from ourselves, from others, from nature and from God (see Chapter 6). But there is really only one form of estrangement for all are subsumed under estrangement from God, since God stands for all that fulfils experience and the possibilities of life not yet experienced by us.

It is important to appreciate that estrangement is a part of the experience of all human beings including those who know what fullness of life means. Jesus on the cross felt forsaken by God. Luther experienced what he described as attacks of utter despair, as the frightful threat of a complete meaninglessness, when belief in his work and message disappeared and no meaning remained. Theologian Paul Tillich would tell his students that each morning until ten o'clock he struggled with his 'demons', meaning those things which threatened to divide his life. Is it then any wonder that we ordinary mortals have our times of estrangement and alienation. Experiences of the 'desert' or 'night' of the soul are frequent among mystics. In his poem 'Desert Places' Robert Frost experiences the desert while wandering in the woods. The animals are comfortable and smothered in their lairs. But loneliness envelops him:

> And lonely as it is, that loneliness
> Will be more lonely ere it will be less
> A blanker whiteness of benighted snow
> With no expression, nothing to express.
>
> They cannot scare me with their empty spaces
> Between stars, on stars where no human race is.
> I have it in me so much nearer home
> To scare myself with my own desert places.

Blaise Pascal in one of the most famous of his pensées confesses to feeling 'engulfed in the infinite immensity of spaces whereof I know nothing, and which know nothing of me, I am terrified ... *The eternal silence of those infinite spaces alarms me'.*

A sense of estrangement comes to many young people when the contents of a religious tradition, however valued and however once loved, loses its power to give content any more. Simple certainties that served us when we were young no longer hold any strong influence over us, except in a negative way. The faith that at one time had no doubts is besieged by doubt. Traditionalists interpret this as a fall from grace. On the contrary, doubt is good. Cardinal Newman struggled with his faith all his life. Looking back over his life, he was able to say 'to live is to change, and to be perfect is to have changed often'. That is a nice definition of perfection.

I have a vivid memory when this first happened to me because of the challenge of science to what was my simplistic faith. As an adolescent I was craving for meaning, for something to make sense. By dint of circumstance I thought I had found it in a fundamentalist faith. I accepted a very simple set of affirmations about God, the world, and myself. As an undergraduate in the University of Melbourne I kept two passions, religion and science, uncertainly together. It was passion rather than thought that governed my life.

With my first degree under my belt I became a research student at the University of Adelaide. I did not find the rigour of scientific experimentation difficult. What I did find difficult was the challenge from my hard-nosed scientific colleagues to my whole edifice of thought. Just about all of them seemed to be agnostic. My immediate colleague had thought his agnosticism through, which was more than I could say of my faith. I was learning more and more about science, but was less and less able to defend my religious convictions. I discovered my religion had foundations of sand. But not all, for I still treasured some deep experiences that had to do with forgiveness, courage, facing loneliness and with other values that had permeated my being.

The beginning of a resolution of my pressing search for meaning came through the Student Christian Movement in the University of Adelaide. It showed me there were alternative interpretations of Christianity to fundamentalism. When reassurance began to re-establish itself, it came like the weaving together of strands. I was conscious of a foundation forming under me. I tried to break it down, partly for moral and partly for intellectual reasons. The strands refused to be broken. The effect was to re-establish a fundamental trust with respect to the meaningfulness of human life. I found that some of the former elements came back, different from the old, no longer borrowed dwellings, for better or for worse they were mine. And that process has continued ever since.

My newly discovered mentors in the Student Christian Movement, especially one of them, urged me to read Whitehead's *Science and the Modern World*. I felt this book was written just for me. That led on to my reading Charles Hartshorne's first book *The Philosophy and Psychology of Sensation*, which really brought the emotive side of life and the cognitive side together.

While I was building a new structure of meaning in my life I had the lurking doubt that perhaps I had got myself onto a false path again. Then something very important happened. The time came for me to leave the University of Adelaide and pursue further research and study in the University of Chicago. In the Department of Zoology in which I was working the most distinguished of the professors was the evolutionary biologist Sewall Wright who happened to be a Whiteheadian! Moreover, Charles Hartshorne was professor in the Department of Philosophy and the Divinity School was full of theologians profoundly influenced by Whitehead. I was torn between my ecology in the Department of Zoology and sitting in on courses in the Divinity School. They were heady days that shored me up in ways I could never have imagined. I had discovered a trust in life through Whitehead and Hartshorne's exposition of the Christian faith. It was later on that Charles Hartshorne introduced me to his former student John Cobb, who became a continuing influence on my life and thought. A more detailed account of my odyssey with science, faith and process thought is given elsewhere (Birch 1991).

My friend and colleague, theologian John Cobb, also had his youthful Christian faith pass through the furnace of doubt. Brought up in a pietistic faith he began to have doubts about Christianity. There were questions about the virgin birth and bodily resurrection, life after death and free will. But there was no question about the goodness of Jesus Christ. As a student at the University of Chicago, more fundamental questions were raised. Whether the Christian message was fundamentally true became for him a matter of deep uncertainty. He was unsure whether the word 'God' had any positive meaning any more. At the University of Chicago he was determined to expose his faith to the worst the world could offer. Within six months of this exposure his faith was in tatters. After about a year he began to take courses given by theologians in the Divinity School. These were men who seemed to Cobb to have taken account of the problems that had destroyed his faith. His openness to these new influences led to a creative reconstruction of faith. It was through the influence of Charles Hartshorne that he was once again able to take the idea of God seriously. Cobb was able to reconstruct his faith in the context of process philosophy and process theology which stemmed from the thought of A. N. Whitehead (Cobb 1991b, pp. 3–10; Griffin 1991). In many respects his venture in faith on the pathway of doubt has similarities to my own.

Faith without doubt is dead. Faith is not to be understood as belief that something is true. I like Paul Tillich's affirmation that faith is the state of being ultimately concerned (Tillich 1957). It follows that real faith is a reaching beyond one's grasp. That gives both an element of certainty and an element of uncertainty. Uncertainty and doubt are consequences of the risk of faith. Paul Tillich used to say that he felt his mission was to bring faith to the faithless and doubt to the faithful! It is to question received dogma and to work out one's own salvation.

To take risks is the safest thing for a Christian to do. The sturdiest faith comes out of a struggle with doubt. One thing I know for sure: in the business of living one must live not by certainties but by visions, risks and passion. Visions: to see the future in hope and expect the best of people and situations. Risks: to venture forth in faith and not to count the cost. Passion: to feel with all one's heart, to show emotion, to share one's deepest experiences. This is to be saved by hope.

In 1927, a 32-year-old man stood on the edge of the lake bordering Chicago's Lincoln Park, planning to drop beneath the waves and drown. His daughter had died, his company had gone bankrupt, his reputation had been ruined and he was becoming an alcoholic. Looking into the lake, he asked himself what one small man in his position could do. Then an answer came to him. He was now free to have a new vision, to take risks and to initiate action on his own. He could help people. He returned home and committed himself to the work that he believed the world wanted him to do, instead of what he had been taught to do. He altered his pattern of living and eventually changed his life completely. But without believing in a vision and taking a chance, his contribution to humanity would never have been made and no-one would have come to respect the name of Buckminster Fuller.

Dietrich Bonhoeffer was asked to lead a service for his fellow prisoners in Flossenburg concentration camp towards the end of the Second World War. As he finished two men flung open the door and told prisoner Bonhoeffer to take his things and come with them. Before going, he entrusted English fellow prisoner Payne Best with a message for his friend Bishop Bell of Chichester: 'Tell him that for me this is the end but also the beginning. With him I believe in the principle of our universal Christian brotherhood which rises above all national interests, and that our victory is certain'. Those were his last words before he was led to the scaffold. That is where vision, risk and passion took him. That is faith.

People feel alienated when they are treated as objects and not subjects. It is to deny their lives richness of experience. Yet in so much of every day, that is what happens to us. This was the basis of student revolts in the 1960s. I happened to be teaching at the University of California at the height of the youth revolt against what they believed was a society that wanted to turn them into cogs in a machine. In the University each student was identified by a number on a filing card. Written in bold type across the card was the phrase 'Do not fold or bend'. The phrase became a catchcry against the administration who were accused of treating students as numbers in a file. The most important thing the administration had to say was not to fold or bend the student card.

There were all sorts of student posters around the campus about doing your own thing and being yourself. I remember vividly my first day on the Berkeley campus. I was in a bookshop on Telegraph Avenue surveying a shelf of books. Right by me was a student obviously enjoying what he was reading from a book he had selected from the shelf. Turning to me, a complete stranger, he simply said 'Look here, this will blow your mind'. I was to learn later that this would be a good thing to happen to me. Jerry Rubin, a student leader at Berkeley at the time, said you are born twice. One is when you are really born. The second time is when you find out who you really are and how you want to live your life.

My own students came to class with balloons and a flower for the teacher. They brought their dogs into class. The lecture was to be a fun thing. And so it was, both for me and for the students. The noticeboards on campus were covered with announcements of 'happenings'. I liked that word as it suggested that something was going to happen to you. It was very existential. The good thing about all this was that students were fulfilling their lives as subjects and not as objects manipulated by a system. Theirs was a cry for humanity. Don't turn me into a number, don't treat me like a thing. Look into my face and behold me as an individual. The phrase on every lip was 'are you for real?'

The 1960s revitalised consciousness, but on the road of excess, by which some sought the palace of wisdom, many lost their minds, lives and careers through drugs, sexual orgies or their constant challenge to authority. Yet something very positive was happening. For many it was an affirmative experience that lived with them as a transforming influence for the rest of their lives. I was reminded of something A. N. Whitehead said long ago, that one of the great advantages of undergraduate life is its irresponsibility. They enjoy the traditional freedom to experiment with all sorts of intellectual attitudes and systems of thought without the restraining influences which bind the fully fledged adult. That this sort of irresponsibility may get out of bounds is no reason for condemning it any more than condemning Einstein because some of his ideas were fanciful.

The opposite of estrangement and alienation is at-one-ment, which is a oneness with self, with one's neighbours, with nature and with God (see also Chapter 6). That is richness of experience. It has two components, zest and harmony (see p. 99). Paul Tillich (1955) has said that if he were asked to sum up the Christian message for our time in two words he would say, 'It is the message of a the *New Being*' (p. 15). The two words come from Paul's second letter to the Corinthians: 'If anyone is in union with Christ he is a new being; the old state of things has passed away; there is a new state of things'. The words point beyond the state of estrangement to participation in a new state of things. It is not this or that religion that matters, not this or that doctrine or practice that is important. These are as nothing besides the question of the 'new being' or the 'new creation' which is of infinite importance. The new being is our ultimate concern. It should be our infinite passion, the infinite passion of every human being. This alone matters ultimately. The sophisticated things do not concern us ultimately. It does not matter whether we understand them or not. But the deep things must concern us always, because it matters infinitely whether we are grasped by them or not. There is always a vacuum when the ultimate question is no longer taken into account. The vacuum fills with quasi-religion, as happened in Germany under Nazism.

The new being involves a transformation of the estranged being in three ways. The first is *re-conciliation.* That means to be reconciled with oneself and all that one is hostile to, consciously or unconsciously. It might be a hostility to others or to our total circumstances. We don't need to do anything but to be willing to be grasped by the lure of the new being as we see it in the fullness of life, as in Jesus and in those who reflect his life. That leads to the second phase, which is *re-union* with the ground of one's existence (which is God) which makes transformation possible. The third mark is *re-surrection* which Tillich is quick to remind us has nothing to do with dead bodies rising out of graves. It is a total redirection of one's life in a new activity that is completely compelling. *Re-surrection* points to what happened to the despondent disciples of Jesus after his death, when all seemed to have collapsed in failure. Instead of turning back to the old state of affairs they set their eyes and their lives on a path of victory. They were *re-surrected!* Their job now was to transform the world. Out of death they discovered *re-surrection* and victory. That is the power of the new being manifest in Jesus and in those who discoverewd that path with him.

## HEALTH AND THE IMPORTANCE OF HOPE AND AFFECTION

The experience of our psyche and mind, be it a rich experience or otherwise, registers deeply within our bodies. This strongly indicates that there are not two kinds of illness, one mental and the other physical. The mental and physical are closely linked, hence the term psychosomatic, meaning mind and body together.

A sense of hope as contrasted with despair and hopelessness is, according to Dr Leonard Sagan, physician and immunologist, critically important for health and well-being in any community (Sagan 1987). Healthy people, he says, are healthy at least in part because they enjoy high levels of self-esteem, commitment to goals beyond their own personal welfare and a sense of community. Entering easily into trusting and strong emotional relationships, they enjoy companionship, but are not at all uncomfortable when left alone. He emphasises the importance of being affectionate and receiving affection, especially when young. Medical science has tended to emphasise the importance of exercise, nutrition and hygiene. Nevertheless, nurturing, love, trust, affectionate contact, self-esteem and the feeling that we are in charge of our lives are important keys to health and well-being. There is a healthy ecology of our internal relations which is reflected in healthy minds and bodies.

Jesus was called saviour (which means healer) because he made people whole (which means healed) in body, mind and spirit. His healings show the relation between bodily and mental disease, between sickness and guilt and between the desire to be healed and fear of being healed. Many of our profoundest insights into human nature are anticipated in the stories of his healings. They tell that becoming healthy means becoming whole, reunited in one's body and psyche. They describe the attitude that makes healing possible, namely a faith in something greater than ourselves that grasps us, transforms and heals. Those who were healed surrendered to this transforming influence. The healers care for the unhealed. The secret of care of the patient is caring for the patient.

There are two ways of living, a sick way which is unauthentic living and a healthy way which is authentic living. In unauthentic living we allow ourselves to be moulded by what we think others expect of us. We convince ourselves that we really do feel what we are expected to feel. We allow our self-image to be constructed by others. Such living is unauthentic precisely because it hides our real self. The unauthentic life may hide itself behind a barrier of assumed confidence, even arrogance. Yet all the while there is a deep inner longing to drop the mask, to be open, real and honest to those around us. The authentic way is to be ourselves and not to lie to ourselves.

It is extremely difficult to relate to the unauthentic person because there seems to be an impenetrable barrier surrounding the unauthentic life. Yet it was these sorts of people who brought themselves to Jesus; split, contradicting themselves, disgusted and despairing about themselves, hateful of themselves, hostile towards everybody else, afraid of life, burdened with guilt feelings, accusing and excusing themselves, fleeing from others into loneliness, fleeing from themselves. Jesus gave them back to their real selves as new beings. They found in him healing.

The word stress was introduced into the medical vocabulary in the 1920s by Hungarian physiologist Hans Selye. He observed that patients with a wide variety of illnesses, when admitted to the hospital, seemed to share many symptoms, including fatigue, loss of weight, and aches and pains in their joints. Only after several days did their symptoms diverge. Eventually he suggested that the symptoms he witnessed in these hospital patients were not a reaction to a specific agent of disease but were a general response to stress.

Selye argued that the body may go through three stages of stress:

◆ **Alarm:** preparation for fight or flight.
◆ **Resistance:** during which some of the original alarm responses are changed or even reversed.
◆ **Exhaustion:** after continuous exposure to stress, symptoms of disease appear that can even be followed by death (Hetzel & McMichael 1987, Ch. 3).

While I am writing these lines a young magpie appears on my balcony for a meal. He doesn't get the meal. His whole body stiffens as he gazes high into a nearby tree where lurks an enemy in the form of a large adult magpie. Food is of no importance to him at this moment. After a minute or two of complete immobility he takes off at high speed pursued by his enemy. He recognised the alarm, prepared for fight or flight and chose flight.

Selye and others were able to demonstrate in experiments on animals that during the alarm phase the amount of two hormones, adrenalin and noradrenalin, increased in the blood. The same phenomenon occurs in humans, as for example among players preparatory to a competitive game. The effect of the hormones is to make the heart beat faster, the rate of breathing increase, blood vessels dilate and bring more blood to the muscles, hair become erect, the sugar content of the blood increase. All of this helps to make greater exertion possible. In addition endorphins, which are natural opiate-like substances, dull the pain as a result of which the discomfort of intense physical exertion is better tolerated. I imagined all this going on in the body of my threatened magpie!

In animals, the alarm phase of stress usually lasts about one hour after the threat has passed. The animal then returns to a normal state. In humans, the stress may be more persistent, as for example in a long traffic jam, being troubled by financial difficulties or a disruptive one-way relationship. All these may cause prolonged anxiety. A prolonged response makes abnormal demands on the body's resources of energy. Hormones continue to be secreted. The body 'gets drunk on its own hormones'. Immunity is reduced, increasing the chance of various ailments developing, such as colds and other infections. There may be other effects as well, such as low back pain and insomnia.

First-year students at Monash University in Melbourne were studied for evidence of stress in their lives. During the first two terms 25 per cent of males and 37 per cent of females reported signs of emotional stress. The stress had largely to do with adjusting to university life compared with secondary school. During the third term, as exams approached, 25 per cent of males and 49 per cent of females sought help from a doctor or student counsellor because of emotional disturbances. During their second year the causes of stress changed. In general the rate of emotional disturbance was higher than in the first year.

This time the causes of stress had to do with three major components of identity problems in late adolescence: career, the opposite sex and philosophy of life (Hetzel & McMichael 1987).

Animals that live in groups, such as baboons, both compete and cooperate to stay together. They form a stable hierarchy of dominant and less dominant individuals that seem to observe the rules of the group and live in relative harmony. Conflict resolution becomes highly ritualised from mock wrist-biting to embracing. When the dominant male is removed by fighting, or in some other way, the remaining males may spend the next several months fighting amongst themselves for dominance. Males that fought for top place suffered symptoms of stress, including biochemical changes. It seemed that when the world of the baboons was secure they were healthy. When insecurity reigned, so did lack of general well-being (Sapolsky 1988).

Circumstantial evidence suggests that in humans there is a higher rate of illness among the bereaved, divorced and lonely, and a higher rate of heart attack among hurried hard-driving people. There is a correlation between stress and a variety of illnesses such as headaches, neck and back pain, and various disorders of the stomach and intestine (Hetzel & McMichael 1987). There is also some suggestion of a relation between stress and the onset of cancer (Brody 1988). The most severe stressful event is the loss of a spouse. Divorce is also high on the list, as is the death of a close member of the family. Major personal injury or illness are highly stressful to many people. Other stresses are of a much less severe nature, such as change in residence or in responsibility at work. Yet all take their toll.

Although there is a great deal yet to be discovered in the whole area of the relation of mind and disease, one conclusion is clear. Healthy, whole relationships with ourselves, our neighbours and our environment make for healthy, whole bodies. Practices such as meditation, relaxation and yoga seem to empower some people to greater mental and physical well-being.

It is important to view the world positively, as a

changing and challenging place, and not as a continuous hazard to life. A young man suffering from AIDS, who at first had a completely negative and despairing approach to the onset of his disease, was greatly helped by Victor Frankl's account of how prisoners in concentration camps who could find some sort of hope survived, when others succumbed to the terrors around them. In particular, he found much help in these words of Frankl: 'When we are no longer able to change a situation, we are challenged to change ourselves'. He did (Adams 1989).

It is now recognised that healing influences exist in the relationships of humans to their pets. Spot, Puff and Trigger are no longer pets. They are 'animal companions' whose affection makes life happier and healthier for their human friends. That, at least, is one of the major premises that form the basis for a new endeavour, the study of the healing influence of pets.

A pioneering study in this field reported by Holden (1981) was done in Yorkshire in 1974 by a student of animal behaviour. He selected a group of forty-eight elderly people of average age seventy-three who lived alone. Half the group were given begonias to care for, and half were given budgerigars (a variety of parakeet). Both groups were assessed by social workers every six months on various factors to do with personality and social adjustment. At the end of three years the 'budgie' owners were distinctly better off emotionally than the begonia owners. They had more friends, more visitors, and generally had more links with the community.

In a later study of the well-being of coronary patients, Holden (1981) reported that ownership of a pet among ninety-three patients was the strongest predictor of survival, stronger even than human relationships. A little more than half the group had pets. After one year a third of those who did not own pets had died, while only three animal owners succumbed. The pets whose company helped in the well-being of these patients were dogs, cats, fish and even an iguana.

These same investigators found that a person's blood

pressure went down when they talked to an animal, whereas it rose when they talked with people! Even gazing at a tank full of tropical fish lowered blood pressure, as in meditation. A number of hospitals now use a variety of animals to improve the emotional well-being of their patients, despite the difficulties of having pets in such institutions.

An ancient account of the therapeutic value of a pet is movingly told to King David by the prophet Nathan in 2 Samuel 12:3. 'The poor man had nothing except a little ewe lamb he had bought. He raised it and it grew up with him and his children. It shared his food, drank from his cup and even slept in his arms. It was like a daughter to him'. When he goes on to tell King David how a rich man killed this lamb for a feast, David was so horrified that he pronounced the dastardly deed as worthy of death. David knew, as well as Nathan, what the pet lamb meant to the poor man.

We can only surmise as to the nature of the influence of a pet on the well-being of its owner. As a cat lover I am deeply aware of an affection that goes out from me to my cat and I think I experience a reciprocal affection extended toward me. He frets for the first day when I go away and leave someone else in charge. On my return he is full of affection. We establish bonds of affection with our pets. They are healing bonds. We become deeply aware of this when our long-time pet companion dies. We lose a friend and suffer the loneliness of grief, not at all dissimilar to the experience of grief in losing a human loved one. I have heard many pet lovers say in this situation that they felt an emptiness in the home. My bonds extend to two lorikeets that visit me every morning at seven o'clock for their breakfast. They have done so for five years. I miss them if they fail to appear, which is quite rare. It is possible to establish bonds of kinship with many other creatures that share our world with us, even though the links may be much less secure than with our pets. Animals who become our pets help us to save us from ourselves.

# THE UNIVERSALITY OF BEING ULTIMATELY CONCERNED

It is my conviction that whoever has a human face can experience richness of experience, at-one-ment, healing and a passionate response to ultimate concern. Paul Tillich's experience and faith in ultimate concern came to him through Christianity. Late in his life he went on a journey to Asia with the purpose of finding out if those who had no contact with Christianity had also discovered the ultimate concern and its manifestation in a new being (Tillich 1961). He discovered that indeed some had. The new being, which Christians find manifested in Jesus, is working in the world, wherever there are human beings who are serious about the meaning and purpose of life.

Early Christianity did not consider itself the exclusive religion but as the all-inclusive one in the sense that whatever is true anywhere in the world is what Christians had found through their tradition. There is only one true justice, only one true forgiveness, only one real courage and these resources are available to whoever has a human face, wherever they are. Yet many Christians are alarmed at the thought that they may not have been granted an exclusive relevation. Should they not rather rejoice that others too have been vouchsafed a revelation that is fulfilling for them? Tillich (1961) refers to what he says is a better translation of 'You must be perfect as your heavenly father is perfect' as, 'You must be all-inclusive as your heavenly father is all-inclusive' (p. 35).

When others performed works similar to the disciples of Jesus, who were outside their circle, Jesus defends them against the complaints of his disciples. When it was reported to Moses that unauthorised persons were prophesying, Moses replied 'are you jealous for my sake? Would that all were prophets'. And although the fourth gospel speaks more emphatically than the others about the uniqueness of Jesus, it interprets him in the light of the most universal of all concepts used at that time, the Logos, the universal principle of the divine self-manifestation. It thus frees

Jesus from a particularism through which he would become the property of a particular religious group. This Christian universalism was not syncretistic. It subjected whatever it received to an ultimate criterion, the image of Jesus as the new being.

In the seventh century the attitude of Christians to other religions changed. For the first time Christians faced the rise of a new and fervent faith in the form of Islam that theatened all Christendom. According to the principle that defence narrows down the defender, Christianity became radically exclusive. The Crusades were the expression of this exclusive hold on truth and the fight to banish its rivals. In the centuries that followed there were swings to and from fanatical exclusivity and tolerant acceptance. Cardinal Cusanus, in the fifteenth century, and the Socinians, in the sixteenth century, both acknowledged the workings of the divine spirit beyond the boundaries of the Christian church. By contrast, and nearer to our own day, the neo-orthodox theologian Karl Barth pronounced that Christianity is based on the only relevation of God that has ever occurred, a view which seemed to be the price paid for a defence against the rise of the quasi-religion of Nazism.

At the present time there are compelling practical reasons that call for the abandonment of the isolationism of Christianity from other faiths and a development of a new genuine openness to learn from them. Perhaps it will be the danger of seeing humanity and nature engulfed by a brutal exploitation that will bring the world religions to a fuller realisation of what they have in common and what they can learn from each other (see Chapter 3).

# SUBJECTS AND OBJECTS

The relations I have discussed so far are those of subjects. By contrast to a subject an object has no felt connections. We should now concern ourselves with why it is important to recognise the difference. The knowledge about the world we have from science is almost exclusively derived from a study of objects or else of subjects treated as objects.

Although a very important part of knowledge, it is a partial knowledge of the world. Therein lies a great danger.

When Galileo sat in a pew in church in Pisa, bored by the sermon, his mind turned to other things. He watched an oil lamp swinging from the ceiling. It must have been set in motion by a puff of wind or perhaps when being lit by a long taper. Galileo put his finger on his pulse, there being no watches in his day. He timed the swings. The average time of the long swings was the same as that of the short swings. He measured it time and again, for the sermon was evidently a long one. He discovered what is now known as the uniform motion of the pendulum which keeps the same time whether it swings a large or small arc. It keeps perfect time. Hence the use of pendulums in clocks from then on. The pendulum is an object. When off centre it is moved by the gravitational attraction of the Earth and tends to move toward the centre of the Earth. The Earth too is an object. The only influence such objects know are those of push or pull from other objects that may set them in motion. In the case of the lamp in the church, this initially was a force such as the long taper that pushed it and then the force of the Earth pulling upon it.

This may seem to be a digression. But it isn't. It is important to recognise the distinction between objects and subjects. Our failure to do so has made an enormous difference to our world for the worse. Science, for the most part, studies objects such as pendulums, steel balls on inclined planes, planets and stars. Science also studies living organisms, but this is almost exclusively a study of organisms as objects and not as subjects. The heart is studied as a pump. The brain is studied as a computer. The procedure of most science is to reduce all it studies to what it regards as the ultimate objects that are supposed to constitute them — atoms, electrons and so on. We are finding now that this exercise, which is called reductionism, while rewarding in answering many questions, is a gross abstraction from reality. The human body is not just an object, nor are its various organs right down to the cells that compose it.

The new physics is telling us that the so-called fundamental particles are not objects either. The myth about matter is built on the fiction that the universe consists of nothing but a collection of inert particles, pulling and pushing each other like cogs in a deterministic machine. The new physics undermines materialism because it reveals that matter has far less 'substance' to it than we have believed (Davies & Gribbin 1991, pp. 8, 229; Davies 1992). The house that science built has to be reconstructed from the ground up. Davies and Gribbin (1991, p. 7) remark that it is fitting that physics, the science that gave rise to materialism, should also signal the demise of materialism. The point for us is not to be so sure that the dominant image of the world given to us by the science of the past, which is called the modern worldview, is a picture of the real world. Of course, we may never know what the real world is. Our concepts of the world are constructs by the brain that filters only what it can handle. At present scientific understanding of the universe is more mysterious than it has ever been before in the history of scientific thought. 'Modern physics,' says physicist Hanbury Brown, 'brings us face to face with mystery' (Hanbury Brown 1986, p. 170).

Subjects have felt connections with the world. They have some kind of inwardness or subjectivity. In this view all individual entities from protons to people are centres of experience and are not simply objects for the experience of others. We are not imputing conscious experience to the proton or the cell but something analogous that can correctly be called subjectivity. Felt connections transform the entity into something it was not but could be. A subject is sentient, it has self-determination, it has freedom to act or not to act. It has what is technically called internal relations.

An object has no felt connections, it has no self-determination, it has no freedom to act or not to act. It is not transformed by its relations with other objects. It has what are technically called external relations, but no internal ones. The distinction between internal and external relations is crucial. When the cue hits the billiard ball, that is an external relation for the billiard ball. The billiard ball remains the same billiard ball. It is not changed in its nature at all. When you deeply love someone you experience an internal relation. Something happens in your inner being, call it your mind or soul or what you will. And that happening changes you. You are now a different person from the one you were before that experience of love. You transcend what you were. You are transformed. The world consists of subjects and objects. I shall, in the next section, identify objects as 'aggregates' of subjects, which aggregates have no self-determination or freedom. A rock, a steel ball, a chair and a planet are examples of objects. A proton, a molecule, a cell, a frog and a human being are subjects.

# THE MODERN PREJUDICE

Why is it we feel
So little for each other, but for this,
That we with nature have no sympathy,
Or with such things as have no power to hold
Articulate language?
And never for each other shall we feel
As we may feel, till we have sympathy
With nature in her forms inanimate,
With objects such as have no power to hold
Articulate language. In all forms of things
There is a mind.
*William Wordsworth, 'Tintern Abbey'.*

The tendency to think almost exclusively in terms of objects that are without sentience in any form and not in terms of subjects that are sentient in some form, is predominant in modern thought. The objects exist side by side, acting on one another externally.

Viewing the world in this way has many consequences. For example, it has led to organising knowledge into separate disciplines such as economics, sociology, physics, biology, religion and and so on. It treats knowledge like the pieces in a jigsaw puzzle. One piece is economics, one piece is ecology. They fit side by side but do not overlap. This is an abstraction since knowledge cannot be so carved up without losing something in the process of fragmentation. The exponents of the disciplines, be they scientists, economists or whoever, cling to their specialities as lifebelts that keep them afloat in a sea of general ideas in which they have lost the capacity either to plunge or to swim. They look with suspicion on those colleagues who stray too far outside their speciality. Each of us tends to understand only one little piece of the whole. We have lost the sense that our little piece belongs to a larger whole that makes some sense out of the little pieces.

Heidegger said 'science does not think', by which he meant that the training in the disciplines does not fit a person to cross the boundaries of the disciplines. The ability to cross boundaries he described as thinking. Some scientists, to be sure, are exceptions to the rule. Einstein was one. He was very critical of many of his colleagues. In an address he gave in 1918 in honour of Max Planck called 'Motives of Research', Einstein asked who these people are who aspire to live in 'The Temple of Science'. He acknowledged that they are mostly 'rather odd, uncommunicative, solitary fellows'. Then he asked what led them into the temple. One of the strongest motives, he said, was flight from everyday life and from the fetters of one's own shifting desires.

> One who is more finely tempered is driven to escape from personal existence and to the world of objective observing and understanding. This motive can be compared with the longing that irresistibly pulls the town dweller away from his noisy, cramped quarters and toward the silent, high mountains ... With this negative motive there goes a positive one. Man seeks to form for himself, in whatever manner is suitable for him, a simplified and lucid image of the world, and so to overcome the world of experience by striving to replace it to some extent by this image ... Into this image and its formation, he places the center of gravity of his emotional life, in order to attain the peace and serenity that he cannot find within the narrow confines of swirling, personal experience.

Einstein's characterisation of the scientist who wants to find a lucid and simplified image of the world is reinforced in our time by the statement of Stephen Hawking (1988) in his *A Brief History of Time,* when he wrote on the final page: 'The eventual goal of science is to provide a single theory that describes the whole universe'. But what Hawking calls the whole universe seems to exclude microbes and humans and falling in love. It is a materialistic image of the universe. In somewhat similar vein Leon Lederman, director of the Fermi Laboratory near Chicago, proclaimed that the objective of physics was to find 'a unified theory of *everything*' so simple it could be written as a single formula that you can wear on your T-shirt (Davies 1989, p. 13). One single formula may unite current disparate theories in physics. Important as that may be for physics, it is not *everything*. It will not tell us about life, love, faith, affection and hope, nor anything else about ourselves as subjects.

I can remember vividly right now a decision I made in my twenties about scientific research as a career. I was standing on a road high on the foothills of Mount Lofty overlooking Adelaide. Immediately below me I could see the Waite Agricultural Research Institute where I had been doing research since I graduated some years earlier. I was getting to know more and more about less and less. I wanted to be doing something that gave me broader horizons and more personal ones than research was giving me. There is a loneliness in research not unlike that of the long distance runner.

On that hillside, on a Sunday long ago, leaning on my bicycle, I said to myself I want to combine research with something that is not so lonely and where people mattered. I decided there and then to strive to become a teacher in a university where I could do both research and be with students. And so in due course I went to the University of Chicago to better fit myself for that role. As with all changes there would be disadvantages, for I knew that university departments then offered nothing like the research facilities of a research institute. However, it was the right decision for me.

The modern scientific worldview, for all its benefits, is an abstraction because its image of the world is made up only of objects. My inner world includes that which cannot be categorised as objects. I was not turning my back against science, but against the dominant worldview derived from science called mechanism or materialism. It led me to combine my first job in a university department with being a vice-master of a college in the same university.

# SUPERNATURALISTIC DUALISM AND MATERIALISTIC ATHEISM

The dominant scientific worldview of materialism became established in the seventeenth century through the influence of men such as Galileo, Mersenne, Descartes, Boyle and Newton. They all agreed that nature is composed of things that could be called material objects. These objects were devoid of self-motion. Each object or thing is moved by other objects or things, by forces external to them. Things are not moved by aims or purposes. They have no internal principles of unrest. They just stay around until some other thing moves them. Every present state of a thing is determined by something else, which in turn is determined by something else, which in turn is determined by something else and so on back. This is the doctrine of complete determinism. It makes prediction possible in principle. So the astronomer Laplace said, if he could know the position and momentum of every particle in the universe he could predict the future of the universe completely.

The doctrine of inertia works well with pendulums and steel balls moving on inclined planes, as Galileo was to discover. These were the objects to which it was first applied. But what about living things, especially animals? Did these founders of the modern scientific worldview believe that everything, including themselves, could be completely understood in purely mechanical and deterministic terms? Was the movement of Newton's mind, through which he discovered the laws of motion, explicable on the same terms as the movement of steel balls on inclined planes? Or is there more to the universe than objects in motion?

That sort of question brings us to a great divide in modern thought. In thinking about this I have been greatly helped by David Griffin's (1990) analysis which is reflected in what follows. There are two versions of the modern scientific worldview: a supernaturalist, dualistic version and an atheistic, materialistic version. They both agree that the fundamental units of nature are bits of stuff wholly devoid of self-determination or self-motion. But they disagree on whether reality as a whole is composed entirely of such things.

According to supernaturalistic dualism there are two sorts of things, inert ones and self-moving ones. Descartes drew the line between human minds which are subjects and the rest of the world made of objects. Dogs are barking machines moved only by other things. The motion of all things other than humans has an external cause; it is loco-motion, meaning the motion from one locus (place) to another. The motion of self-moving things (subjects) is internal; it is internal becoming. Descartes said he can move himself from this place to that in space or in his thinking because he has an inner reality, his mind, which is different from inert things. As a subject it has some degree of self-determination. For Descartes the most real things about himself were his feelings and thoughts that inert things and non-human creatures do not have.

Where does God come into the picture of supernaturalistic dualism? Matter, which is inert, is in motion because God put it in motion at the creation of the universe. God is called the first mover which is the main description of God in this discourse. All power of motion was restricted to God and to self-moving created things, namely human beings. This was the dominant view amongst those who first formulated the mechanistic view of nature in the seventeenth century.

By the second half of the following century the dualistic view became transmuted into scientific materialism. By the end of the nineteenth century that view became dominant throughout the scientific world.

There were many reasons why supernaturalistic dualism was so unsatisfactory. There was the mind–body problem of how could mind and matter, being so different, interact? (Birch 1990, Ch. 2). Secondly, there is the problem of evil. If God is omnipotent, and if God is also good, how come there is so much evil in the world? There has been more double talk on this conundrum by theologians than about anything else. Some evils are the consequence of human wickedness. Other evils are not. A genetically malformed baby with amaurotic idiocy never has a chance. It is destined to live a very short and very painful life. The same is true of many other genetic diseases. These are natural evils because they inhibit the development of a full human being. These are real problems for those who think God could prevent these diseases but does not. There is no way out of this dilemma while retaining a belief in the omnipotence of God. This dogma is one of the worst of all theological mistakes (Hartshorne 1984, pp. 10–16; Birch 1990, pp. 93–6).

For these and other reasons, supernaturalistic theism transmuted into atheistic materialism. Some thinkers have returned to a dualistic view while rejecting God. But they still provide no answer to how mind and matter interact. Dualism, be it supernaturalistic or atheistic, is a problem, not a solution.

In the worldview of atheistic materialism, the world contains only one type of thing. It has no principle of self-moving or self-determination but is entirely moved from without. The only kind of movement is locomotion. There are no beings with an inner reality with capacity for self-movement. This is claimed in the face of the acknowledgment that humans do have thoughts and purposes and are conscious. But these are regarded as epiphenomena, as the rattling of the train is to the motion of the train, or else phenomena equated with chemical and electrical activities in the brain. Varieties of these interpretations are elaborated in a straightforward way by Churchland (1984). There are many problems with materialism, the greatest of which is its denial of mind or the reduction of mind to matter. How can things that are subjects evolve out of things that are mere objects?

Given that supernaturalistic dualism and materialistic atheism are unsatisfactory, a third way suggests itself. It is to reject the mechanistic view of matter and make the radical proposal that there are more subjects in the world than were ever dreamed of by any mechanistic theory. It is the proposition that sentience in some form and self-determination in some degree go all the way down the evolutionary scale from humans to protons and the like. Sentience in this context does not mean consciousness, but the inward taking account of the environment.

This overcomes the problem of the evolution of mind from no mind. The evolutionary sequence from protons, molecules, cells, plants and animals to people would be interpreted as an increase in complexity of experience and degree of self-determination. On this scale humans would have a richness of experience and a degree of self-determination vastly different in degree, though not in kind, from the proton. There are then no absolute differences in kind in individual entities, only differences in degree. All are subjects. This is a panexperiental or panpsychic (from the Greek for 'all' and 'soul') view of nature. It is an interpretation of 'experience' that applies up and down the line from protons to people. It is a view that challenges all dualistic concepts which happen to be the dominant concepts today.

There is however a proviso. This discussion concerns *individual entities* such as protons, molecules, cells and humans. An individual entity is something that 'feels' and acts as one. There is another group of things that are *aggregates* of individual entities. They are objects, not subjects. A rock is an aggregate of molecules and as a rock has no individual centre of sentience or action. For a more detailed account of this important distinction see Birch (1990). It is helpful to realise that the objects of scientific investigation are, for the most part, in the category of aggregates. And in so far as science investigates subjects such as animals, it leaves out of account their subjective aspects.

Science has had no way of dealing with subjects as such until quite recently, when the new physics and some biology have had some success in dealing with Thomas Nagel's (1979) question about subjects: 'What is it like to be a bat?' (essay 12). There is no reason in principle why the whole world of inner experience should not be included in the domain of science. Ours is a transition period of an incomplete, unbalanced science that has yet to allow for internal factors. But that would be to call for a re-enchantment of science (Griffin 1988).

# THE ALTERNATIVE ROAD

There is now a growing realisation that science, as such, does not require a mechanistic worldview. The reigning wisdom is under attack. Much evidence, especially from the new physics, suggests a less deterministic, more organic and subjective interpretation of nature. There is a 'within' of things which is what things are in themselves and to themselves. The stuff of the world is 'feelings' or relations clothed in 'emotion'. Subjectivity is everywhere in nature. The evidence for this is discussed by Birch (1990), Griffin (1988; 1990), Cobb and Griffin (1976), Sheldrake (1990) and by others to whom they refer.

Furthermore, this postmodern worldview opens the way to a non-dualistic interpretation of theism. God acts in the world, not through external causes as postulated in the doctrine of the first mover but in another way which I now discuss. Just as Saint Augustine said that our hearts are restless because of their inherent ineradicable relation to God, so too to some degree is that true of all subjects from protons to people. There is an eros in the universe persuading and luring and meeting the eros of the subjects of creation. 'Eros' is the name in Greek mythology for the life-giving qualities that turned a world that was barren and lifeless into a world full of vibrant life. It is therefore appropriately used for the lure that creatures feel in their lives, transforming them from moment to moment to fuller life.

What does God do in the world? In supernatural theism discussed above, God acts in the world first by creating the world out of nothing, establishing and maintaining its natural laws and subsequently by intervening at points in the history of the world to effect special results. This is the mistaken notion of divine omnipotence. Much of the history of the Judeo-Christian religion has been interpreted this way. This view inevitably retreats before science. Science leaves little for that sort of God to do. We need to turn our minds to another sort of causality. Indeed it is a very familiar one which I have discussed earlier in the context of felt connections.

Suppose I am deeply involved in a discussion with a colleague on the issues of this paragraph. Let us further suppose that each of us is completely present. We are really serious and we bring to bear all our concerns in a serious way. I am becoming influenced by my colleague. Influence means to flow into. His ideas are flowing into my mind. Indeed they become so critical that I am changed as a consequence. My orientation to life becomes different. It has a different focus that is transforming. Something my colleague has communicated to me has become a constitutive part of my being. A scientific observer would be limited to observing my outward behaviour. He might even put some electrodes to my brain and register electrical impulses, say in some part of the cortex. But none of this reveals the primary causal relationship that is going on. Internal relations are involved. They are relations within my mind and soul which I can feel but which you cannot see as an outside observer. What has changed me is a succession of internal relations associated with ideas I am sharing with my colleague. There is an ecology of personal well-being that has to do with getting our internal relations right.

It is one of theologian John Cobb's important contributions that he points so clearly to this kind of causation, which we know so well, as providing a much better way of conceiving of God's causality in the world than the concept of a God who intervenes through external causation. Rather, God participates in the constitution of the events of the creation from protons to people (Cobb 1983). There is an ecology of God which we can think of as God's internal relations with the creation. God's use of persuasion, as opposed to omnipotent coercion, which is so often attributed to God, is not based on a voluntary self-limitation. God could not choose from time to time to intrude here and there in the world. This point, as Griffin has so clearly argued, is at the heart of the difference between supernatural theism and the postmodern theism of process theology (Griffin, 1989 p. 140).

I expect that most who have read thus far will probably be willing to accept the proposition that all that we have met is a part of us. Our present state of well-being or otherwise reflects the happenings of the past as a result of the internal relations we have experienced. It logically follows that we are a part of all that we are meeting now, right at this moment.

In addition to the antecedent world in our experience there is another reality that enters into each moment which we can respond to. This reality is future possibilities. They are to be conceived as causes in the present. This is the meaning of purposive activities. This reality is given the name God in process thought. I do not think the proposition that future possibilities as causal in the present is contestable, though some will object to the use of the word God in relation to the reality of future possibilities and their lure upon the world.

My next point therefore will seem contestable to some. It is that the reality entering each moment, which is called God, is a *realm* of possibilities. All possible values are parts of cosmic value which abides. Whatever is present in some degree in every creature is maximally present in God. God confronts the world with what is possible for it at every moment. In our lives, each of us intuitively differentiates these values as we choose the next step. Call it conscience or what you will, we have within us a capacity to make that differentiation such that we choose that value which is relevant for us at this moment. When we are young and immature our intuitive instrument is blunt. Indeed, we let a lot of decisions be made for us by others. To grow into maturity is to sharpen our intuitive instrument and to become more independent of parents and authorities in making decisions. We become free.

For example, the most important value I may need to experience right now is forgiveness. I have been hurtful to someone and I have a deep sense of guilt. I may harbour up that feeling until it bursts out in all sorts of negative ways. That is an immature response to the value I need in my life at that moment. Alternatively I may go to the one I have harmed, admit my guilt and ask that we may begin all over again as though that bit of the past is, in some sense, blotted out. He forgives me. But more, I myself experience forgiveness as a new quality in my life. The burden has been lifted. My internal relations have a new harmony. I have a sense of wholeness again. The image is of John Bunyan labouring along the road with a huge bundle on his back. As he tells us in *The Pilgrim's Progress*, he eventually reaches the foot of the cross on his journey. There the bundle falls from his back to the ground. He is free.

Or go back a little in Bunyan's journey when he is wading across a swiftly flowing river. The bottom of the river seems to be deep with mud that will engulf him if the river itself does not sweep him away. He panics and is afraid. What does he most need at that critical moment of his life? His desperate need is for courage, the courage to be when his life is threatened. Courage enters into his being. He says to his faithful partner, 'I feel the bottom and it is sound'.

One cannot remove anxiety by simply arguing it away. One needs an inner strength to face the situation in a new spirit that can overcome all circumstance. Bunyan's anxiety was an awareness of a conflict between turning back and going ahead with the possibility of a new hope. Our anxiety might be between emotional drives and

repressive norms, between different drives trying to dominate our personality, between our hope to achieve in our
studies or profession and a lack of confidence in ourselves,
between the desire to be accepted by others and the experience of being rejected, between our real selves and the
image of ourselves we try to give others or between our
sense of loneliness and the need for friendship. All these
conflicts make themselves felt as anxiety. Anxiety turns us
toward courage, because the other alternative is despair
(see Chapter 6).

The experience of loneliness is a cause of pain for
many people. When in England Mother Teresa agreed
there was poverty in India, then added, 'but here you have
a different kind of poverty, the poverty of loneliness, and
that is the worst disease in the world today'.

The writer of the twenty-fifth psalm says 'Turn to me
and be gracious, for I am lonely and afflicted'. I recall the
preacher of the Temple Church in London, Leslie Weatherhead, giving this account of a friend who was under nervous strain knowing not which way to turn. He was staying
at Weatherhead's house previous to speaking at a big meeting. He felt terribly alone, despite being surrounded by lots
of people at that moment. Noticing that he looked tired,
Weatherhead asked him if he would like to escape all the
chatter and rest in a room upstairs. So he left the crowded
room to retire to a comfortable room upstairs. In his loneliness he turned to a Bible seeking comfort in Psalm 59 verse
10. In the margin opposite this verse someone had written
in pencil the following rendering of this verse: 'My God in
his loving kindness shall meet me at every corner'. It was
light in a dark place. He no longer felt alone in the world
with his anxiety. He experienced the affirmation: when I
am alone I am not alone. His loneliness turned into creative solitude.

Loneliness is to be distinguished from solitude. Ultimately, loneliness can only be conquered by those who
can bear solitude. The emptiness of loneliness can be filled
for a time with friendship. But for much of our time we are
destined to be alone. That is certainly the lot of those who

choose to be students. Tillich (1963) said loneliness expresses the pain of being alone but solitude expresses the glory of being alone. He went on to say that today human beings, more intensely than in previous periods, are so lonely that they cannot bear solitude. In their desperation they try to become part of a crowd.

Solitude allows us to accept, upon reflection, our fears and inner turmoil. It enables us to find a way to cope with life's ordeals. In solitude we meet ourselves and the possibilities of ourselves. We meet God as friend and sustainer. An indefinable longing is met by the ultimate concern for that moment. Perhaps that is the thought behind that much quoted (and much misunderstood) statement of Whitehead (1930) 'Religion is what the individual does with his solitariness' (p. 37). Whitehead was referring to solitude, not to loneliness.

During the First World War a soldier in the trenches saw his friend out in no-man's land, between the trenches and those of the enemy, stumble and fall in a hail of bullets. He said to his officer, 'May I go Sir and bring him in?' The officer refused. 'No-one can live out there', he said. Disobeying the order, the soldier went to try to save his friend, for they had been like David and Jonathan. Somehow he got his friend on his shoulder and staggered back to the trenches. But he himself lay mortally wounded and his friend was dead. The officer was angry. 'Now I have lost both of you. It was not worth it'. With his dying breath the soldier said, 'But it was worth it Sir'. 'Worth it', said the officer. 'How could it be? Your friend is dead and you are mortally wounded'. The boy shrank from the reproach. But looking up into the officer's face he said, 'It was worth it Sir. He wasn't dead when I reached him and he said to me, "Jim I knew you'd come"'.

It is not a matter of chance that I select forgiveness, courage and the friendship of solitude as examples of values I meet in my moments of anxiety. They happen to be three of the most vivid and transforming experiences in my life. These experiences carry with them a certain conviction that I do not create these values or any others. The realm of values is not a sort of pantry from which I choose. They choose me. My part is to be receptive and open to whatever value is relevant for me now. The experience of appropriating values is real. It is personal. It is transforming. It is to feel a claim upon me. It is what Christians down the ages have meant by the influence of God in human experience. That is what I mean by the reality of God in life.

For this influence there are many metaphors: the treasure in the field, the pearl of great price, the light on the hill, the good shepherd searching for the one sheep that is lost. All convey the idea of overriding value, of clear purpose and, above all, lure. God is the great persuader pressing upon us, ever-active, only blocked by us. It is for Paul Tillich 'ultimate concern' which beckons within us the only response possible of 'infinite passion'. We meet God when values flood into our lives in our solitude or through others, as happened in the case of the dying soldier whose last words met a response in his courageous friend. This is the divine eros flooding into the world. God is to the world as self is to the body.

There is a second aspect to the divine love which is the consequence to God when God's love becomes concretely real in the world. What happens in the world makes a difference to God. God feels the world in its joys and suffering as the world feels God. This is the divine passion. It is the doctrine of panentheism (all in God) as distinct from classical theism (Birch 1990). This way of thinking about God cannot be contained in the old images of God as ruler, king, potentate and patriarch. God is the supreme instance of sensitivity, receptivity, responsiveness, relatedness and creativity. God takes all experience into the divine experience, preserves it everlastingly with no loss. The very nature of the divine is unconditional love and acceptance. Sallie McFague (1987) has suggested new and vivid metaphors for God, such as lover, friend and mother, that come much closer to the new understanding of God as divine eros and divine passion. Our response to God's acceptance of our lives into his/her life provides a powerful sense of the meaning of life and a profound sense of the intimacy of the human and the divine. It enhances our capacity for intimacy in all our internal relations, be they with others, the non-human world or God.

'There is ... in the Galilean origin of Christianity', wrote Whitehead (1978), 'a suggestion ... which does not emphasise the ruling Caesar, or the ruthless moralist, or the unmoved mover. It dwells upon the tender elements in the world, which slowly and in quietness operate by love; and finds purpose in the present immediacy of a kingdom not of this world' (p. 343). Whitehead's 'present immediacy' is put in quite personal terms by Cobb (1983):

> It is by virtue of the presence of God that I experience a call to be more than I have been and more than my circumstances necessitate that I be. It is the call to transcendence that frees me from simply acting by habit and reacting to the forces of the world. In short, it is by God's grace that I am free. ( p. 53)

This is a freedom of the present moment, making the present an ultimate experience that transcends past experience. It is an end in itself without the need to project what later experience might be.

The relation of God to humans is in principle the relation of God to all subjects in the creation from protons to people. None is self-sufficient. None is merely stuff. Each has some degree of self-determination or freedom, negligibly small though this must be at the lower levels of creation. All individual entity from protons to people are responding, valuing, creative subjects. The world feels God as God persuades the world to be what it could be. But God is not the world and the world is not God. God affects creatures, not by determining them from without, but by persuading them from within. 'God is not *before* all creation but *with* all creation' (Whitehead 1978, p. 343). Hence William Blake's epiphany in his 'Auguries of Innocence':

> To see the World in a Grain of Sand,
>     And a Heaven in a Wild flower;
> Hold Infinity in the Palm of your Hand,
>     And Eternity in an Hour.

Some events in the history of the cosmos, including human history, have more significance than others. There are peak events. This is not because God intervened in these events and not in others. To interpret significant events as special acts of God is to turn God into an agent of mechanical intervention. It is to replace persuasive love by fiat, acting according to some preordained plan.

Significant events are significant because they open up new realms of possibility heretofore closed. The history of the Jewish people is rich in such events. The life of Jesus is such an event. It opened and still opens up for humanity new possibilities of compassionate understanding, creativity and human fellowship. Christians today, as with the first disciples, look at Jesus and look through him to discover something true about God. The followers of Jesus spoke of discovering 'the light of the knowledge of the character of God' in his face. And they spoke of God being in him, reconciling the world to himself. What is highest and greatest in human life is deeply grounded in the universe. God is like that. It was an affirmation of the creeds of the early church that humanity is the vehicle of the divine. That is the meaning of incarnation.

# CONCLUSION

The new consciousness is the discovery of new felt relationships of compassion between ourselves and other people, with other living creatures, with the whole of creation and therefore with God. It emphasises the subjective as real and determinative in life. Key concepts in the new consciousness are: subject, felt relations, internal relations, sympathy, richness of experience, creative solitude, hope, faith, affection, new being, ultimate concern ( = God), compassion and God's action in the world as internally related to all individual entities from protons to people. These concepts lead to critical attempts to understand our lives and nature as the scene of interplay of two contrary tendencies of disordering and ordering. That which disorders and divides is evil. That which orders and unites is good. We live under both influences at the same time.

This vision of the world stands in strong contrast to supernaturalistic dualism and materialistic atheism. It is not provable in the way in which a mathematical proposition might be proved. It stands or falls by its adequacy to account for and illumine all experience. But it requires imagination to see it. The world is not as tame as our sluggish, convention-ridden imaginations tend to suppose. There are three classes of people: those who see, those who see when they are shown, and those who do not see.

For those who see, this vision has profound implications for how they act and what they do with their lives. That is the subject of the next chapter.

# CHAPTER 2
# A NEW WAY
# OF LIVING

We need new ethical and practical ideas to mediate between ultimate ideas and our concrete situations.

*Charles Hartshorne (1983, p. 223)*

The belief that human beings have value for themselves,
and that they are valued by God, becomes in process
thought the grounds for ethical attitudes toward all actuali-
ties.

*John Cobb and David Griffin (1976, p. 77)*

he new consciousness discussed in Chapter 1 stands in strong contrast to the dominant and accepted tradition in Western thought. In that tradition the dominant model of life and its relations to the world is a mechanical one. It is also dualistic. It makes hard and fast separations between psyche and body, reason and feeling, objective and subjective, human and non-human, supernatural and natural and the world and God. For the most part the individual entities of creation are objects. They have no inner aspects, no internal relations and their only value is their value to us.

By contrast, the new consciousness cuts across dualisms. It sees every dualistic concept as a gross abstraction from reality. The emphasis is on internal relations which constitute the inner aspect of all individual entities. It is an *experiential* view of reality, as contrasted with the image of reality consisting of objects only. It finds the world a much more feeling place.

There is a compelling connection between the way the world is conceived (metaphysics) and what is held to be good and bad, what sort of behaviour is right and wrong and what responsibilities and obligations we have as individuals (ethics). In the quotation from Joseph Campbell in the front of this book, he says that people say they are seeking a meaning for life, whereas what they are really seeking is an experience of being alive. That may well be true of our priorities. We want to feel alive in the world. But we are unlikely to achieve that state, or anything like it, unless we discover some meaning for life. Philosophy and ethics depend on each other, so too does meaning of life and the experience of life.

Differences in consciousness make all the difference in how we order our lives in relation to our fellow humans and to the rest of the creation. The dominant Western view has turned the world into a factory for producing things for ourselves. Technology is not simply the use of tools. It is first a vision of reality. The use of tools follows. It turns the people who work in factories into parts of the machinery. Consumption becomes an overall aim, a form of salvation.

The image is of 'Faustian man' who celebrates his day by seeking gratification here and now. Therefore one lives dangerously at one's own and whosoever's expense, even if that means ruining the world and its ecology in the process. Its economics has produced so-called 'economic man' whose desire to consume is the only basis of value of other things. The overall objective is to increase production of goods and services.

In this process, other creatures who share the earth with us, together with the environment in which they and we live, take a terrible beating. Somewhat belatedly, while species and countryside around us disappear under the onslaught, we begin to think of ways of protecting them and the environment, provided they contribute to our own existence. They are not protected for their own sake or because they are seen as having value in themselves to themselves or to God. We look after nature because nature looks after us. The ethic of the dominant Western worldview is thus highly anthropocentric. But even its anthropocentric nature is warped because of its male dominance and patriarchal nature.

The relationship between the productive system, the economic system and ecological system in the dominant Western view is quite different from what would follow from the new consciousness. Its economic system (emphasising growth) determines the nature of the productive system with little, if any, reference to the ecological system on which production depends. Yet any arrangement beween these three systems that takes the individual value of humans and other subjects into account would have to be different.

It would be logical to ask what are the needs of human beings for food and housing and other necessities; then to decide which productive systems can produce the needed goods; then to organise an economic system that can lead to the production of the needed goods, while taking the well-being of the ecological system into account. But this is not what happens.

In the new consciousness the world is replete with subjects. To be a subject is to have feelings, self-determination and therefore freedom to act. It is precisely the knowledge that other human beings enjoy and suffer, have value in and for themselves and have some degree of self-determination that grounds our sense of obligation toward them. The belief that there are many levels of reality, many individual entities that can also enjoy some degree of experience, provides the basis of our obligation directly to them.

In traditional Christianity there is a double ground for ethical attitudes toward other human beings; the belief that human beings have value in themselves for themselves and that they have value to God. It follows that other subjects besides humans have value in themselves for themselves and to God. There is thus a twofold ground for our obligation to them. Yet traditional Christianity, despite the views of its founder, has been reluctant to extend human obligation this far. Animals are left out of ethical account.

When we speak of our obligation to all individuals who are subjects we are not saying that this obligation extends to everything that exists. A distinction is made in Chapter 1 between subjects who feel and aggregates which do not feel. Rocks and tables are aggregates of low-level subjects (atoms and molecules). Our attitude to them is very different from our attitude to a dog or a fish.

*The first ethical principle is the distinction between individual entities that feel and that are properly called subjects and those that do not feel, such as rocks and tables.* Failure to make the distinction leads, as we shall see, to a confused ethic.

*A second ethical principle is to treat other humans as ends in themselves and not merely as means to our own ends.* Likewise we should, to the appropriate degree, treat other subjects as ends and not merely means to our own ends.

*A third ethical principle is the recognition of a gradation of value amongst subjects.* We are not supposing that all subjects have equal value. There is a gradation of value. If we do not presume some such gradation we have no basis for treating a human being differently from a mosquito. Oddly enough this is a controversial issue in environmental ethics. To these last two ethical principles we now turn.

# ENDS AND MEANS AND INTRINSIC VALUE

The worst thing we can do to fellow humans is to treat them as means only and not as ends in themselves. We may cultivate the acquaintance of someone solely because we think they could be useful to us in our career or in some other way. Even more damaging, people use others for ulterior motives. That damages all concerned. I think of a street kid who was picked up by some youths at the Wayside Chapel in Sydney. They invited him to lunch, where I met him. They were being real friends and were extending compassion to him. But he couldn't understand that anyone would be kind to him for any other than an ulterior motive. That had been his experience with adults in his whole life until then. As a result he was unable to accept love and affection when it was offered to him. His life had been deeply damaged by others who had used him to their own ends.

To treat a person as a means only is to value that person solely in terms of their usefulness to us or to others, that is, in terms of their instrumental value. It is to treat the person as an object and not as a subject. Any human being is an end in himself or herself because every human being has value in his or herself and for one's self and therefore to God, the source of all value. It is the same thing to say that every human being has intrinsic value.

What confers intrinsic value? Only feeling does. Wherever there is sentience and feeling there is intrinsic worth. I am aware that there are other views on what constitutes intrinsic value. The reader who is interested in pursuing these alternatives can find a full discussion in Fox (1990, pp. 161–76). To the extent to which this discussion is relevant to this chapter, it is referred to again in later sections.

The appropriate response to intrinsic value, when we meet it, is respect. We respect other people because their life is of value to them as they experience it. There may be times when the value of a person's life to that person may so dwindle that the person prefers suicide to living. That is a pathological state, induced by terrible tragedy, seemingly unbearable suffering and an awful sense of meaninglessness or a sense of total separation from the real self and from others. Normal life seeks more life, not less.

This section has been about the consequences of recognising human beings as ends in themselves. The principle is that human beings and other subjects are to be respected as ends in themselves because they have intrinsic value to themselves and to God, irrespective of any use they may have to others. This is not to deny that we are of use to others and that we are also means to ends. The bus driver is an end in herself, and as well a means to the well-being of others. So it is with all professions. But we need to continuously ask if our use of people as means to our ends is inhibiting them from enjoying a richness of experience that might otherwise be possible for them.

So we ask, does the end justify the means? Does the end of getting people to their work and homes on time justify the methods we use to achieve that? This is an extremely important question. Yet our answer cannot be arrived at by simply looking at the values in the means used or the values in the ends of those concerned. We have to regard as a whole the values involved in the situation from beginning to end and compare them with those attaching to alternative courses of action.

The role of women in a patriarchal society is very much that of being a means to the ends of the husband and family. To be sure, it is hoped that the mother will find the home a place where she will discover her own worth. But often the set-up deprives her of the possibility of really pursuing her own chief interests, be they professional or otherwise.

# THE MEANINGS OF LOVE

The word that describes the attitude that promotes human beings as ends and not just means is love. Compassion, as Lynn White says in the quote at the beginning of this book, is what one does to actualise love. Love has many meanings. Some of them, such as the state of 'being in love' when individual boundaries of the person seem to disappear, are not real love (see Chapter 1). Real love recognises individual freedom to develop one's individuality. I say I love that person who ministers to my deepest hungers and desires. I love that person for my sake and for his or her sake. Each feels a sense of fulfilment in such a relationship, provided neither partner uses the other in a purely selfish way.

There are lots of things that can block the healthy relationship of love. We may repress our feelings. For example, the repression of feelings of anger and emotional pain can lead to the repression of feelings of affection and tenderness. If we try to control our actions too tightly by our rational will, others will not feel warmth and affection from us. By becoming more comfortable about ourselves and all our feelings we can become more outgoing and expressive toward others.

Can we love with real concern those who make us feel uncomfortable, whose complacency exasperates us, who are in many ways revolting to us? Jesus exhorted his followers to love their enemies. What can we love in such people? It can't be to love what they are, as we see them right now in front of us. We are challenged to love their possibilities, to seek to promote their well-being and potential and to have faith that they can be transformed by love.

It is difficult to know to what extent our own self-reference remains in such love. Compassion may never be completely disinterested. Reinhold Niebuhr (1941) underscored his conviction that self-love pervades even the most seemingly altruistic thought and action. An historian of antiquity recorded that in the year 1250 two Arabic-speaking Dominicans in Damascus saw a woman holding in one hand a bowl of fire and in the other a jug of water. When they asked her why she did so, she replied: 'With this fire I would burn Paradise, and with the water quench Hell, so that none should do good for hope of Paradise or fear of Hell, but only for the love of God'.

Four types of love were distinguished among the

Greeks (Cobb 1967, p. 127). There was *desire.* That was attending to the other as that which gave satisfaction. Its goal was possession. The object might be things, prestige, success, power or sexual possession.

Second there was *adoration.* This was not possession of but surrender to the object of love. It was a case of being possessed. Adoration might be directed toward another person or a deity. Adoration was the word that immediately sprang to my lips when I was asked in an radio interview in Moscow, what was my strongest impression of life in the Russian Orthodox Church? The adoration of a thousand or more peasants, all in black, celebrating the Liturgy in the heart of the Russian steppes. That was my most memorable experience — the look on their faces as they sang their praises and looked upon the bishop as he robed and disrobed his finest vestments, then disappeared into the holy of holies before emerging again in simpler garb to share with them the bread and the wine. Their lives were surrendered for those moments, nay hours, to something ineffable and altogether adorable for them.

A third type of love for the Greeks was *aesthetic admiration.* Here there was no attempt to gain possession or to be possessed. A distance was maintained between the object of love and the lover. The object of love could be a work of art or a human being's beauty of physique or of character.

Fourth was *friendship.* It differed from the others as being only between human beings and it had to be mutual. Friendship might be based on desire of one for the other or admiration of excellence of one another's character. Seeking friendship was synonymous with seeking happiness.

Each of these four sorts of love could lead to pain, suffering and disappointment. Hence, in later Greek thought, the absence of love in all four senses, which is apathy, was a much approved state of mind. The opposite of love is not hate but apathy. There are similarities in the Greek idea of apathy to Buddhist thought which values detachment from clinging and the cessation of desire.

In Hebrew thought the concept of love centred on

mercy and justice. God extended these according to the deserts of his people. The Hebrews knew that obedience to God could be at personal cost and without expectation of reward. Obedience and law were their key concepts.

In Christianity these limitations were broken down. God sends his 'rain' to fall upon the just and unjust alike. All are recipients of a love that is unconditional. The unacceptable are accepted in spite of their unacceptability. We are to love ourselves and our neighbours as ourselves and and in so doing we love God. As the verse says:

> I was looking for God, but he withdrew from me.
> I was looking for my soul, but I did not find it.
> I was looking for my brother, and I found all three.

Hence, 'if someone says, I love God, but hates his brother, he is a liar. He cannot love God if he does not love his brother' (1 John 4:20).

John Cobb points out that there are two conflicting images of what is involved in following the Christian way (Cobb 1991b, p. 84). One is the image of following a blueprint already given in a set of rules, commandments or a fixed set of guidelines. This is the way of legalism. It is the way of much conservative Christianity. The second image is that of trusting the Spirit of God that leads us into the truth about life, responding to opportunities as they arise, opening ourselves to the limitless persuasion of the Spirit that presses in on our lives, only to be blocked by us. Henry James said the great thing in life is to be *saturated* with something, adding that he chose the form of his saturation. The way Jesus offered was one of being open to surprise and new perceptions, not clinging to established guidelines and inherited patterns. Human love is to reflect the outgoing, limitless, ever-active love of God that floods into the world. The greatest love possible is an altruistic love that leads one to lay down one's life for one's friends. That Jesus did.

I find in the sequence of Greek, Hebrew and Christian concepts of love a development of meaning. One could also trace the meanings of love in Eastern religions such as

Hinduism and Buddhism. There are both similarities to and profound differences from Western images of love (Cobb 1982).

The Western tradition culminates in the Christian concept of altruistic love. In contrast to such altruistic love of one's neighbour is erotic love. By its nature it is not universal but exclusive. Its object is sexual union with one other person. Yet the more powerful need is not for sex *per se* but for intimacy, acceptance and affection. There is a distinction between the sexual desire and the striving for intimacy. The two are often confused. We experience sexual desire and think it is genital satisfaction that we need, when actually the sexual desire represents the need for intimacy. If the need for intimacy is met and satisfied, the need for physiological genital experience becomes less dominating. One can have intimacy without sex.

One of the most beautiful of intimate friendships in recorded history, that between David and Jonathan, seemed, from the account, to be of that sort. We are movingly told 'Jonathan became one in spirit with David, and he loved him as himself' (1 Samuel 18:2). And after Jonathan was slain in battle David, in the agony of his grief, says 'I grieve for you, Jonathan my brother; you were very dear to me. Your love for me was wonderful, more wonderful than that of women' (2 Samuel 1:26).

I recall a bikie who was having no success with maintaining a relationship with any of a succession of girlfriends. His approach was first to get his girlfriend into bed. He hoped the rest would follow. It didn't. He failed to satisfy his hunger for companionship and intimacy. As with many adolescents, he was attempting through sex to meet a more encompassing need. The biological drive is so powerful that he focused on it and nothing else. Integrating his biological drive with affection and mature love seemed to exceed his present capacity. When sexual gratification is the primary or only aim, the consequences for a relationship can be devastating. Too often in the past a set of rules has been promulgated by churches and other institutions in an attempt to lay down a norm for sexual behaviour. Responsibility, not rules, should become the moral principle for sexual ethics. Responsibility relates to what specific actions do to oneself and how they affect another.

The 1991 report of the US Presbyterian's Special Committee on Human Sexuality made this principle central when it stated: 'Rather than inquiring whether sexual activity is premarital, marital, or post-marital, we should be asking whether the relation is responsible, the dynamics genuinely mutual, and the loving full of joyful caring' (Lindermayer 1991, p. 163). The report eschews any easy formulas such as 'celibacy in singleness' and 'fidelity in marriage'. The committee which produced this report has been accused of selling out to the prevailing culture. On the contrary, it appears to have realised that often Christian ethics fail to transform the world because they refuse to come to grips with key aspects of human reality; victims of sexual violence who cannot find comfort, let alone justice, in the church; gay men and lesbians whose reality is not acknowledged in their churches and who feel they must hide (see Chapter 6); male pastors who experience sexuality as a compulsion and some who violate counselling relationships for the sake of sexual satisfaction; women who manipulate men to get what they want and men who adopt the prevailing patriarchal sexual code. 'Although sexuality is a good' says John Cobb (1991a, p. 96) 'it is a limited good. A limited good treated as a final good becomes an idol. Sexual fulfilment as an end in itself, separated from other concerns, becomes idolatrous and, therefore, demonic'.

The 'other concerns' are manifold. Sexuality enters into many aspects of life: in the developing child, in the search for identity with its special crises in adolescence and in maturity. Its energy, psychic qualities and affective tone may alter, enrich, or debase everything in experience. I recall a professor of Italian saying that translating a Pirandello play from the Italian onto his typewriter was an erotic experience. We can recognise the omnipresence of sex without asserting its omnipotence.

There is a threefold involvement of love, be it altruistic love, brotherly love, motherly love, self-love, erotic love or love of God. It is the ultimate ethical principle expressed in the 'with all' injunction: to love with all of one's *heart, mind* and *strength.*

First is the involvement with all of one's heart. This is Paul Tillich's 'with infinite passion'. It is the total involvement of our feelings, emotions and being. 'The heart has its reasons that reason knows not', said Blaise Pascal. This is the love that connects hearts. It involves the whole person in relationships of self-awareness, vulnerability, openness and caring. It is a yearning to be as richly related as is possible and therein to discover the fullness of life (McDaniel 1989, p. 128).

Second is the total involvement of mind and will. We love our neighbour with our mind as well as with our feelings when we subject our desires and feelings to careful thought. Are we single-minded or confused? Are our motives unalloyed? We love God with our mind when we let faith and doubt work together as we probe the ultimate mysteries. Mind includes will which is resolution and determination. It involves our imaginative participation in the coming day's possibiliities. It includes the capacity to organise one's self on the basis of these images. The person who lacks will becomes anxious and uncertain.

Jesus, time and time again, stressed the importance of endeavour. Having put your hand to the plough, don't look back. To the man who decided he wanted to follow but not yet, as he would first have to bury his father, Jesus replied, 'let the dead bury the dead'. The story referred to the young man's inability to detach himself from ties to parents and home. Jesus told another to be first reconciled to his brother, then come and offer his gifts.

The full involvement of heart and the mind lead to priorities for the will. Some things have to be sought first and single-mindedly. Others will follow. You cannot serve more than one master. Most of the objects of our youthful enthusiasms must be sacrificed for a few, and the few must be approached with soberness. Personal initiative and resolution are essential to true living.

Living is a process of continuous rebirth. Paul said

that when he was a child he thought as a child and behaved as a child, but when he became a man he put away childish things. That means cutting adrift from some of the anchors that tie us to the past and venturing forth to farther horizons. The child in the womb has no experience of breathing until the umbilical cord is cut. We are torn between two tendencies since the moment of birth, one for certainty and the other for adventure, one for protection and dependence, the other for the risk of independence. The tragedy is that so many people die before they are fully born! To be fully born is to be born anew, not just once or twice in our lives, but every day, and to relive these tensions at a deeper level.

Third is the principle of loving with all of one's strength. We love life and others by putting life to full use. But the labourers are few, though the harvest is plentiful. Why are the labourers few? Their feelings, mind and will have not been brought to bear on the tasks at hand. Perhaps we think we have few talents and we despise ourselves and bury those talents we do possess. We fail to recognise the principle of action that when we use such talents as we possess, they grow.

In his autobiography Charles Darwin tells of how he lost some of his talents because he did not let them grow but he gained others because he used them assiduously. He says he became more skilful in guessing the right explanations and in devising experimental tests due to mere practice. He had difficulty, he says, in expressing himself clearly and concisely. This difficulty caused him much loss of time. But it forced him to think long and intently over every sentence, which gave him a fine capacity for seeing errors of reasoning, both in his own writings and those of others. In the end Darwin produced his great work on *The Origin of Species,* now regarded by many as the last great scientific work to be totally accessible to the lay person.

On the other hand, Darwin tells of talents he lost because he did not use them. Up to the age of thirty he got great pleasure from reading the works of Milton, Byron, Wordsworth, Coleridge, Shelley and Shakespeare. As well, both music and art gave him great delight. But now in his later years he says that he cannot endure to read a line of poetry. Shakespeare he finds intolerably dull, even nauseating. Music generally sets his mind thinking too energetically on what he has been working on, instead of giving him pleasure. He refers to:

> this curious and lamentable loss of the higher aesthetic tastes ... my mind seems to have become a kind of machine for grinding general laws out of large collections of facts, but why this should have caused the atrophy of that part of the brain alone, on which the higher tastes depend, I cannot conceive ... if I had to live my life again, I would have made a rule to read some poetry and listen to some music at least once every week; for perhaps the parts of my brain now atrophied would thus have been kept active through use. The loss of these tastes is a loss of happiness, and may possibly be injurious to the intellect, and more probably to the moral character, by enfeebling the emotional part of our nature. (Darwin 1887, p. 31)

We do not know if Darwin's failure to use some of his talents caused an atrophy of part of his brain, as he suggests. What is sure is the principle in the parable of the talents: what we do not use we lose and what we use grows by that use. Any deep relation to a human being needs to grow, otherwise it is taken away from us. Perhaps that is why marriage counsellors tell their clients that marriage is hard and steady work.

The parable of the talents (Matthew 25:14–39) has a deeper religious meaning. The master who distributes the talents is God. The purpose of a person's life is to serve the claims of God upon that life which are the enrichment of that life and the life of God. Apart from such service, life is ultimately meaningless and worthless. The reward of such service is opportunity for further and larger service. The worst punishment for failure to serve is to be deprived of the opportunity to serve at all. Because we did not let our earlier encounters with ultimate concern grow, it slowly disappeared, leaving an empty space. We became unconcerned, cynical and indifferent.

The parable of the talents ends with an even more tragic state assigned to those who fail to use the talents they have. They find themselves in hell! What springs to mind here is the earlier story of the man possessed by a demon, namely that which divides and separates. It is not enough to get rid of the demon and clean the house out. For an empty house is just the sort of place that can be home, not to one but to many demons. The last state of that person is worse than the first. The darkness of evil lurks in all existence. It fills the empty spaces. Love becomes distorted so that even 'acts of self-sacrifice' can be nothing but vengeful attacks on others or a way of deluding others to do our will. When love is blocked it opens the floodgates to the demonic passion of fanaticism, self-worship and arrogance. What then can that person do? The void must be quickly filled with a positive motivation to serve higher values. We have to believe that the unaccepted in us is acceptable because love can enter into life, irrespective of one's deserts.

We participate in each other's having and we participate in each other's not having. When we become aware of this involvement of our lives in that of others, something happens. The fact that others have not changes the character of my having. It undercuts its security, it drives me to give, to share, to help. The fact that others fall into crime and misery changes the character of the richness of experience I may possess. The awareness that others who could have become fully developed human beings and never have, changes my consciousness. Their early death makes my life and my health a continuous risk. I could have been them. It is part of the Christian message that God participates totally in the suffering of the dying child, in the condemned criminal, in the disintegrating mind, in the starving ones and in those who reject ultimate concern. To the schizophrenic, God says, mad or sane you are one of my sheep. A youth with AIDS asked a priest, 'If I give up my homosexuality will God save me?' The priest replied, 'God loves you as you are'. There is no situation into which the divine does not reach. This is what the cross, the symbol of the most extreme of all human conditions, tells us. Williams (1968) puts it this way:

> There are two ways of existing, the inauthentic and the authentic. Inauthentic existence is to allow ourselves to be moulded by what others expect of us. We feel what the advertisers want us to feel. We tell ourselves that we really do feel what we are expected to feel. We allow our self-image to be constructed by others. Such existence is inauthentic precisely because it is not our existence. We become separated within ourselves and this can be the beginning of self-rejection and despair. The authentic way is to be ourselves, to affirm our humanity, not to lie to ourselves about how we do feel and think. (p. 149)

# COMPASSION FOR ANIMALS

There is perhaps no statement on ethics more anthropocentric than the famous dictum of the Sophist Protagoras about the middle of the fifth century who said 'Man is the measure of all things'. Nearer the mark is the view that everything has its own measure. We live in a world inhabited, not only by humans, but by countless other creatures who share the world with us. What should our relationship to these other creatures be?

According to an ancient story handed down by the Hebrews, a man by the name of Balaam arose early in the morning, saddled his ass, and went on his way. But the ass stopped short in his path and turned off the road. Balaam struck the ass to turn her back onto the road again. But the ass again refused to go on and pressed Balaam's foot against a wall. So he struck her again. Yet a third time the ass refused to move. Balaam struck her again with his staff. But then the ass spoke to Balaam. 'What have I done to you that you have struck me these three times?' And Balaam said to the ass, 'Because you have made sport of me. I wish I had a sword in my hand, for then I would kill you'. And the ass said to Balaam, 'Am I not your ass upon which you have ridden all your life long to this day? Was I ever accustomed to do so to you?' And Balaam replied, 'No'. According to the story the ass stopped because she saw an angel standing in the road with sword drawn. It was not until Balaam had replied to the ass that his eyes were opened and he too saw the angel with his own eyes. He was given a dressing down and told that if the ass had not turned back it would have been Balaam who would have been slain, since he was on a no-good errand on his ass (Numbers 22:21–33).

A critical element in this story is that the ass is presumed to have experiences not unlike its master. She says to Balaam, in effect, 'You have hurt me. How would you like this done to you?' That is the correct context within which to think about our attitude to animals. *Would you like this done to you?* Biology emphasises our likeness to our nearest relatives among the primates and our kinship with all animals. There is every reason to infer that they too have feelings of joy and sorrow.

We are told in Proverbs (12:10) that a righteous man has regard for the life of his beast. Why should we have regard for the life of the animals who share the world with us? There are two reasons.

First, there is an empirical reason for being concerned about animals and other living organisms. In the long run we look after ourselves by looking after them, because they look after us. They do this in two ways. They provide resources and services which we use, whether rightly or wrongly. As well they form part of the life-support systems of the Earth on which all life, as well as our own, depends (see Chapter 3). These are instrumental values of creatures to us and to other organisms.

Instrumental values may be quite subtle. Human beings find aesthetic values in nature. In North America there are some thirty million regular birdwatchers. Indeed, birdwatching is said to be the most rapidly growing sport on that continent. People often find the plants and animals in their natural settings intriguing. They feel impoverished when they disappear. What is behind the longing of city dwellers for parks, pets, birdwatching and nature films? In posing this question Paul Ehrlich (1984) quotes three biologists who wrote in the *Bulletin of Atomic Scientists,* 'We are ... as likely to be programmed to a natural habitat of clean air and varied green landscape as any other mammal. To be relaxed and healthy usually means simply allowing our bodies to react in the way for which one hundred million years of evolution has equipped us' (p. 93). This human bond to other species has been given the name 'biophilia' by E.O. Wilson in his book of that name (1984). The world for humans is richer for the presence of an environment formed by other species. Many religions have recognised this. The carefully tended gardens around Buddhist temples in Japan are tributes to this human need. The main argument of conservationists for the preservation of nature are instrumental arguments. They are good as far as they go. But they do not go far enough. It is to treat non-humans as means and not as ends in themselves. We see them as objects and not as subjects. This is to deny them intrinsic value to themselves and also to God.

Second, intrinsic value is contrasted with instrumental value. It resides in the experiencing of value. Only feeling gives intrinsic value to anything. (There are other views of intrinsic value which are discussed by Fox, 1990, and Mathews, 1991, which I pursue on pages 98 and 102.)

We recognise intrinsic value in humans because they are experiencing entities. We are not simply objects, but subjects. We are not just means but ends in ourselves. Precisely the same arguments apply to non-human animals. They, like us, have a tremendous urge to live. What motivates them other than their realisation that life is valuable for them? There is just as much reason for recognising experience and feelings of joy and suffering in chimpanzees and dogs and cats — and why not also fish and snakes and frogs — as there is to recognise experience in other human beings besides ourselves. Hence the relevance of the question Voltaire posed to the vivisector: 'You discover in it all the same organs of feeling that are in yourself. Answer me, machinist, has nature arranged all the means of feeling in this animal so that it may not feel?' (quoted in Regan & Singer 1976, p. 68).

Most people are willing to grant that their pets experience joy and suffering. Responsible owners of pets do their best to enhance their pets' quality of life. But why draw the line with those animals we know best? Bird lovers include birds as sentient creatures (*sentient* derived from the Latin *sentire*, meaning to feel). Wherever we find a nervous system we may suppose there is something akin to what we know as feeling. The intensity of feeling and therefore the degree of richness of experience of life may be correlated with the complexity of the nervous system. There is neurophysiological evidence to support pan-experientialism in animals. For example, the anti-anxiety agents benzodiazepines have similar effects on non-human animals as on humans. Furthermore, sensory receptors for these chemicals have been found in all vertebrates except cartilaginous fishes such as sharks. This would suggest that a wide range of vertebrates may experience some sort of suffering akin to anxiety in humans. Also a wide variety of vertebrates are known to have 'reward circuits' in their brains. These are pathways of nerves involved in feelings of pleasure when given a reward.

The importance of all this is that the recognition of intrinsic value in creatures besides ourselves makes an ethical claim upon us to recognise our obligation toward them. In this sense we can speak of animals having rights that we should recognise and work to uphold (see Birch &Cobb 1981, pp. 153-62). The argument that rationally grounds the rights of humans also grounds the rights of animals. 'Save the whales' is now a moral rather than an empirical imperative. There is no resource provided by whales that cannot now be provided from some other source. We can say that whales have 'moral considerability'. So do all animals. An ethic based on such considerations is a biocentric ethic as contrasted with an exclusively anthropocentric one.

'Our task', says Cobb (1973), 'is to decide which general statement, from among several alternatives, is correct' (p. 312). He proposes the following possibilities (Cobb 1973, p. 312): (a) so act as to maximise value for yourself in the present; (b) so act as to maximise value for yourself in the rest of your life; (c) so act as to maximise value for all humanity for the indefinite future; (d) so act as to maximise value in general.

The first is hardly to be viewed as an ethical principle at all. It says eat, drink and be merry, for tomorrow we die. The second principle is a maxim of selfish prudence. The third is the utilitarian principle of the greatest good for the greatest number of people. But why limit action to human value? Humans are not the only pebbles on the cosmic beach. Therefore only the fourth principle is sufficiently encompassing to be acceptable. If we adopt the principle of seeking to maximise all value (not just human value) for all time (not just our lifetime) we are extending the utilitarian principle as it is usually stated.

Peter Singer has consistently argued for a utilitarian ethic that includes all animals. The ethical task for Singer is to reduce unnecessary suffering in the world. He strongly advocates vegetarianism for all on the grounds that eating animals is one of the greater causes of animal suffering in the world today (Singer 1991). Laudable as is Singer's objective, it is not enough. Even if animals in factory-farms were anaesthetised, and thus could not suffer, there would still be reason to protest at depriving them of their natural fulfilments. The responsible owner of a cat or dog is not only unhappy when their pet suffers pain but is concerned to enhance its general enjoyment of life.

Richness of experience is more than the experience of reduced suffering. It has a positive component as well. We should seek to be neighbour to non-humans in a way analogous to the way we seek to be neighbour to our fellow humans; to succour those who fall by the wayside, to try to remove the causes of suffering and to provide a room in the inn.

The central principle of a biocentric ethic is that we deal with living organisms appropriately when we rightly balance their intrinsic value with their instrumental value. Elephants have a negative instrumental value to humans outside national parks in Rwanda where they damage crops and take up space that is needed for cultivation. The state of Rwanda decided that elephants were a pest. But they did not kill them. They airlifted them by helicopter to a neighbouring state that was prepared to put them in a national park.

The grey kangaroo and the red kangaroo are two species that are abundant across a wide area of arid and semi-arid Australia which coincides with areas where sheep are farmed. About 10 million kangaroos share this part of Australia with 120 million sheep. A century or more ago the kangaroos and Aborigines had the area to themselves. Today kangaroos have a negative instrumental value to the farmer. They are regarded as pests. They have a positive instrumental value to people who hunt them for their pelts and carcasses. They have a positive instrumental value to the native vegetation as compared with sheep. The hard hoofs of sheep cause great damage to the vegetation and its regeneration. The kangaroo has intrinsic value to itself for itself. Sheep have a positive instrumental value to the farmer who sells their wool and a negative instrumental value to the vegetation as already mentioned. They have intrinsic value to themselves. Here is a complex of ethical issues. How are they to be balanced out?

Conservationists tend to be on the side of the kangaroos. Farmers are on the side of the sheep. The solutions proposed depend upon the relative values attached to each of the items mentioned. But we have virtually no rules to go by in sorting out the issues. How, for example, is one to balance intrinsic value with instrumental value? The solutions proposed vary from getting rid of all the kangaroos and having sheep only to getting rid of all the sheep and having kangaroos only, by converting the whole area into a national park for kangaroos. In between there are several other options. In view of the rudimentary nature, as yet, of biocentric ethics in practice, perhaps the most we can do initially is to stress that in the equations kangaroos are given an intrinsic value above zero.

Ethical issues in the treatment of animals have to do with many areas including animal experimentation, farming of animals and their use for food, zoos, circuses, gladiatorial shows, hunting and genetic engineering and animals in the wild. A number of these are discussed in Birch, Eakin and McDaniel (1990).

The Judeo-Christian scriptures warrant any of three human attitudes towards animals. The dominant one in Western Christian thinking is the assumption of our absolute rule over nature. This is based on Genesis 1:26–28 and Genesis 9:2–3. It assumes that all things are created for human use and for no other purpose. A second related attitude derived from Genesis 2:15 is that humans are trustees responsible to God for the care of their fellow creatures. Adam is placed as a gardener in Eden to 'to dress and keep it'. A third attitude was adopted by St Francis: that we are fellow companions of other creatures, all of whom rejoice in the beneficence of God. It is based on Genesis 1 and several Psalms such as Psalm 96:11–13 where all the earth 'sings a new song'.

These three attitudes can be summarised in three words: exploitation, stewardship and compassion. In exploitation we ascribe only instrumental value to non-human creatures. While stewardship adds an element of responsibility, it still ascribes no more than instrumental value to non-human creatures. Only the third attitude ascribes intrinsic value to nature, yet it has been the least dominant attitude in Western Christianity. There are various reasons for this. One reason is the doctrine of *imago Dei* which can be traced back to Genesis 1:26. It is the idea that humans, and humans alone, are created in the image of God. The biblical story does indeed single out human beings as those for whom God is peculiarly concerned.

The Christian habit of accenting only this reflects, as Cobb (1991a) points out, 'more an arrogance that is not commended in the Bible than a balanced reading of the story' (p. 22). The particular significance of humans is placed within a context that has been largely lost in the course of Christian thought. The context focuses on the goodness of the whole creation. God pronounced that the whole lot was 'very good'. That can surely mean none other than to say that non-human creatures have their own intrinsic value to themselves and to God. In the Genesis account, God finds goodness in things before, and quite apart from, the creation of Adam. Later anthropocentric exegesis interprets this as meaning that it was good in the context of yet to be created humans. But this is not in the text. The assertion of the text, and many others, is that other creatures, quite independent of their usefulness to humans, have intrinsic value. As John Passmore has so persuasively argued, it was Greek influence, and later that of Descartes and Bacon, not the authors of Genesis, which propagated the view that humans can do as they please to nature with impunity (Passmore 1974).

The story of Noah and the flood emphasises the preservation of species. 'Keep them alive with you' (Genesis 5:19) is the injunction to Noah. Moreover, the covenant God establishes with Noah includes 'every living creature that is with you, the birds, the cattle and every beast of the earth with you'. And we are told that a rainbow in the sky is the symbol of that covenant.

In the teaching of Jesus, a human life is said to be 'of more value than many sparrows' (Matthew 10:31). That does not warrant the conclusion that a sparrow is worth nothing at all. Instead, it implies that if a human being is worth many sparrows, then a sparrow's worth is not zero. Luke adds, 'and not one of them is forgotten before God' (Luke 12:6). Here the implication is that, if God cares for the sparrow, how much more must God be concerned about a human life? We live in a community of subjects. They should therefore be treated, not merely as means, but as ends in themselves. The clear implication of the intrinsic value of all creatures is the expansion of compassion and justice to all of them.

Despite these affirmations about non-human life, Christians have tended to interpret their scriptures anthropocentrically denying value and rights to non-human life. A second reason for the reluctance of Christian churches to accept responsibility for the whole creation is their prior concern for the poor and oppressed. But why cannot they hold together a concern for humanity and for the creation? This does not require a lesser concern for the poor. Shakespeare said in *Julius Caesar*, Act 111, 'Not that I loved Caesar less, but that I loved Rome more'. It is not that we should love the poor less but that we should love the non-human creatures more than we do.

While Christian churches and theologians have been slow to move toward a concern for the whole creation and to recognise the intrinsic value of non-human creatures, there are exceptions. One in particular is the eco-justice movement in Protestant churches in the USA which brings together concern for injustice with an environmental concern. The World Council of Churches has had for a decade and a half a program on the just and sustainable society, but as yet little has trickled down to the churches. Amongst theologians who are stressing a biocentric ethic are John Cobb, Jurgen Moltmann, James Gustafson, Sallie McFague and Jay McDaniel. Their ideas, together with those of others, are brought together in the book *Liberating Life* by Birch, Eakin & McDaniel (1990).

A sympathetic identification with nature is powerfully expressed in Buddhism and in the art that it inspires. In Buddhism the idea of individual persons is an illusion. The self as an encapsulated ego is a myth. To think of self as cut off from the rest of nature by one's skin is to think anatomically and not realistically. Buddhist reality is profoundly ecological. All things, including humans, exist by their participation in other things. This has similarities with transpersonal ecology (otherwise known as deep ecology), as interpreted by Warwick Fox (1990). Further, the doctrine of reincarnation leads the Buddhist to ask is that bird my mother or my father? It is obvious that such questioning would lead to a caring for other creatures. The caring goes deep, for the Buddhist objective is to be freed from this endless round of reincarnation.

The key to this way of salvation from the suffering of all creatures in the world is the doctrine of non-attachment. It is the cessation of clinging. We humans suffer because we are attached to things, we desire to cling to them. When we cease to cling we become free. Christianity also urges against a craving for worldly security and reputation. But the Buddhist idea is more radical than anything in the West. Apparently the self has to completely disappear and then only is the state of Nirvana attained. Since the self exists only in its connection with the rest of creation, this seems to be the Buddhist way of saving the creation as a whole.

There is in Buddhism a very close relation between humans and nature and between the salvation of both. It is John Cobb's view that Christians can learn from Buddhists, particularly from their concept of ourselves existing by participation in other things and the concept of cessation of clinging. Cobb calls Christians to go beyond dialogue in their relations to other religions and to seek to learn from them. We may then discover new elements of value to us or rediscover old elements of Christian thought that have been lost in the convolutions of historical tradition (Cobb 1982).

There is an analogous attitude within Hinduism to the Buddhist attitude to nature. In India there are tribal religions as well that have a profound reverence for nature. The Bishnois are a tribal people in the desert areas of Rajasthan in North India. Their religion forbids the cutting down of trees and the killing of animals. They are vegetarians and practise non-violence. On 9 September in 1730 in a Bishnois village the Maharaja of Jodhpur had planned to construct a palace for himself. Limestone and red stone needed for the building was available in plenty, but the brick kilns needed firewood which was a scarce commodity in this desert area. The lieutenant in charge of the project decided to cut down the trees in the sacred grove in the village. The villagers pleaded with the workmen not to fell the trees. They turned a deaf ear and proceeded to cut down the trees, one by one. Enraged, the villagers rushed into the grove and everyone, women, men and children, went into the grove and hugged every tree. The axes fell, and along with the trees three hundred and fifty-three defenceless villagers who hugged the trees were hacked to death. The news of the massacre spread like wildfire and more Bishnois from nearby villages poured into the grove. Fear gripped the workmen and they took to their heels.

On hearing the news the maharaja rushed to the village, made peace with the villagers and enacted laws forbidding anyone from felling trees around the Bishnois settlement. To this day the Bishnois are known for their zeal in protecting trees and animals at the cost of their lives. The tradition of the Bishnois and their sacrifice finds its symbolic expression in the 'hug the tree' movement in the Garwhal region of the Himalayas. This is but one example of how religion in India is vitally linked with nature.

Australian Aborigines of the Aranda in Central Australia have major totemic sites for the red kangaroo that coincide with the best habitats of the species. When Aboriginal people approach kangaroo totemic sites, they do so in silence and reverence and with eyes closed. Hunting is forbidden near these sites and weapons have been laid down some way off. Thus red kangaroos are protected near their best habitat (Newsome 1980). In hunter-gatherer societies such as this, no strict hierarchy exists between human and non-human species.

# CONCERN FOR THE WORLD APART FROM ANIMALS

We are not the first generation to be concerned about the way humans manipulate the environment with little regard for the consequences. Job has this to say (Job 28:9–12):

> Man's hand assaults the flinty rock
> and lays bare the roots of the mountains.
> He tunnels through the rock;
> his eyes see all its treasures.
> He searches the sources of the rivers
> and brings hidden things to light.
> But where can wisdom be found?
> Where does understanding dwell?
> *Man does not comprehend its worth.*

There is a wisdom to be found that will help us to relate to the whole world, both living and non-living, in a creative and non-destructive way. It requires a new attitude to the whole of nature, some entities of which are subjects and others are objects only. Isaac the Syrian of the early Christian church described the compassionate heart as:

> A heart which is burning with love for the whole creation, for humans, for birds, for beasts, for demons, for all God's creatures. As he calls them to mind and contemplates them, his eyes fill with tears. From the great and powerful feeling and compassion that grips the heart, and from long endurance, his heart diminishes, and cannot bear to hear or to see any injury or any tiny sorrow in creation. This is why he constantly offers prayers with tears for dumb beasts, and for the enemies of truth, and for those who hurt him, that they may be protected and shown mercy; likewise he prays for the race of creeping things, through the great compassion which fills his heart, immeasurably, after the likeness of God. (Yannaras 1932)

The living world consists of a great array of living organisms other than animals which were discussed above, such as microorganisms, fungi, trees and other plants. Some of them, such as microorganisms, are individual entities which we can regard as subjects. Others, such as trees and other plants, come in between individual entities such as an animal and aggregates of individual entities. It is difficult to conceive of them in the same terms as we conceive of an animal because they have no centre for acting and feeling as one entity.

Whitehead thought of plants as democracies of individual entities, the cells. The point of this brief excursion is that for the most part we can best value plants in terms of their instrumental value to other organisms in the habitats where they live. They are also of great instrumental value to us in so far as they contribute to the life-support systems of the planet and to the resources we need for our lives.

The same sort of argument applies to valleys, mountains, landscapes, rocks and ecosystems. Their value is their instrumental value to the organisms that live there.

This scheme of environmental ethics contrasts with both transpersonal ecology (deep ecology) and Aldo Leopold's 'land ethic'. Transpersonal ecology is not interested in the distinction between intrinsic value and instrumental value. Rather, it gives value to anything that has an 'interest' which in this context means the maintenance of a particular state of organisation. The animal has an interest in remaining alive, therefore it is of value. The tree has an interest in maintaining itself as a tree. The ecosystem such as a lake has an interest in self-regulation so that it remains a lake with its array of organisms. All these and many other things are classed together (Fox 1990). But the meaning of the word 'interest' is very different in the case of an animal compared with an ecosystem.

While this approach has the advantage of covering just about everything in the environment, it is flawed by failing to make a distinction between those things that are sentient and those that are not. The distinction is important because of the special value of those things that feel. My relation to a rock is very different from my relation to my pet cat. Transpersonal ecology is not interested in differences in value. What it wants us to do is to relate ourselves to all that has value (in its meaning of value).

Aldo Leopold's land ethic has had a considerable vogue in environmental ethics. Leopold enlarged the boundaries of the 'moral' community to include soils, waters, plants and other things as well as animals. Leopold's (1949) land ethic states: 'A thing is right when it tends to preserve the characteristic diversity and stability of an ecosystem (or the biosphere). It is wrong when it tends otherwise' (p. 224–5). Leopold's proposition is a maxim rather than an argument and it lacks any analysis. However, it does point to the need to extend our concern beyond humans to nature in general.

I return to the beginning of this section and reiterate that the new consciousness of concern for humanity and nature is best served by making the distinction between intrinsic value as defined here and instrumental value, despite the criticisms of this approach from Fox (1990) and others.

# A GRADATION OF INTRINSIC VALUE AND A DIVERSITY OF RIGHTS

In the discussion thus far I have assumed that not all organisms have equal intrinsic value. A human being has more intrinsic value than a mosquito because a human being has a greater richness of experience than a mosquito. A human being has a richer psyche because of greater freedom, self-reflection, capacity to wonder, to attribute worth to (worship) that which is of ultimate concern, greater creativity and communication by language. As well, it is only humans who have a moral responsibility to other organisms. It is only we who can be held morally blameworthy when we fail to take responsibility.

McDaniel (1989, p. 80) recognises two components of richness of experience. One is *harmony,* which is a feeling of accord and affinity with ourselves, with other people, with other creatures and with God. A second component is *zest* or energetic vitality, enthusiasm and passion.

Within human beings there are differences in degree of richness of experience, that is of a sense of harmony and zest. There are moments when my richness of experience is greater than at other moments. Richness of experience may change as we go through lifestages from childhood to old age.

Until modern medical technology stepped in, most grossly deformed children died in infancy or early childhood. Now they can be kept alive for an indefinite period. One of the most critical ethical questions for modern medicine is, does the poor quality of life of some of these survivors warrant the use of medical technology to keep the sufferers alive?

There is, for example, a growing practice of making decisions as to whether to treat vigorously or not treat vigorously babies with spina bifida on the basis of some assessment of the quality of their life. Peter Singer cites the example of John Lorber, one of England's leading physicians in this area. Lorber examines the nature and location

of the opening in the spine, and takes account of other conditions. He has worked out a kind of scale which guides
him as to whether or not the baby should be treated vigorously. For some time he had simply treated all babies as
vigorously as possible, producing a large increase in the
survival of babies with spina bifida, but with a quality of
life so poor that he decided he was not doing the right
thing. Lorber's present practice of assessing the likely quality of life of the baby means that fewer babies survive but
those that do have a much better quality of life, on average,
than used to be the case when all survived. Those that are
not vigorously treated generally die within about nine
months at the most (Singer 1992, p. 42).

For some people, richness of experience virtually disappears if their life reaches a senile stage as in late
Alzheimer's disease and other forms of dementia characteristic of some elderly people. The proportion of such people is increasing in the community. The ethic of allowing,
even forcing, people to live as long as possible comes into
question as we increase our ability to keep alive people in
a chronically disabled, handicapped, and painful condition.
Bates and Lapsley (1982) quote a doctor who writes:

> As one who has had a long, full, rich life of practice, service
> and fulfilment, whose days are limited by a rapidly growing
> highly malignant sarcoma of the peritoneum, whose hours,
> days and nights are racked by intractable pain, discomfort,
> and insomnia, whose mind is often beclouded and disori-
> ented by soporific drugs, and whose body is assaulted by
> needles and tubes that can have little effect on the progno-
> sis, I urge medical, legal, religious, and social support for a
> program of voluntary euthanasia with dignity. Prolonging
> the life of such a patient is cruelty. (p. 17)

The controversial ethical issues involved in such
human tragedies are discussed with great sympathy by
Cobb (1991a, Ch. 2) on 'The right to die'. Cobb points out
that recourse to the phrases 'the sacredness of human life'
and 'the infinite value of human life' have obfuscated the
discussion. It leads to an absoluteness that fails to take account of the varying quality of life of human beings. Fur-

thermore, it tends to the absolutest conclusion that only human life has intrinsic value. Cobb also argues that Christians who have supported the absolutist ethic are not being faithful to their own scriptures. The doctrine of 'made in the image of God' is not equivalent to the sacralising of human life. In biblical terms only God is sacred. It is not human beings alone, but all creatures who are described in Genesis as 'very good'. Cobb writes: 'Athough Christians are committed to a teaching that affirms respect for every human being simply as human, they are not committed to the sacralising of human life or to the affirmation of the infinite value of each human life' (p. 53).

The point of this last discussion is to affirm that quality of life or richness of experience in human beings is not the same for everybody and at all times. There is a scale of richness of experience which we need to recognise when we try to work out a life ethic.

Compared with a human being a mosquito has a lesser degree of richness of experience in its life. It may have a harmony like that of a contented cow as it chews grass in the field. And it may have some zest akin perhaps to that of the happy carefree dog. But these are lesser levels of harmony and zest than can be experienced by humans. We appropriately criticise a fellow human whose contentedness is no more than that of a cow eating grass to its heart's content. A fish which gives up swimming is no longer a fish. A human being who does not anticipate and work for the possibility of a fuller life is either protracting infancy, anticipating senility or just vegetating. As John Stuart Mill advocated, it is better to be Socrates dissatisfied than a fool satisfied. Henry David Thoreau went to the woods to escape the life of 'quiet desperation' he saw as the plight of his New England neighbours. They seemed to him to have given up living.

We can in imagination appreciate the differences in richness of experience of different human lifestyles. But we do not know what it is like to be a mosquito. Even so, we might try to imagine what it might be like to be one, as we do with other people. It is no doubt a little easier to imagine life as a chimpanzee than a mosquito. I would say a chimpanzee has greater intrinsic value than a mosquito and in this way consider there to be a gradation of intrinsic value in nature. On the basis of that understanding it is possible to begin to establish some sort of bioethic in practice, as was suggested in the case of the kangaroos earlier. This seems to me intuitively obvious. But it is not so to others.

Some exponents of deep ecology (transpersonal ecology) promote a principle of 'biocentric egalitarianism'. This is variously interpreted. Devall and Sessions (1985) state that 'all organisms and entities in the ecosphere, as parts of the interrelated whole, are equal in intrinsic worth' (p. 67). On the other hand Fox (1990) interprets biocentric egalitarianism to convey no more than a non-anthropocentric attitude, not the equal intrinsic value of all organisms. Keller, King and Kraft (1991), from another standpoint, argue for 'the acceptance of equal intrinsic value of all of life against the concept of degrees of intrinsic value' (p. 29). Taylor (1986, pp. 129–56) has a long argument against a gradation of intrinsic value. The crux of his position is that such judgments are made from a human standpoint. If we knew the mosquito's standpoint, decisions about intrinsic value would be different. No doubt if the mosquito were able to tell us, that would be the case. But what capacity has the mosquito to judge moral and spiritual values? I suspect rather little, if any at all. Of course, human judgments are made from a human standpoint. Nevertheless they can be informed by sympathetic understanding of other creatures as exemplified by Jane Goodall's sympathetic empathy with chimpanzees in the wild.

It is hardly surprising that Arne Naess, the founder of deep ecology and originator of the phrase 'biocentric egalitarianism', said on a visit to Australia 'I'm not much interested in ethics or morals. I'm interested in how we experience the world' (Fox 1990, p. 219). That is to be consistent, for it is difficult indeed to imagine how a biocentric ethic could be built on the idea that all creatures have equal intrinsic worth. The successful campaign of the World Health Organisation to rid the world of the vaccinia virus that causes smallpox was no doubt undertaken in the belief that humans were more important than the vaccinia virus. But if someone authorised a campaign to eradicate elephants from the earth we would adopt a very different attitude to that adopted in the eradication of the vaccinia virus. Yet if viruses and elephants are of equal value, why the fuss?

A practical ethic recognises the intrinsic value of animal life as being greater than that of plant life and the value of human life as greater than that of other animal life. So our responsibility is differentiated. Grades of intrinsic value imply a diversity of rights of creatures. It is right and proper that we give major concern to the poor and oppressed and amongst other creatures to chimpanzees and whales and porpoises, whose feelings seem to be particularly rich.

The Genesis account of creation implies an ordering of value of animals above plants and humans above other animals. Otherwise the authors would hardly have considered it morally acceptable for animals to eat plants and humans to eat plants and animals. According to the account of God's covenant with Noah, recorded in Genesis 9:3: 'Everything that lives and moves will be food for you. Just as I gave you the green plants, I now give you everything'.

The view of a differentiated human responsibility to the creation provides a better direction for ethical reflection than any alternatives. McDaniel (1989, p. 73) makes the point that to adopt a biocentric ethic is to be informed by three 'moral virtues'.

The first moral virtue is *respect* (or reverence) for life. This is the recognition of subjects as ends in themselves. It involves a recognition of grades of intrinsic value amongst creatures.

The second moral virtue is *reduction of suffering.* It is to avoid inflicting pain and to refrain from taking life, except when the taking of life is to avoid unnecessary suffering.

The third moral virtue is to exercise *active goodwill.* In the case of non-human creatures, this is not simply to avoid harm. It is the active fostering of opportunities to enable the animal to realise its interests.

Transpersonal ecology stresses the existential, rather than the ethical, aspect. It is for the expansion of a sense of self beyond the personal ego to the rest of nature. It is a question of our relationship to all things, hence the term transpersonal. There is a sense in which most of us can identify with our pets.

Fox (1990) calls for a non-anthropocentric identification of that sort, but a much wider one. How then can we realise that? Fox refers to three sorts of identification: personal, ontological and cosmological. Personal identification refers to experiences of commonality with other entities with which we become personally involved. Ontological identification comes from a deep-seated realisation of what things are. This involves an almost mystical sense of belonging to a wider world. Cosmological identification comes from a realisation that we are, and all entities are, aspects of a single unfolding reality, as in the worldview of many indigenous peoples. We can be grateful to transpersonal ecology for its emphasis on the value of the non-human creation and to the extent to which it engenders in its followers, through its own approach, a concern to save the world. The ethical task is to develop the implications of a biocentric ethic and attempt to implement them in relation to issues such as methods of raising and transporting farm animals, hunting animals for food and fur and the use of animals in laboratories and for entertainment (see Birch, Eakin & McDaniel 1990).

Maybe in our own time there will be relatively few people who are willing to become ambassadors for a new consciousness toward their fellows and other species who share the Earth with us. That puts the onus even more squarely on those who are committed and on churches and other organisations whose commitments should lead them in this direction.

The great achievement of the Enlightenment was to build a theory of human rights that made possible enormous advances towards social justice. A great achievement of our time could be to extend the concepts of rights and justice to all living creatures, not only in theory, but in the practice of a non-anthropocentric, biocentric ethic. This leads us to a profound acceptance of human responsibility for the fate of the Earth which is the subject of Chapter 3.

# CONCLUSION

We live in a community of subjects which includes all creatures who share the Earth with us. The first ethical principle is that we should treat subjects as ends in themselves and not merely as means to our own ends. A subject has intrinsic value. Only feeling confers intrinsic value on anything. A subject has sentience. It is this which we respect.

The word that describes the attitude that respects human beings as subjects, and not just as objects, is love. Love has many meanings. It has meant different things for the Greeks, the Hebrews and Christians. The highest principle of love is to value one's neighbour as oneself and to love God in the process. The fullness of love involves all our emotions (with infinite passion), all our will and mind, and all our strength in active participation.

Compassion is to be extended to all creatures who share the Earth with us. Here again we should respect other creatures because of their intrinsic value and not simply because they are useful to us.

Not all organisms have the same intrinsic value. A human being is worth more than a sparrow, but a sparrow's worth is not zero. The gradation of intrinsic value implies a diversity of rights. The greater the richness of experience of the subject the greater the rights. We may not be able to measure richness of experience, but we know its two components, harmony and zest.

Within a human life richness of experience, and therefore its intrinsic value, changes from conception to death. This raises complex ethical issues towards the beginning of life and towards its end, which eventually must be faced.

We also have a responsibility to the non-animate world. Its value is its instrumental value to us and to other living creatures. It is important to make the distinction between those things which have intrinsic value, such as living organisms and those which do not have intrinsic value, such as rocks and valleys. Otherwise our environmental ethic becomes confused and impractical. We need to develop a non-anthropocentric, biocentric ethic, which extends the concept of rights and justice to all living creatures.

# CHAPTER 3
# THE WORLD IS TO BE SAVED

Unless we change we'll get where we're going.
*Anon.*

Because of the strain on resources it creates, materialism simply cannot survive the transition to a sustainable world.
*Lester R. Brown (1990, p. 190)*

**R**eligious pietism promotes a fallacious image of the relationship of the individual to the world. A jigsaw puzzle has a picture of a human being on one side. On the other side is a picture of the world. The puzzle is solved by putting the image of the human being together and, lo and behold, when you turn the picture over you find the world is put together also! The moral this purports to convey is that to save the world you save the individuals in it.

The image is fallacious because you can no more build a new world by planning to make everybody good than you can build a perfect house by collecting a pile of perfect bricks. You may have the best bricks in the world, but they won't make a house unless a number of other conditions are fulfilled. The foundations have to be secured on rock or some other suitable base. There has to be a plan of the building. Engineers need to see that stresses are evenly placed so that the walls do not collapse. Beams have to be provided to support the roof, windows and doors. Good cement has to be prepared to stick the bricks together according to the plan.

The bricks are the people in society. The plans of the building, and everything else besides the bricks, are the structure of society — its economics, its politics, its industries, educational institutions and so on. There are good structures of society and bad ones. Even the best people will not attain the best potential of their lives when they live in a very imperfect society; for example a society that does little about the way industry pollutes the air and water and whose transport system is inadequate.

Bricks that look perfect on the surface have defects within. None of us is unambiguously good. Even what appears to be the most altruistic act of a good person is alloyed with some degree of self-interest. Even amongst the most enlightened people, the will to live truly is transmuted into 'the will to power'. The same person who is devoted to the common good may have desires and ambitions, hopes and fears, which set them at variance with their neighbour and the world.

The will to power inevitably justifies itself in terms of the morally more acceptable will to realise our true nature. This means that corruption of universal ideals is a much more persistent factor in human affairs than any simple moralistic creed is inclined to admit. Reinhold Niebuhr (1944) held that 'evil is done, not so much by evil men, but by good men who do not know themselves'. He refers to the 'incorruptible' Robespierre, the Jacobins of the French Revolution, Cromwell and Lenin (p. 93).

The distinction between justice and injustice, virtue and evil is not always sharp. In the parable of the 'last judgment', with the separation of the sheep and the goats, Jesus says that the righteous, who stood on the right hand of the judge, protested they were not really virtuous, while the unrighteous, who were on the left side of the judge, were equally unconscious of their deeds of omission and commission. The story prompted Blaise Pascal to say, 'The world is divided between saints who know themselves to be sinners and sinners who imagine themselves to be saints'.

No society of perfect individuals has ever existed, so far as we know. Between the years 1500 and 1700, during the great period of the Renaissance, the Reformation and the Scientific Revolution, over 50,000 people were executed as witches A similar number were tried on the charge of witchcraft and none was acquitted (Bartlett 1991). In our own time millions of innocent people died in gas chambers because they were of Jewish descent. The children of light and the children of darkness operate in the same society. Rules have to be made to help keep behaviour within some sort of acceptable boundary. The problems of the world do indeed have to do with the problems of imperfect, ignorant and wicked people. They are always with us.

Just as you need a lot of information to build a house, so you need a lot of information to build a society that functions properly. Things don't simply fall into place without a deliberate plan. The world's problems have to do with management on a huge scale. To begin to see what the problems are we need a lot of information on ecology, science, technology, economics and politics. If we do not have this information, people with the best will and determination in the world will not be able to rectify mistakes. We need wisdom as well as righteousness.

In contemplating the revolution needed to move toward an ecologically sustainable society, global modellers speak of information as the key to the transformation. It will be information that flows in new ways and to new recipients. Secondly they recognise that major obstacles to any such transformation are the structures of society that resist changes in flows of information such, for example, as government bureaucracies (Meadows, Meadows & Randers 1992, p. 223).

We cannot save the Earth without a change in consciousness. Yet advances are made without converting the whole of the world's people to some chosen norm. The fact of the matter is that the creative advance of any generation rests upon the responsiveness of a small margin of human consciousness. The pitifully few are called to be a leaven in the loaf.

The world is sick. Its healthy relationships have been broken and corrupted. It is groaning in agony to be saved. As theologian Joseph Sittler once said, the whole of Lake Michigan groans in agony waiting to be set free from its bondage of decay. For biblical and early Christianity salvation was a cosmic matter (see Chapter 6). Contemporary Christianity, with its emphasis on individual salvation, has lost sight of that.

# THE FATE OF THE EARTH

Our generation has a litany of crimes against the world to its record. Topsoil disappears at the rate of one football field each second. Arable land is covered with concrete at the rate of three football fields each minute. Forests disappear at the rate of four football fields each minute. Species disappear at the rate of one hundred a day. Add to this the greenhouse effect and the hole in the ozone layer and it becomes obvious that our present treatment of the Earth cannot continue for ever.

The world is dying. We are on an unsustainable course. A flashing red light tells us that the scale and nature of human activity has grown out of proportion relative to the capacity of the Earth to sustain it. Half the world is poor, deprived, sick and dying of malnutrition and other preventable diseases. Our relations with other living creatures is that of a despot. We are fast destroying the environment on which all life depends.

From an emphasis on concern for individuals in the first two chapters we turn to the fate of the Earth as a whole. It is not only individuals who have to be saved, but the Earth as well. This will involve a change in tune in the sense that we will be dealing with more factual information in this chapter than in the previous ones. It is therefore a little technical, but not heavily so. I have attempted to put the issues in such a way that anyone who cares to read may understand.

A new consciousness leads to a new way of living. A new way of living leads to the concept of a new sort of society whose values are different from those of the consumer society designed around the factory.

The objective of that new society can be stated quite simply. Its end result is the opposite of sick people in a dying world. The new objective is for healthy (whole) people in a healthy environment, with healthy relations to that environment. The emphasis is on the quality of life or richness of experience of the inhabitants of the Earth, for this and future generations.

How then can we hope to move from the unhealthy world to a healthy one? We need first to recognise the tremendous tension between technological progress and the health of the environment, including all organisms in it. Secondly, we need to recognise the tremendous tension between social injustice in the world today and social justice. So destructive are these two tensions that many now wonder if what we call progress will eventually lead to our demise and that of the planet. The modern worldview and

its conception of the future has dead-ended in wars, genocide, the exploitation of Third World countries, increasing
pollution, the disappearance of resources and the spectre
of omnicide. The sort of progress we have become accustomed to is the forerunner to the clanging of a funeral bell.

Modernity has failed to point a way beyond injustice
and destruction of the environment. Indeed it seems impossible to attain a vision of a viable future within the para-
meters of the modern mind. As Erwin Laszlo (1990) has
commented: 'Coping with mankind's current predicament
calls for inner changes, for a human and humanistic revolution mobilising new values and aspirations, backed by
new levels of personal commitment and political will' (p.
12). He went on to say that humanity's true limits relate to
inner values and attitudes, not to outward resources. Yet so
often technocrats and others believe that technology will
provide the answers.

The economist Julian Simon says 'the ultimate resource is human brains', implying that human technical ingenuity and prowess will solve all problems of resources
and pollution. Such technological optimists seem to think
that the economy is a flow in a single direction between
two infinities; infinite resources on one side, and an infinite hole on the other side into which we can dump all our
wastes.

The life of nature has been maintained over aeons because life is based not on linear systems of resource use
and production of pollution but on recycling of resources
and the breaking down of pollutants. These are circular
flows, not linear ones. The answer is not to be found in
some technological fix. Indeed the technological perspective is largely the cause of the problem, not the cure.

There is an alternative vision. It requires different social goals from those the modern worldview demands. Its
emphasis is on care and justice for all inhabitants of the
Earth. The emphasis of the modern worldview has been on
continuous and increasing production and consumption.
The same aim is paramount in programs of development
in the developing world. Yet there is increasing evidence

that if the whole world were to become rich like the rich world, in the way the rich world became rich, the effect would be lethal for the planet.

The fundamental causes of environmental decline and poverty are inextricably linked. As Jose Lutzenberger, when Minister of Environment in Brazil, said: 'If development is to be the continuation of the present mode and we must help the developing countries to reach our level of affluence, while the developed countries must still continue developing to even higher levels of consumption, then what we are doing is suicidal' (1991, p. 11).

The resolution of the problem of injustice requires a fundamental re-examination of the relationship between the one billion people, or 20 per cent of the world's population, who live in industrialised countries and who use 80 per cent of the world's resources and the majority of the world's population in poor countries who have to make do with 20 per cent of the world's resources.

How can we look after the needs of the poor and deprived and at the same time preserve the ecological integrity of the Earth? How can we achieve both a healthy people and a healthy environment? There is an increasing awareness that only a reversal in the direction of production and consumption and the economics and politics that determine that direction will save the future. The changed objective is for an ecologically sustainable society that is also a just society. As the quotation at the head of this chapter indicates, because of the strain on resources it creates, materialism simply cannot survive the transition to a sustainable world. In other words, materialism is deadended, not just because it fails to lead to a decent quality of life for all but because it destroys the Earth on which all life depends.

I was present at the birth of the phrase the 'ecologically sustainable society' at a conference in Bucharest organised by the World Council of Churches in 1974 on Science and Technology and Human Development (World Council of Churches 1974). Jorgen Randers (an author of *The Limits to Growth*) and I were conducting a workshop at the conference on that subject. The objective of the workshop was to demonstrate that the Earth was finite in its resources, including its capacity to absorb the pollutants of industry. That being the case, we have to learn to live within limits if we and the Earth are to remain a home for people and its other inhabitants, many of whom are essential for our own lives. The workshop was getting nowhere with delegates from the developing world. Indeed, they were hostile to the idea. They argued that the rich countries had had their share of growth. Now it is their turn. Don't talk to us about limits to growth, they said, when what we need is to grow as the rich countries have grown.

At a coffee break Jorgen Randers said to me: 'We have to find some phrase other than limits to growth that is positive in its impact. Limits has a negative connotation. Other suggestions such as a stationary state, an equilibrium society and a steady state society are too static'. Then he suggested: 'What about the ecologically sustainable society?' meaning the society that could persist indefinitely into the future because it sustained the ecological base on which society is utterly dependent.

We went back to our workshop with this suggestion. Of course, they said, we want an ecologically sustainable society. How can we move toward that end? So we discussed requirements. All came to realise that the concept was radical indeed. Yet it was accepted by the plenary meeting of the conference. The phrase then spread around the world like wildfire. Its time had come. It became incorporated into the seven-year program of the World Council of Churches called the Just, Participatory and Sustainable Society.

The Worldwatch Institute in Washington was established in the 1970s to alert the world to increasing threats to human well-being and to the environment. Its director, Lester Brown, caught on to the concept of the ecologically sustainable society and wrote *Building a Sustainable Society* (1981) in which he diagnosed the present state of global unsustainability and suggested paths to sustainability. In 1984 the Worldwatch Institute produced its first *State of the World* report with the subtitle 'A Worldwatch Institute Report on Progress Toward a Sustainable Society'. Each year since then it has produced a *State of the World* report. In addition, it publishes Worldwatch papers and books on critical environmental issues.

The 1987 report of the World Commission on Environment and Development (WCED 1987), also known as the Brundtland report, dropped the phrase 'sustainable society' for 'sustainable development'. As Herman Daly has argued, this is a contradiction in terms. For many it has come to mean sustainable economic growth. But sustainable growth is an impossibility. Sustainable development makes sense for the economy only if it is understood as development without growth, that is a qualitative improvement of the economic base without an ever-increasing throughput of energy and other resources (Daly 1991). Further landmarks in the recent history of moves toward an ecologically sustainable society are documented by Young (1991).

Concern for ecological sustainability and human justice for the poor and oppressed are, as I have already indicated, closely linked. Yet justice and ecological sustainability are sometimes seen as alternative human concerns. Those who emphasise human justice sometimes see ecological sustainability as the cry of those who benefit from the present structures of society and who want to distance themselves from the abuses of power within it. Yet justice and sustainability must ultimately be linked into a single vision of life-giving hope for a richness of experience of life for all people in the world (see Birch, Eakin & McDaniel 1990, pp. 2–4).

# ECOLOGICALLY UNSUSTAINABLE SOCIETIES

There have been plenty of societies in history that proved to be ecologically unsustainable and perished. They give us clues to the sort of society that renders itself extinct. The decline of the Mayan civilisation in the lowlands of

Gautemala was almost certainly due to severe soil erosion
and deforestation. For seventeen centuries the population
doubled every 400 years, reaching a density by AD 900 comparable with that of agriculturally intensive societies of
today. At this peak the civilisation suddenly collapsed.
Within decades the population fell to less than one-tenth of
what it had been. They didn't know how to look after the
Earth.

The collapse of the civilisation that occupied the Euphrates River basin of the Great Fertile Crescent was also
probably a consequence of humanly induced environmental deterioration. Extensive irrigation without adequate
drainage led to salination and waterlogging of the soil. The
ancient Chinese also recorded deforestation, followed by
floods and droughts and other environmental changes in
densely populated areas. They are still problems in China
today.

It has been said that forests precede humanity, deserts
follow. It is no accident that the fallen columns and broken
statues of past civilisations often lie on devastated ground.
The ruined cities of North Africa, once flowing with olive
oil and honey, lie stagnant in the sand. The bare hills of At-
tica were mourned by Plato as 'skeletons' of what they had
been. The Maowu desert of Inner Mongolia overtook the
lush pasture land alive with deer that Genghis Khan chose
for his tomb. All testify that when land is exploited by
greedy and ignorant people, everything collapses.

No civilisation, however, has set about devouring its
own future with such enthusiasm as our own. The difference between us and the Mayans is that we know we are
on an unsustainable path. We may not have seen the collapse of whole civilisations in our day in this way, but we
have seen the disappearance of large areas of formerly
habitable earth. Environmental degradation, resulting in
desertification of once productive sub-Saharan Africa, has
created millions of 'environmental refugees' in the decade
of the 1980s alone. The United Nations Environmental Program warns that one-third of the entire land surface of the
world is now in danger. In the world as a whole, topsoil dis-

appears each year in an amount equivalent to the total top-soil of the entire vast wheat belt of Australia which covers 113,000 square kilometres.

# CHANGING DIRECTION TOWARD AN ECOLOGICALLY SUSTAINABLE SOCIETY

The first major effort to understand the needed changes was made by the Club of Rome in its report Limits to Growth (Meadows, et al. 1972). The report was based on a computer model for long-term global trends. It was not a prediction but a projection as to what would happen if the direction were not changed. It drew three main conclusions.

The first was that if existing trends in population, food production, industrialisation, resource use and population were to continue unchanged, limits to growth would be reached within a century. Everything that has happened since then, including the greenhouse effect and the hole in the ozone layer, makes it clear that a future world could not sustain a population of even the present number at a higher level of industrial development without reaching environmental limits. This conclusion has become known as 'the impossibility theorem' — the high rate of consumption and pollution of the rich would be impossible for the whole of the world. That immediately poses a problem of justice.

The second conclusion of the Club of Rome was that it is possible to alter present trends and establish conditions of economic and ecological stability that could be sustained indefinitely. We have a choice. We can either stabilise the number of people, and levels of use of resources and levels of pollution, or we carry on at the risk of overtaxing the environment.

The third conclusion was that if the people of the world wish to achieve an ecologically sustainable future, rather than pursuing the delusion that present levels of growth can be continued indefinitely, the chances of achieving that goal will be improved by starting sooner rather than later. The longer we delay, the more serious are the problems.

After surveying the debate, triggered twenty years ago by *Limits to Growth,* Eduard Pestel (1989), who was much involved in global modelling, said that the most important result was that it drove into the heads of more and more people the urgent need for long-term, anticipatory thinking and learning at a time of precipitous change and 'opened our hearts and minds to the urgent necessity of a radical change of values, at present so dominated by material aspirations' (p. 160).

There have been twenty or so projects of global modelling since the report of the Club of Rome on limits to growth in 1972. Ninety per cent of the conclusions are held in common, though the public perception from the media is that there is little agreement. Even the somewhat crude projections of the 1972 report have been borne out, to a greater or lesser degree (Van Ettinger 1989). Twenty years after the publication of *Limits to Growth* three of the original four authors (Meadows, Meadows & Randers 1992) reworked all the models with the latest data, taking into account technological advances in efficiency in the use of resources and pollution control. After computing some dozen or more variants of the model they concluded that the present way of doing things in the world is unsustainable. Although in some twenty years some options for sustainability had narrowed, others had opened up as a result of technological advances. The three conclusions of the *Limits to Growth* referred to above are still valid and only needed strengthening (p. xv). We turn our attention now to the critical issues of a world at risk and how we might change direction.

# THE LIFE-SUPPORT SYSTEMS OF NATURE

For millions of years the thin envelope of life around the earth, which we call the biosphere, has sustained the resources necessary for life in a wonderful and complex way. We know only in part the complex relations involved. Some of them can be understood by considering what are called 'the life-support systems of nature' or 'the cycles of nature'.

A life-support system is analogous to the engineering system that maintains the environment inside the space vehicle to support the life of the cosmonauts. They need an atmosphere to breathe, which means that the appropriate amount of oxygen and other gases have to be kept at a constant level, despite being constantly used up while carbon dioxide is constantly exhaled from breathing. They have other requirements that have to be provided, such as appropriate temperature, air pressure and food. Wastes have to be disposed of as they are produced.

It is appropriate to regard the Earth as a spaceship where the environment is maintained in such a way as to sustain life. Much of the science of ecology is concerned with finding out how this is done. Until recently we did not have to bother about this problem. The Earth looked after itself. But as the number of humans increased and their activities became industrialised we found we were disturbing the ecology of the Earth in disastrous ways. The life-support systems were being threatened.

Just six elements — carbon, oxygen, hydrogen, nitrogen, phosphorus and sulphur — constitute 95 per cent of the mass of all living matter on Earth. Since the supply of these elements is fixed, so life depends upon their efficient cycling through the rocks, soil, water, the atmosphere and living organisms. These cycles are part of the life-support systems of nature. In recent years human activity has significantly disrupted these cycles, particularly those of carbon and nitrogen.

Atmospheric oxygen is essential for the life of all organisms except for a few microorganisms that are called
anaerobic organisms. Yet the cycle of oxygen is one we do
not need to worry about. The oxygen in the atmosphere
comes from plants. It is carried by winds across the Earth.
Every breath we take includes about a billion oxygen molecules that have been, at one time or another, in the lungs
of every one of the fifty billion humans who have ever
lived. The simple act of breathing links us in this curiously
intimate way with every historical figure and the most ob-
scure of our forebears in every epoch. Before there were
plants there was probably no oxygen, or very little of it, in
the atmosphere. That was about two billion years ago. The
oxygen that is today removed by living organisms, including humans, is replenished by plants. The proportion of
oxygen amongst the various gases of the atmosphere remains remarkably constant at 21 per cent. That means that
oxygen is produced at about the same rate as it is removed
from the atmosphere and all is well. Not so with the carbon
cycle.

Carbon dioxide is taken from the atmosphere by
plants to make their plant tissues. It is returned to the atmosphere in the decomposition of plants and animals. A
second smaller source is volcanoes. Some of the carbon
dioxide in the atmosphere is absorbed by water in oceans
and rivers. Not all animals and plants that die are decomposed. Some of them have in the past been converted into
coal and oil. When we burn these fossil fuels, or for that
matter the trees in forests, carbon dioxide is returned to
the atmosphere.

The balance between what is taken out of the atmosphere and what is returned has been remarkably constant
over the ages until recently. Since 1958, when measure-
ments were first made, the carbon dioxide content of the
atmosphere has been increasing. The combustion of fossil
fuel now augments the atmospheric carbon dioxide by 0.7
per cent each year. A doubling of the concentration of carbon dioxide over its pre-industrial level may occur by the
middle of the next century.

The increase in carbon dioxide that is now occurring is expected to have dramatic consequences for life on Earth as a result of the so-called greenhouse effect which will make the Earth hotter. Should the carbon dioxide level reach double pre-industrial levels, the Earth's average temperature may rise between 1.5° and 4.5°C. Such a change could have profound effects on the climate of the world. (For details of the greenhouse effect see Henderson-Sellers and Blong 1989.)

That presents huge ecological problems for the future. Immediate and enormous steps need to be taken to reduce the amount of carbon dioxide we produce. Increases in the price of fossil fuels since 1979 have meant that less has been burned and less carbon dioxide has been added to the atmosphere. But the decrease is well below that required. Increasing the efficiency of production and use of energy would also be beneficial. The destruction of forests causes an increase in carbon dioxide in the atmosphere due to the decomposition and burning of the forest and the fact that there are fewer trees to remove carbon dioxide from the air.

A 1980 study by the World Bank of West African countries showed that the demand for wood for fuel exceeded the estimated sustainable yields of forests in eleven of the thirteen countries surveyed. In both Mauretania and the mountainous areas of Rwanda, the demand for firewood is ten times the sustainable yield of remaining forests. In Kenya the ratio is five to one; in Ethopia Tanzania and Nigeria, demand is 2.5 times the sustainable yield and in the Sudan it is roughly double (Brown 1986, pp. 23–4).

Besides the burning of wood for fuel, forest fires add carbon dioxide to the atmosphere. Fires in the Amazon region are entirely man-made. For trees to burn in the wet tropical forest they have to be felled and left for two or three months to dry. They are then ignited by people who want to clear the land. Satellite surveys have shown that at the peak of the burning season, from the end of August to early September, there are as many as 8000 separate fires in a single day throughout the Amazon region.

Deforestation is second only to fossil fuels as a human source of atmospheric carbon dioxide, almost all of which comes from the tropics and overwhelmingly from Brazil.

Reforestation is one way of helping to restore the balance in the carbon cycle. This is being done on a large scale in South Korea and China, where enormous areas of land have been denuded of forests. But the largest contribution to restoring the carbon balance will be a reduction in world population since every person who lives makes a contribution to the carbon dioxide in the atmosphere by his or her use of the products of industry or by burning wood for fuel. On the average each person contributes two metric tonnes of carbon dioxide a year of which one tonne gets into the upper atmosphere to contribute to the greenhouse effect. Small increases per person can have an enormous effect when multiplied by huge numbers of people, as for example in China and India, if, as they propose, they increase their use of fossil fuels in the near future. There is probably no practical way to achieve the necessary reduction in greenhouse emissions (chiefly carbon dioxiode and methane) without controlling the numbers of people in the world (Ehrlich & Ehrlich 1990).

Why does the carbon dioxide increase as a result of the burning of fossil fuels, yet the oxygen which is used up in this burning is not significantly depleted? The reason is that the proportion of oxygen in the atmosphere (21 per cent) is very much larger that the proportion of carbon dioxide (about 0.03 per cent). The combustion of fossil fuel that increases carbon dioxide by 0.7 per cent per year decreases the oxygen by only 0.001 per cent per year (Ehrlich, Ehrlich & Holdren 1977, p. 79).

Nitrogen constitutes 78.1 per cent of the atmosphere. It is also circulated in cycles in nature. It is removed by microorganisms which pass it on to plants. Some plants, notably the blue-green algae, 'fix' it directly from the atmosphere. Animals get their nitrogen for making proteins from plants. When animals and plants die and decompose, nitrogen is released back to the atmosphere. Some bacteria also return nitrogen directly to the atmosphere. Industry, which includes factories that make nitrogenous fertilisers, take nitrogen from the atmosphere and return it to the environment as nitrates. Automobiles, power plants and industries release oxides of nitrogen into the atmosphere. In the United States the quantity of nitrogen oxides released in this way doubled between 1950 and 1973 (Postel 1987).

This is a matter of much concern as nitrogen oxides are greenhouse gases. They now constitute quite a substantial proportion of the nitrogen that goes from the atmosphere into the soils and waters of the Earth. We do not know yet what the consequences of this are. Nor are we sure what the consequences would be if chemicals we add to the environment killed off important microorganisms in the nitrogen cycle.

All other elements that are necessary for life have their own cycles in nature such as, for example, the phosphorus cycle and the sulphur cycle. We intervene in the phosphorus cycle by mining rock phosphate and adding it to soil as fertiliser. Phosphorus is also used in detergents, animal feed supplements, pesticides and many industrial activities. The most critical aspect of our use of phosphorus is that the supplies will run out in the long run since we are doubling the amount used every fifteen years. In the meantime, excess phosphates from fertilisers get leached into rivers and lakes. There they provide nutrients for algae which increase in numbers in what is called algal blooms. The change is quite undesirable, as the bloom depletes oxygen in the waters, killing off fish and other animals. There are other cycles in nature, such as the water cycle, in which water circulates between the atmosphere and the soil and oceans and rivers. When forests are destroyed more water runs into rivers and is wasted and there may be less rain when trees are removed.

The greatest human influence on the sulphur cycle comes from industrial activity, mainly the combustion of coal and oil and the smelting of sulphur-bearing metallic ores. These sources produce sulphur dioxide. When sulphur dioxide gets into the atmosphere and meets nitrogen oxides, compounds are formed that lead to acid in the rain.

This has disastrous effects on forests, killing trees in many parts of the world. Likewise, nitrogen oxides and sulphur dioxide react with other chemicals in the atmosphere under the influence of intense sunshine to form ozone, which is a main ingredient of photochemical smog. Besides being hazardous to human health, smog is also disastrous to trees. Huge areas of pine forests in the mountains east of Los Angeles are dead because of smog from Los Angeles.

A cycle which incorporates all these cycles is the food cycle. In any community of plants and animals, the basis of the life of the community life is the plants that convert the energy from the sun, the minerals from the soil and the carbon dioxide from the air into plant tissue. Plants are called producers. Animals feed on plants and are known as herbivores or consumers. Then there are predatory animals that feed on the herbivores, known as carnivores. There may even be, in some cases, predators of predators. So in the plains of Africa the grass in the plain is eaten by herbivores, such as antelopes, and the antelopes are eaten by lions. But in this case the lions have no major predators other than parasites and other organisms that cause diseases. All organisms eventually die and are decomposed by microorganisms which return the mineral nutrients, that are broken down from their tissues, back to the soil or river or sea.

Ecologists investigate the amount of energy that exists at each food level, say over a hundred hectares. A rough rule of thumb is that if green plants capture 10 000 units of energy from the sun, only about 1000 units will be transformed into herbivores and only 100 units will have got into the carnivores. There is a loss of 90 per cent of energy at each step of the food cycle.

There are two important implications of this information. The first is that ten times as many people can survive eating a corn crop as can survive eating cattle that have been fed on the corn. It is not surprising therefore that peasant farmers in Brazil, for example, have a staple diet of rice and beans. Far more people could be fed with the food the world produces if less of it were not converted into pigs, sheep and cattle. It seems certain that in the future more and more people will, by necessity, become vegetarian if they are to survive. Human beings use up some 40 per cent of the planet's potential plant production either by direct consumption or in indirect ways by suppression of plant production. This not only represents a huge impact on what is available for humans, but it is a disproportionate share for only one of 30 million or so species of animals! (Ehrlich & Ehrlich 1990, p. 36) As the Ehrlichs point out, this is a frightening figure for ecologists, yet they are even more concerned about the rising fraction of potential plant production that is being lost for all life, including ourselves. Humans have become a globally destructive force increasingly threatening the habitability of the Earth.

A second consequence of the features of the food cycle is that when toxins such as the insecticide DDT get absorbed by plants, they get concentrated at each successive food level. This is because the herbivores have to eat ten kilos of plants to produce one kilo of flesh. And the predators of herbivores have to eat ten kilos of herbivore to produce one kilo of their flesh. A consequence is that many predators throughout the world, particularly predatory birds, get lethal concentrations of toxins in their flesh. The problem applies particularly to the pesticides that are called persistent. They do not readily break down and so persist for long periods unchanged. Persistent pesticides, such as DDT, are a serious cause of disruption of food cycles even in places far removed from where they were used. Even the flesh of Antarctic penguins contains DDT.

All cycles of nature constitute part of what is called the life-support systems of nature. They have been going on for millions of years without much perturbation until humans began to alter the cycle through industrial activity. Nature's global society has been kept sustainable because the molecules keep moving through these cycles. Indeed, in some cases the molecules are kept moving with very little loss along the way. A mature rainforest community of plants and animals recycles virtually all materials used as resources. Apart from water and carbon dioxide the only resource that comes in from outside is the energy of the sun.

Trees and other plants absorb minerals from the soil with great efficiency. They turn them into their own tissues. Their leaves and branches fall to the ground or are eaten by animals whose waste products fall to the ground as well. They die and decompose and produce waste products, all of which go back to the forest floor to be decomposed by bacteria and fungi that turn them into minerals. They are taken up by plants again with such efficiency that the water that runs from the undisturbed Amazonian rainforest is virtually the same as distilled water in composition. The rivers are called black rivers because the water looks black compared to the white rivers which drain eroded areas and are full of clay and other minerals. A paradox of the great Amazon rainforests is that most of them live on impoverished soils, yet they sustain more than 500 tonnes of living material on each hectare. Moreover, the underlying rock is so far beneath the surface that roots of trees do not reach it to get minerals from there. For a long time this remained a mystery until the amazingly efficient recycling of minerals in the forest was discovered.

## THE CARRYING CAPACITY OF THE EARTH

A sheep farmer speaks of the carrying capacity of the farm for sheep in terms of one sheep per hectare or perhaps ten sheep per hectare. This means that the farm can sustain indefinitely up to that many sheep. Exceed the carrying capacity and the quality of the farm deteriorates. Every natural habitat has a carrying capacity for the sorts of organisms that live there, whether they be kangaroos or buffaloes or lions.

In many years the numbers of inhabitants of a region may be well below the carrying capacity because of unfavourable weather or other unfavourable features of the environment of the organism in the habitat. In a series of good years the carrying capacity may increase and so too may the number of inhabitants. When lean years return there may be too many inhabitants to be catered for. The carrying capacity will have been exceeded. The consequence is that many of the inhabitants will go short of resources and may perish.

Exactly the same situation applies to the human inhabitants of the Earth, which has a limited carrying capacity for people. Exceed that capacity and two things happen. The quality of the environment (its carrying capacity) deteriorates and human life is threatened along with that of other species.

A leading economist pronounced 'no-one has ever died of overpopulation'. The American journal *Science* responded with an editorial under that title. Just at that time disastrous floods in the delta region of the river Ganges in Bangladesh had taken the lives of thousands of villagers and left countless others homeless. What killed these hapless people? The editorial argued quite correctly that they died from overpopulation. The region is prone to periodic disastrous flooding. It should not be populated at all. But it is populated because suitable living places in Bangladesh are already overcrowded. So the poor are forced to live in perilous places. After each flood they go back again because they are denied safe space elsewhere.

The semi-arid belt of the sub-Saharan countries known as the Sahel, which stretches from Mauretania in the west to Ethiopia in the east, was until recently inhabited largely by nomadic peoples. Their agricultural practices, learned over the centuries, conserved the soil and its vegetation for continued pastoral use. This changed in the 1950s and 1960s. Nomads were restricted in their movements and so stayed in areas longer than before. New strains of cotton and peanuts were introduced to increase production from the land. Attempts were made to boost this intensive agriculture by sinking wells to irrigate the land. Overgrazing followed. In drought years disaster ensued. The desert extended further south. The region was now overpopulated. Production of food per person declined. Its carrying capacity was lower than it had ever been. People either died on their farms or they joined huge numbers of 'environmental refugees' seeking some haven to the south.

This sort of thing is happening in many parts of the world to a lesser or greater extent. In the last decade productive land the size of the twelve countries of the European Community has been turned to dust because carrying capacity has been exceeded. One-third of the entire land surface of the Earth is now in danger. The foundations of civilisation in these places crumble to sand.

A sustainable society will respect the limits of the Earth, which is finite, in three respects. It has a limited capacity to produce renewable resources such as timber, food and water. It has a limited amount of non-renewable resources such as fossil fuels and minerals. And it has a limited capacity for providing its free services for the maintenance of the life-support systems such as its pollution absorption capacity. In the 1980s emphasis moved from limits of resources to the sort of limits which are referred to as 'sink limits'. This was because of the serious threat of greenhouse gases and secondly of chlorofluorocarbons to the ozone layer.

These three limits determine the carrying capacity of the Earth for people. Growth in population coupled with industrial growth reduces the carrying capacity of the Earth because of the environmental impact on both renewable and non-renewable resources. Figure 3.1 illustrates this relationship. Suppose that today the human demand on the environment is equivalent to only 5 per cent of the carrying capacity of the Earth, which is surely an underestimate. Take into account the overall environmental impact, which, according to the American study SCEP (1970, p. 22) is growing at 5 per cent per year. The environmental demand would reach the saturation point in fifty-five years, even if the carrying capacity itself were not reduced by growth.

A group of twelve economists, including two Nobel prize economists, have issued a critically important working paper published by the World Bank in which they argue

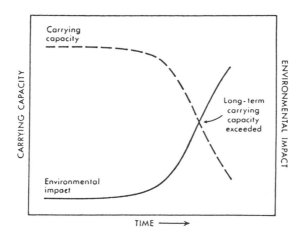

**Figure 3.1**
*The generalised relationship between economic growth and the carrying capacity of the Earth. Growth results in environmental deterioration with consequent reduction in carrying capacity.*

that the world's economy cannot grow any more (Goodland, Daly & El Serafy 1991). If the poor are to be fed and housed and if the global environment is to be saved, the rich must reduce their economic growth. Ecologists have been saying this for years. But this has been anathema for traditional economists. They have held to the opposite view that the rich must grow richer if the poor are to become richer. Furthermore, economists have shown singularly little concern for the deterioration of the global environment. So why should economists, some of whom are on the staff of the World Bank, have produced such a document? After all, the bank is well known for financing huge projects in developing countries that have made it an accomplice in the pollution of rivers, the burning of forests, and the strip mining of huge areas. The basic argument of the twelve economists is that there are limits to growth which have now been reached on a global scale. They do not speak for the World Bank but to the World Bank. The critical issues they identify are as follows:

◆ The 'sink restraints' are now considered to be more stringent than the resource constraints. They have become of immediate critical concern for the global community. Global emissions of carbon dioxide from the use of fossil fuels are estimated to have to be reduced by 75 to 80 per cent. This means that the use of fossil fuels must be reduced by 75 per cent. That means the global industrial economy has to be reduced drastically.

◆ The WCED (1987) or Brundtland report argued that the poor world could only be helped if there were an increase in the world economy from between five to ten times the present world economy. This is not possible. All the resources used by humans, with the exception of minerals and petroleum, are dependent upon four ecological systems: grasslands, croplands, forests and fisheries.

Of all the plant material produced on land each year in the world, humans use 40 per cent. This has been a frightening figure for ecologists. It has now frightened the twelve economists who wrote the World Bank working paper. The critical question they ask is, how big can the human economy be relative to the total ecosystem? Two more doublings sees us using over 100 per cent of the world's ecological production. So the World Bank paper argues that an increase of five to ten in the world economy recommended by the Brundtland report is ecologically impossible.

◆ The World Bank paper finds that the Brundtland growth plan fails also because it argues for a lifting of the bottom (the poor) rather than a lowering of the top (the rich). The poor cannot be lifted unless the top falls. The rich must live more simply that the poor may simply live. Yet that seems unacceptable to the rich world which considers that its difficulties, such as inflation and unemployment, can only be remedied by increasing economic growth.

It is neither helpful nor ethical to expect poor countries to cut their development, though we can expect them to drastically curb their population growth. Therefore the rich world, which is responsible for most of today's envi-

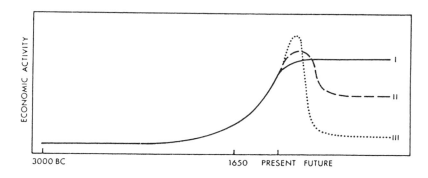

**Figure 3.2**
*The generalised ecological history of the world, past, present and future.*
*I,    direct transition to high-level sustainable state;*
*II,    belated transition to somewhat lower-level sustainable state;*
*III,   reversion to a pre-modern agrarian way of life.*

ronmental damage, must take the lead. More growth for the poor must be balanced by less growth for the rich. The cake of limited size must be carved up more equably. 'We cannot grow our way into sustainability' (Goodland, Daly & El Serafy 1991, p. 6). This conclusion was also reached by economists and ecologists in an international symposium on ecological economics edited by Robert Costanza (1991).

Both the World Bank paper and the 1991 report from the Club of Rome (King & Schneider 1991) argue that only a change in heart will suffice. Economic rationalism must fly out the window and let ecological realism in. The consequences would be a drop in living standards of the rich, though an increase in their quality of life. For example, to stop the contribution of the Netherlands to acidification of forests and lakes the Dutch would have to reduce the number of motor car kilometres and farm livestock by half. The quality of the rain would be better but the standard of living would be lower. The spectre is also raised of increased unemployment when economic growth does not continue. However, this need not be the case, as is well argued by Renner (1991).

# WHEN TO GROW AND WHEN NOT TO GROW

The momentum of growth and the lag in social response to deterioration of the environment predispose the world system to overshoot the level that would be sustainable over a long period. The inevitable consequence of overshoot is collapse. The options open to us are shown in Figure 3.2. Throughout most of human history, growth in economic activity has been very low. It began to skyrocket after the Industrial Revolution and has continued ever since. Policy option I in Figure 3.2 is an early and direct transition to a sustainable steady state. Policy option 1 illustrates the literal meaning of 'to grow', namely to spring up and develop to maturity. Daly (1977 p. 99; 1991) makes the important point that the notion of growth therefore includes some concept of maturity beyond which physical accumulation gives way to physical maintenance. Growth gives way to a steady state.

Not everything is held constant in the sustainable society. As a sustainable society develops, its development is not dependent upon quantitative growth. The sustainable society differs from a growth economy in aiming at maturity. It will have plenty of scope for development in services, such as education, health and welfare, to improve the quality of life. But the services will be such as to reduce the use of energy by, for example, promoting rail over motor cars. A significant degree of decoupling economic growth from energy throughput appears substantially achievable. Witness the 81 per cent increase in Japan's output since 1973 using the same amount of energy.

There is a phase of growth in the life of every organism. This is followed by a phase of no further growth in size in which resources are used for the maintenance of maturity. This rule of healthy life is disobeyed in cancerous growth in which parts of the body continue to grow at the expense of the organism as a whole. The organism dies from overgrowth.

The global human society has been in a growth phase

all its history. Parts of the body, namely the rich countries, have cancerous growth which is destructive to other parts of the body, namely the poor countries, which still need to grow in material goods. This concept was developed in the second report of the Club of Rome (Mesarovic & Pestel 1974), where it is called organic growth as distinct from undifferentiated growth. In undifferentiated growth every nation has as its goal continued growth. A global society that promoted organic growth would eventually conform to option I in Figure 3.2. Indeed it would be similar in its pattern of growth to that of the trees in the Amazonian rainforest. There is a growth phase as young trees approach maturity. That is followed by a no-growth phase in a mature forest where the total mass of living trees remains much the same from year to year at about 500 tonnes per hectare.

The Earth can be visualised as a hollow vessel with an inlet and an outlet. For population the inlet is the birthrate. The outlet is the deathrate. For a steady state no-growth population, birthrate and deathrate are equal. Both should be as low as possible, perhaps around 11 per 1000 people per year.

Similarly with goods or material wealth in the world. The inlet is the production of goods. The outlet is the consumption of goods. One should equal the other, giving a constant level of material wealth. The level at which people and wealth stabilise is largely an ecological problem. Traditional economic systems that encourage growth, aim to maximise throughput of goods and materials, whereas in a sustainable state it would be minimised.

If option I in Figure 3.2 is not taken, overshoot will occasion a fall to a lower sustainable state (option II). This is the situation in a run-down farm. It is probably characteristic of many countries in Africa, where population still grows at a phenomenal rate. The production of necessities, such as food, does not keep pace with a growing population. Other renewable resources, especially timber, become unrenewable and agricultural land deteriorates. Option III indicates what happens when the overshoot is even greater than in option II. This could be tantamount to a pre-agrarian way of life as seems to be happening in much of sub-Saharan Africa. It is the way of those societies like the Mayans whose civilisation became extinct.

Meadows, Meadows & Randers (1992) give detailed examples of the three options in Figure 3.1. On their global model they set finite limits to non-renewable resources of 200 years at 1990 rates of extraction. They also set optimistic limits to land that could be brought under cultivation for agriculture and to the pollution absorption capacity of the environment (p. 117). In models represented by options II and III in Figure 3.2, overshooting the sustainable capacity of the Earth occurs soon after the year 2000 with collapse occurring 100 years or so before resources run out. One lesson from these models is that in a finite world, if you remove or raise one limit and go on growing, you encounter another limit. The next limit occurs surprisingly soon. You do not of course have to resort to a computer model to come to the conclusion that in a finite world exponential economic growth in use of resources will sooner or later lead to collapse. What the models tell is something about the rate of collapse and what has to be done if we are to move to option I in Figure 3.2.

# THE ENVIRONMENTAL IMPACT OF HUMANS

The impact of human beings on the environment probably began 10,000 years ago with the Agricultural Revolution in Asia Minor and the Near East. At a slightly later time similar events happened in Central America and perhaps in the Andes, in South-East Asia and in China. From these centres the new way of life, the farm, spread to the rest of the world. As a consequence the human population grew from about 15 million before the invention of agriculture to 200–300 million, some 2000 years ago. During this period forests were cut down for fuel, land was cleared for farming and irrigation began to be practised by diverting water from rivers to the fields. As farmers produced more food than they needed for their own families, cities came into existence. The first were in Mesopotamia. The growth of cities in the Middle East culminated about 2500 BC in the Sumerian city-state of the Tigris and Euphrates valleys in what is now Iraq. The Sumerian culture was based on irrigation. One cause of its demise is believed to have been the result of centuries of irrigation with consequent salination of the soil and silting of rivers.

The next major impact of human beings on the environment came with the Industrial Revolution from about 1850. There had been increased growth in human populations in the 200 years prior to the Industrial Revolution which was due to improved hygiene. But the Industrial Revolution had an even greater impact. Deathrates fell in countries undergoing industrialisation and the numbers of people in the world began to soar. It was not until the nineteenth century that birthrates began to fall in industrialised countries.

The Industrial Revolution improved the standard of living for many people. However, it began a new phase of environmental deterioration with its great and increasing dependence upon non-renewable resources such as fossil fuels and on renewable resources such as timber and food. The question of what are the limits to the use of these resources became a critical one, while the whole time industry increased pollution of the atmosphere, the soils and waters of the Earth. Add to that the threat of war and the possibility of a nuclear holocaust and it is now widely recognised that humans have in their hands the instruments of vast environmental devastation.

Instead of thinking of the environmental impact of humans as a long list of components, we get a much better picture from a synoptic approach. By far the best proposal is that of Ehrlich, Ehrlich and Holdren (1977, p. 720), which was used as a basis for their later book on the population explosion (Ehrlich & Ehrlich 1990, p. 58). The impact of humans on the environment is viewed as a product of three components: (a) the number of people; (b) a measure of the average person's consumption of resources (which is also an index of affluence); and (c) an index of environmental disruptiveness of the technologies that provide the goods consumed. This component can also be viewed as the environmental impact per quantity of consumption. Hence:

$$\text{Impact} = \text{Population} \times \text{Affluence} \times \text{Technology}$$
$$\text{OR}$$
$$I = PAT$$

Each of these components can in principle be measured. For example, resource use could be measured in terms of units of energy used per person. The T factor is difficult to measure, but one index might be the grams of sulphur produced per kilowatt hour of electricity generated.

The equation shows that the components are multiplicative in their effect. Suppose that population, consumption of some commodity and the impact of technology per unit of consumption each increase threefold. The total impact increases twenty-seven fold. The contributing components in this example are equally important, but each seems quite small compared to the total. Slowly growing components, when they multiply each other, lead to rapidly growing totals. Suppose we want to know whether population growth or rising consumption per person played the greater role in the growth of total energy consumption in the United States between 1880 and 1966. In this period, total energy consumption increased about twelvefold while the population increased fourfold. It may therefore appear that consumption per person was a more important component than population growth. It was not. Consumption per person increased threefold, versus a fourfold increase in the population. The twelvefold increase in the consumption of energy arose as the product, not the sum, of the fourfold increase in population and the threefold increase in consumption (Ehrlich, Ehrlich & Holdren 1977, p. 720).

In poor countries P is large and A and T are small. In rich countries A and T are large and P is much smaller. The total impact can be reduced by reducing one or more of these components. In the case of the attack on the ozone layer by chlorofluorocarbons, the impact could be made negligible by operating on the T factor alone, that is, ban the offending chemical. This might result in a slight decrease in affluence if substitutes were more expensive. On the other hand, the injection of the major greenhouse gases, carbon dioxide and methane, into the atmosphere is not so easily corrected.

The concentration of greenhouse gases in the atmosphere is tightly tied to the size of the population. Small per person changes can have enormous effects when multiplied by enormous numbers of people. There is probably no practical way to achieve the necessary reduction in greenhouse emissions without population control. Ehrlich and Ehrlich (1990, p. 113) have calculated an interesting example that illustrates this principle.

Suppose the United States decided to cut its contribution to the carbon dioxide emissions by terminating all burning of coal. Suppose also that China's population remained at 1.1 billion. Suppose secondly that China scaled back its development plans so that it only doubled its per person consumption of coal. That would raise China's per person use of energy to some 14 per cent of that in the United States. This modest advance in development by China would more than offset the reduction of carbon dioxide emissions achieved by the total abandonment of coal by the United States.

The P component of the PAT equation is critical here. Poor nations are at present relatively minor contributors to the carbon dioxide generated by burning fossil fuels. Industrialised countries with less than a quarter of the world's population are responsible for about three-quarters of the carbon dioxide released by burning fossil fuels. But that could change when China and India, for example, increase their energy consumption by using their vast reserves of coal.

When people in Brazil are persuaded by their government to migrate away from the coastal areas to take up farming on a plot of land in Amazonia, they cause great destruction. The land is made available by cutting down forests and burning the trees, and in many cases only one crop is obtained from the land. The native Indians have been doing this for centuries without any serious environmental impact. In each case the plot of forest destroyed is quite small per person. But whereas the P component is small in the case of the Indians, it is very large in the case of overpopulated modern Brazil. The situation is more complex than that because of the combination of technology with so-called development in modern Brazil. Small farms in remote areas need access. That is provided by building huge highways through the forests. Also dams are built across streams for the farmers. The total effect is an enormous increase in soil erosion and in some cases the farms have to be abandoned, so great is the environmental impact.

The amount of firewood burnt by a single family in India or in Africa is quite small. But the P factor in both continents is so high that forests are disappearing at an unsustainable rate in many places. One could also argue that the number of cardboard boxes each one of us uses in a year is not that great, but multiply it by the population of Japan and its customers and we get huge areas of forest in Australia destroyed by the woodchip industry. Attempts are made by the forest industry to regenerate the forests, which is to their advantage. However it is not the original forest, with its varied inhabitants, that is regrown any more than is the case in Brazil when rainforests are cut down.

Piping sewage into the sea is a cheap way of disposing of it. It worked in the case of the city of Sydney without causing much environmental impact while the city had relatively few inhabitants. But when the population of Sydney grew to 3 million the P factor results in an unacceptable environmental impact as Sydneysiders have discovered to their chagrin. Acceptable alternatives are very expensive.

# **P**OPULATION

Population is the P factor in the PAT equation of environmental impact. Some people claim there is no global problem of overpopulation, only problems of mal-distribution and faulty technology. Examples above illustrate how population in our day is always a component of total environmental impact. The people who think that population is no longer important point to the growth of population in Western countries which has slowed, with zero growth in thirteen countries. And some Asian countries have managed to reduce their rate of population growth in recent years.

What these people fail to appreciate is that, despite this, the annual global increment in population in 1990 was an all-time high of 95 more million people added to the planet. The fact remains that the 1990s will see the greatest increase in human numbers of any decade in history. If by some way humanity were able to reduce the environmental impact of all its technologies by 10 per cent and there were no increase in per-person affluence, world population growth would return the collective impact of humans to the previous level in about five years. Just about every step forward in the A and T items of the PAT equation is negated by population growth.

The world's population in 1992 was estimated to be 5.4 billion. It is likely to reach 6.3 billion by the end of this century, nearly the equivalent of adding another China. More than 90 per cent of the increase is in poor countries. That poses an immense problem for the rich and poor world alike.

The average birthrate in industrial countries of 1.9 children per woman is below replacement level. But this does not mean the industrial countries have not a population problem. Indeed it can be argued that because of their high level of A and T in the PAT equation, their impact is enormous. Perhaps the impact of one person in the rich world is 50 times that of one person in the poor world.

The 1980s saw a slight slackening in the rate of growth of the population of the world. But this does not herald an end of the population explosion as some have proclaimed. The slowdown has been from a peak annual rate of 2.1 per cent a year in the early 1960s to 1.7 per cent in 1992. To put this in perspective, the doubling time of the human population has been extended from thirty-three years to thirty-seven years from 1950 to 1987. The largest jump in population numbers from 5 to 10 billion in well under a century is still ahead of us.

If every woman in the world from this year on had no more than 2.2 surviving children, which is replacement reproduction, the world's population would still grow. This is because population growth has a momentum such that it takes about two generations before curbs applied now have a major effect. Some European countries have expressed a concern at having reached replacement reproduction. Yet these same countries cannot avoid a 20 to 30 per cent increase in numbers, even if they maintain replacement reproduction. To achieve zero population growth in the twentieth century, even in the most developed countries, birthrates would have to fall well below replacement levels. This seems unlikely. If replacement reproduction for the developed world as a whole had begun in the 1980s, the population would still increase by more than a quarter, adding some 300 million more people.

The reason for the population momentum is the relative youth of the growing population. It is young people who have most of the children and deaths occur primarily in old people. So if a population has a high proportion of young people, one has to wait for the average age of the population to increase before deathrates catch up with birthrates. That takes about sixty years in poor countries. That is why it is so important to reduce birthrates as soon as possible, if population growth is to be curbed. A reduction in the birthrate now takes many years to be reflected in numbers of people. The concept of population momentum may be a difficult ecological concept to grasp, but it is not difficult to understand its effects. That understanding should be far more widespread than it is. Precisely because population growth is slow to be controlled, it is the issue to tackle now.

A sustainable world will have a population whose size is commensurate with global carrying capacity and which size does not increase unless carrying capacity increases. Zero population growth is an inevitable component of the sustainable world of the future. If we do not deliberately work for a smooth transition we shall arrive there through overshoot and catastrophe. What then is a sustainable population for the world as a whole? The question is a complex one with no simple answer. Any assessment must depend upon an estimate of the environmental impact of people on the planet. Indeed some would argue that the world is already overpopulated, that the existing 5.4 billion people are causing such a deterioration of the environment that this cannot continue for much longer without a severe lowering of the carrying capacity of the Earth. For example, Ehrlich and Ehrlich (1990) conclude that 'Earth cannot long sustain even [the 1990s figure of] 5.3 billion people with foreseeable technologies and patterns of human behaviour' (p. 238).

If civilisation is to survive, population shrinkage below today's size eventually will be necessary. Population shrinkage would require below replacement reproduction to be continued beyond the point when zero population growth had been reached. Below replacement reproduction would not be unprecedented. It prevails in most European countries and the United States today. China has for some time recognised that all its problems become more intractable the larger the population grows. The gradual reduction of the population after reaching zero population growth has been an explicit part of China's policy. Thirteen countries have already achieved zero population growth, so it is not utopian to expect others to follow.

When is an area overpopulated? That depends upon the carrying capacity of the area. When a population cannot be maintained without rapidly depleting its nonrenewable resources and without degrading the capacity of the environment to support the population, that area is overpopulated. Africa is overpopulated because its soils and forests are rapidly being depleted such that its carrying capacity for humans in the future will be lower than now. The United States is overpopulated because it is depleting its soils and water resources and contributing greatly to the greenhouse effect. Europe, Japan, and the republics that used to constitute the Soviet Union are overpopulated along with other rich nations because of their massive contributions to the greenhouse effect and the deterioration of their soils and waters.

The population of the People's Republic of China increased 64 per cent between 1949 and 1973. In the late 1970s China's leaders were jolted to discover that there were almost 100 million more people living in China than had been thought. The Deng regime claimed that high rates of population growth, lower deathrates caused by modern medicine and a generally poor and badly educated population had forced China to spend too much on housing, food and employment, and fresh water was becoming a limiting factor. The resources drained for these purposes could be used, so Chinese officials argued, to develop and 'modernise' the country. The government concluded that China could support no more than 800 million people on a sustainable basis at a decent standard of living. China's population had already reached one billion when this conclusion was reached.

To arrest population growth the Chinese regime created a program of mass 'ideological education' and a system of economic incentives to encourage people to have fewer children. According to the guidelines set by the Ministry of Health, the number of children should not exceed one per family. The government set targets for each province. China became the only nation in the world with the goal of not only ending population growth as soon as possible but also of reducing its population by a substantial amount. The number of children per family is approaching replacement level, slightly more than two per family. But the momentum of population growth caused by high birthrates in the recent past means that the population will grow to a peak of about 1.2 billion or more before it begins to fall.

Australia, by contrast with China, is now almost unique among developed Western nations in its continued commitment to population expansion. The only evidence of a sustainable population in Australia is the population of Aborigines which lived there for 40,000 years or more. Modern Australia is overpopulated because of the very high levels of A and T in the PAT equation. People who do not know better think of Australia as a vast land waiting to be populated far and wide. But Australia is mostly desert. It is the second driest continent on earth after Antarctica.

Water the Australian desert as the Israelis do, people say. But there is a catch. There is no permanent water in the vast deserts other than artesian water in some places which is fast being used up. So-called development of vast inland spaces is limited by shortage of water. That is the main limiting resource of Australia. It is the reason why most Australians live on the coastal fringe. The population of Australia in 1992 was 17.8 million. If we make the reasonable assumption that one Australian has an environmental impact equivalent to fifty Indonesians, the total environmental impact of Australians would be the equivalent of about one billion Indonesians!

The present rate of growth of the population in Australia of 1.6 per cent a year is the highest in the industrial world. Almost half of this comes from immigration. At this rate the population will reach 30 million by about the year 2025. And what is good about that? It is quite ridiculous to have an immigration policy without a population policy.

As Paul Ehrlich commented on a visit to Australia, it is like someone asking you to design an aircraft that can take sixty people on board a minute but not telling you how many passengers it is going to fly with! Senator John Coulter has made a humane proposal that he believes could lead to a sustainable population in Australia. Immigration would be restricted to compassionate grounds; migrants for family reunion would amount to 50,000 per year, refugees would amount to 20,000 per year. Migration on the grounds of skill, wealth and business ability would be eliminated for the most part. Such a program would result in the Australian population gradually rising to a plateau of about 25 million people by the year 2055 (Coulter 1990). It is a better prospect than continuation of the trend of the 1980s, but many of us think it is still too large and will extend the damage to the already beleagured Australian environment, unless Australians discover ways of making a smaller environmental impact than they do at present.

Overpopulation is deleterious because:

◆ It reduces the chance that all the people in the world can be adequately fed and housed. The increase in production of food in the world following the Green Revolution has hardly done more than maintain the existing amount of food per person because of the continuous increment in population.

◆ It increases the pressure on most other resources, many of which are difficult to obtain.

◆ It accentuates the problem of urbanisation. Increased population means more people migrate to already overcrowded cities such as Sao Paulo and Calcutta.

◆ It negates the effect of economic development in poor countries and in rich countries it exaggerates still further their disproportionate consumption of the world's resources and their disproportionate contribution to pollution. Overpopulation in rich countries presents a much greater present threat to the health of the environment than does population growth in poor nations. The rich countries, for example, are responsible for about 80 per cent of the carbon dioxide injected into the atmosphere.

◆ Population growth in the poor countries increases the misery of the poor. According to a study of the Food and Agriculture Organisation about 700 million people in the rural areas of the poor countries live in absolute poverty and their lot is not improving

The 1990s is now regarded as the crucial decade which will determine population trends over the next century. Immediate action is required on a number of fronts. Rapid population growth is now widely recognised as a hindrance to development in poor countries. In the 1970s there was a widespread notion that 'development is the best contraceptive'. We now know that this is an oversimplification. Such traditional measures of development as GNP per person and urbanisation seem to have little or no relation to birthrates and therefore population growth.

On the other hand, certain kinds of development do foster reduction in the birthrate. 'Social development', as opposed to 'economic development', seems to hold the key here. For example, adequate nutrition is important. Some people in the past have argued that the more food the poor get the larger will be their families, that extra food is converted into extra babies. The fact is that denying people food will not lower birthrates. It increases deathrates. Providing food in conjunction with the improvement of socio-econiomic conditions actually lowers birthrate. Improved socio-economic conditions can be identified that motivate parents to have fewer children. These conditions are: parental confidence about the future, improved status of women, literacy, better health and sanitation. These are measures that lead to a sense of greater security and they are effective in lowering birthrates. Increased economic equality greatly accelerates the process as does land reform. It is not necessary that per capita GNP be very high, certainly not as high as that of the rich countries during their gradual demographic transition from high rates of growth to low rates. In other words, lower birthrates in poor countries can be achieved long before the conditions exist that were present in the rich countries in the late nineteenth and early twentieth centuries. At the same time vigorous family planning programs become effective when they were ineffective before these measures were taken (Murdoch 1980; Murdoch & Oaten 1975).

At least thirteen developing countries have managed to reduce their birthrates by an average of more than one birth per 1000 population per year for periods of five to sixteen years. Such a reduction would bring birthrates in poor countries to replacement level by the turn of the century. These countries include Taiwan, Singapore, Costa Rica, South Korea, Egypt, Chile, China, Cuba and Sri Lanka. To stop population growth worldwide, birth control would have to grow from about 50 per cent to 70 per cent of couples, and average family size would have to decrease from about four to two children.

# AFFLUENCE: THE CONSUMPTION OF RESOURCES

This is the A factor in the PAT equation. It is little appreciated that four biological systems — croplands, forests, grasslands, and fisheries — provide all the resources for the economy, except for fossil fuels, minerals and water. Croplands supply food, fibre, vegetable oils and such like. Grasslands provide meat, milk, leather and wool. Forests provide timber, lumber and paper.

The share of the land planted to crops increased from the time agriculture began until 1981. Since then the area of newly reclaimed land has been offset by that lost to degradation and conversion to non-farm uses. The area of grassland has shrunk since the mid-seventies, as overgrazing converts it into desert. Forests have shrunk for centuries, but the losses accelerated in the middle of this century and even more from 1980 onwards. The combined area of the three biologically productive systems on land is shrinking, while what is left, wasteland and areas covered with human settlements, are expanding (Brown 1990).

Until world population reached 3 billion in 1960 the yields of the four biological systems expanded more rapidly than population. By the time the population had reached 4 billion in 1976 the per capita production of forest wood and the products of grasslands (beef, mutton and wool) began to decline and have continued that trend ever since. The fish catch had been growing at a record rate for two decades prior to 1970, but since 1970 the fish catch per person fell by 13 per cent or over 1 per cent per year. Then fifteen years later, in the mid-1980s there was an upturn of nearly 20 per cent due largely to the recovery of the depleted Peruvian anchoveta fishery.

Turning from per capita production to total global production, the total production from forests has been declining for several years (Brown 1991). There was an enormous growth in grain production from croplands between 1950 and 1984. But it fell sharply in 1987 and that fall has continued. Per capita grain production varied from region to region. During the 1950s and 1960s, grain production exceeded population growth on every continent, diets improved almost everywhere. Beginning in the 1970s, however, production in Africa fell behind population growth, leading to a fall in production per person of about one-tenth. During the 1980s, Africa has been joined by Latin America, whose decline dates from 1982, the year the debt crisis began. In Japan, Taiwan and South Korea, production of grain has been declining since 1967. Japan's historically excellent, productive and sustainable agricultural system is being destroyed by deforestation, development, pollution and pesticides. From a peak production in 1967, Japan's production of grain fell by more than one-quarter in ten years (Brown 1988).

It is clear that human demand is now outstripping the sustainable yield of the natural biological systems that support the world economy. The concept of sustainable yield is an ecological one. It refers to the yield that can be sustained without causing a deterioration of the carrying capacity of the resource and therefore a reduction in the yield. For example, intensive studies of the effect of fish catch on yield led to the conclusion in the early 1970s that the total global fish yield could be sustained at around 100 million tonnes a year. That projection may have to be reduced (Brown 1981, p. 53).

The principal determinant of whether food production per person is rising or falling in various regions is the rate of population growth. Where population growth is slowest, Western Europe, per capita food production is rising most rapidly. In the two regions where population growth is fastest, Africa and Latin America, it is declining. In these latter areas and throughout the poor world increasing population is pushing farmers onto lands too steep to sustain cultivation or too arid to protect them from winds when cultivated.

The deterioration of land in Third World countries often starts with growing demand for firewood. Forests are destroyed and villages start to use crop residues and animal dung for fuel. This sets in motion two processes of degradation. The land is deprived of nutrients and organic matter which is essential for maintaining productive soil-structure. Second, as soils become more compact more rain runs off, soil erosion accelerates, less water is absorbed into the soil and soil moisture for crops diminishes. Water tables fall and wells dry up. Eventually not enough soil is left to support even subsistence-level agriculture. At that point villagers become environmental refugees, migrating to cities and relief camps. In India about 40 per cent of the nation's land is now degraded. It is losing some 5 billion tonnes of topsoil each year (Brown 1988).

The deterioration of soil on agricultural lands is worldwide. The world as a whole loses 113, 000 square kilometres of topsoil each year which is equivalent to the topsoil of the entire wheat belt of Australia being lost each year. The United States is in the midst of a program to convert at least 16 millon hectares of eroded cropland, 11 per cent of the total, to grassland or woodland before it loses more. Much agriculture in the United States is unsustainable, that is to say present practices are causing soil deterioration with reduction in crop yields. The causes are manifold including overuse of chemical fertilisers that tend to destroy soil structure, salting from irrigation and wind erosion.

Likewise, much of existing agriculture in Australia is unsustainable. The Centre for Farm Planning and Land Management in the University of Melbourne estimates that 60 per cent of Australian agricultural land requires treatment for land degradation, salinity, erosion and tree decline. For every hectare of land used for cropping, between 50 and 300 tonnes of topsoil is lost each year. The cost is at least $600 million each year. Former Prime Minister Bob Hawke said that 'none of Australia's environmental problems is more serious than the soil degradation ... over nearly two-thirds of our continent's arable land' (Brown 1990, p. 60).

Soil erosion in Australia has been called the quiet crisis because it creeps upon a farmer often unnoticed. It has increased in recent years because of the pressure for the farmer to produce more from each hectare. Another problem is that short-term costs of combating soil deterioration often exceed the short-term benefit in some places by three times. Rangelands provided about a quarter of Australia's grazing country for sheep. Overstocking and subsequent invasion by inedible shrubs, such as hopbush, and inedible annual grasses has resulted in nearly 3 million hectares being completely 'shrubbed out'.

Deserts are expanding as a result of inappropriate human activity in Africa, south-central Asia, Australia, the western United States and southern South America. In China between 1949, when the Communist government came into power, and the year 2000 it is estimated that the total area of desert will have doubled (Ehrlich & Ehrlich 1990, p. 129).

The deterioration of natural productive systems in the many ways so far discussed exemplifies the ecological principle that over-use converts renewable resources into non-renewable ones. It uses them faster than they can be renewed. When this happens soil becomes unsustainable for cropping and forests do not regenerate. Another example of this principle is the extent to which water is being taken out of underground stores (aquifers) many times faster than it is being replaced by nature. This is happening to the aquifer underlying the great plains of the United States, to the artesian basin of Central Australia and possibly also to the great underground stores of water in the Sahara desert fed from the Atlas Saharile mountains in north western Algeria. Likewise the rate of net withdrawal of water from the Colorado River is now about equal to its flow.

Most irrigated land in the Soviet Union gets its water from two great rivers, the Syr-Darya and the Amu-Darya, that flow into the land-locked Aral Sea. As a result of excessive withdrawal of water from the diversion of these rivers, the water in the Aral Sea has fallen some twelve metres. The sea has shrunk to half its size. Its port city of Muniak is now fifty kilometres from the shoreline. The dry bottom is becoming a desert, the site of sand storms that may drop up to half a tonne per hectare of a mixture of sand and salt on the surrounding fields to damage the cotton crops. In addition the irrigated fields have severe problems of salination due to evaporation of surface waters that leave salt behind in the soil. Restoration of the irrigated lands might be possible by using crops that need less water and by using drip irrigation which is so expertly used in Israel. The Aral Sea used to support a fishing industry and had fourteen species of fish. Now only one species survives and is not commercially useful (Brown 1988, p. 27; UNEP 1991, p. 10).

A major biological resource that is being drastically depleted as a consequence of human activity is the diversity of life of microorganisms, plants and animals. The depletion of the diversity of species is referred to as the reduction of biodiversity. We do not really know how many species there are, possibly over 30 million (Wolf 1987). We do know that the tropics provide the richest array of plants, insects, birds and mammals. More than a third of all known species of flowering plants are native to tropical America. Tropical rainforests that cover just 7 per cent of the Earth's land surface may contain more than 40 per cent of all living species of plants and animals. A single hectare of Peruvian rainforest has 41,000 species of insects in the forest canopy. One isolated ridge-top in the Andean foothills of western Ecuador, only twenty square kilometres in area, lost as many as ninety unique plant species when the last of its forest was cleared to plant subsistence crops (Wolf 1987).

We do not know which are all the critical species involved in the life-support systems of the planet, nor those that might be useful in the future for creating new crops and new medicines. A probable estimate is that about one hundred species are becoming extinct each day. This is a tremendous loss in the diversity of life of the planet. Most of this loss is due to the destruction of habitats such as forests, especially those in the tropics. The rate of tropical deforestation in 1989 was almost double that in 1979, with roughly 1.8 per cent of the remaining forests disappearing each year (Ehrlich 1990).

Wolf (1985, p. 124) makes the pertinent comment that if Charles Darwin were writing today his subject would not be *The Origin of Species* but *The Disappearance of Species*. Paul and Anne Ehrlich (1981) have written that book with a one-word title, *Extinction*. They commence their account with their now famous parable of 'The Rivet Poppers'. You are walking toward your airliner from the terminal and notice a man on a ladder prying rivets out of its wing. You inquire why he is doing this. He replies that he is working for the airline Growthmania Intercontinental which has discovered that it can sell these rivets for a couple of dollars apiece. But you ask, won't that fatally weaken the wing? The rivet popper tells you not to worry as he has taken out lots of rivets so far and the wing hasn't fallen off yet. You realise that you are not compelled to fly on that airliner. So you go back to the terminal to find another airline with its planes intact. But unfortunately all of us are passengers on a very large spacecraft on which we have no option but to fly. And it is swarming with rivet poppers behaving in ways analogous to the rivet popper of Growthmania Intercontinental. These rivet poppers are not consciously malign. They are just uninformed.

Rivet popping on spaceship Earth consists of doing things that cause the extermination of populations of non-human organisms and even whole species. The Tasmanian tiger, the pig-footed bandicoot, the brown hare wallaby and the Darling Downs hopping mouse are some of the mammals that became extinct in Australia following European settlement. On the endangered list are twenty-three Australian mammals, eighteen birds and two reptiles (Ovington 1978) as well as very many other animals and plants. Elsewhere there are current threats to the continued existence of the chimpanzee, mountain gorilla, right whale and Californian condor, to mention but a few. Added to these lists are about 20,000 species of threatened plants and over 400 invertebrates (Wolf 1985, p. 143).

It is possible that a dozen or so rivets lost from spaceship Earth might never be missed. On the other hand the thirteenth rivet popped from a wing, or the extinction of a key species in the cycling of nitrogen, for example, could lead to a serious malfunctioning of the nitrogen cycle. In most cases an ecologist can no more predict the consequences of the extinction of a given species than an airline passenger can assess the effects of the loss of a single rivet. But no sensible policy could condone the continuous loss of either rivets or species. Acknowledging the limits of our understanding may be the first step toward conserving the diversity of life.

The parable of the rivet popper is particularly applicable to the threat of human activity to the cycles of nature such as the nitrogen cycle or the carbon cycle, which are part of the life-support systems of nature. Much more ecological research needs to be done before we are in a position to know the nature of the real threats to these cycles.

The loss of diversity of life has additional serious consequences. Agriculture has been greatly dependent upon wild varieties for genes that increase productivity, give resistance to disease and enable varieties to be produced that can withstand drought, cold and other extremes of weather. The wild relatives of commercial varieties, ranging from tomatoes to wheat, have provided genes worth billions of dollars in higher crop yields.

Recognition of this had earned these wild relatives the label 'the newest resource'. They become increasingly important as advances in biotechnology make possible the transfer of genes, not just from one variety to another but, from one species to another. Genes of known existing varieties are now being preserved in 'gene banks' set up in thirteen international centres. The seeds and cuttings of a wide range of crops are stored at low temperature. The idea is also being explored of establishing 'gene parks' where crop species can be kept under cultivation (Wolf 1985, p. 134). In addition to the preservation of wild strains of crop plants there is the possibility of discovering altogether new crops. Only a few of the more than a quarter of a million kinds of plants that exist have been investigated for this purpose (Ehrlich & Ehrlich 1990).

Since most of the loss of species is a consequence of destruction of habitats it is clear that the prevention of further losses means that this sort of activity has to be severely restricted. Instead, reserves for the preservation of habitats need be created such as the two hundred and fifty-two reserves established in sixty-six countries under UN-ESCO's Biosphere program. Acts of parliament need to be passed, as in the state of Victoria in Australia, that provide for the preservation of species by preserving critical habitats. The size of the preserved habitat is critical because of the ecological principle that increasing habitat size increases the chance of survival. There is a direct relation between the area of a natural habitat and the number of species it can sustain. One of the tragedies of clearing the Amazon rainforest in Brazil is that the forest in many places has been reduced to a series of islands too small to act as reservoirs of species that were at one time common.

In addition to habitat destruction, the disappearance of species is associated with other forms of deterioration of the environment. There is evidence that species of amphibians (frogs and the like) are becoming rarer throughout the world. In some cases this is due to local destruction of their habitat. But declines are occurring in the absence of destruction of habitats, suggesting other causes such as pollution from pesticides, acid rain and increases in ultraviolet exposure or even change in climate (Blaustein & Wake 1990). The possible effect of future change in climate is one of the big unknowns in the future of the diversity of life on the planet.

An indispensable strategy for saving our fellow living creatures is to diminish the scale of human activities. Both the size of the human population and the environmental impact of the average individual must eventually be reduced well below what it is today. Unless we can move in that direction, all other efforts will eventually be for naught.

In addition to biological resources discussed above, the life of human society is at present dependent upon non-renewable resources, notably fossil fuels and minerals. These are appropriately discussed in the next section on the impact of technology on the environment.

# TECHNOLOGY: ITS ENVIRONMENTAL IMPACT

The environmental disruptiveness of technologies used to produce the goods consumed by society is the T factor in the PAT equation. They include the production of toxic substances both from the normal operation of industry such as ionizing radiation and from disasters such as the Chernobyl nuclear explosion, and products of industry such as pesticides and chlorofluorocarbons. By far the most important source of disruption of the environment comes from the use of fossil fuels for energy. Coal was the main offender soon after the Industrial Revolution began. In the middle of the nineteenth century coal began to be displaced by oil and later oil has been complemented with natural gas.

At its peak in the 1970s oil and natural gas accounted for nearly 70 per cent of the world's use of commercial energy. The World Energy Conference in 1989 concluded that by the year 2020 the world, on present trends, would be using 75 per cent more energy, and that most of it would be supplied by coal, oil and nuclear power. At present rates of use the accessible reserves of both coal and oil will be consumed within a single generation. Ours is essentially a petroleum culture. But it is not the exhaustion of fossil fuels that is the primary concern. It now seems certain that we shall have to phase out the use of these sources of energy well before the reserves are gone if we are to make the transition to the ecologically sustainable society. The reason is their disruption of the environment.

This began to be appreciated worldwide with the realisation that carbon dioxide from the burning of fossil fuels was disrupting the carbon cycle and leading to the greenhouse effect. This is potentially so disastrous that a number of nations have agreed to drastically cut their emission of carbon dioxide. Some have already done so. Between 1973 and 1984 energy efficiency in the United States rose by 23 per cent despite economic growth. This saved 10 million barrels of oil a day. Western Europe, starting with substantially more efficient economies, realised a 16 per cent increase in energy efficiency. Japan was even better. On the other hand, in Greece and Australia the use of energy was less efficient during this period (Brown 1986, p. 84). In addition to carbon dioxide there are other distruptive products from the use of fossil fuels such as the nitrogen oxides that have already been referred to.

The energy component of the transition to a sustainable society has two dimensions — a shift to renewable sources of energy such as solar energy and wind and increase in the efficient use of energy. Energy conservation is the way to increase energy efficiency. It should now top the list of all efforts to prevent further environmental disruption in the rich nations. Even quite small changes in technology can have dramatic effects in reducing environmental impact. In the United States the Reagan administration relaxed the efficiency standards of automobiles that had already been met by Chrysler. If these regulations had been kept in place, within a decade or so the amount of petrol saved would have been equivalent to the entire amount of oil estimated to underlie the Arctic National Wildlife Refuge. That single step could have both removed a threat to one of the last really wild places on Earth and would have reduced pollution in cities (Ehrlich & Ehrlich 1990, p. 320). Likewise, simple steps such as better insulation and more efficient heating and cooling systems in houses, are effective ways of conserving energy.

# CONCLUSION

The world needs to be saved because it is moving in an ecologically unsustainable path. The global economy cannot continue to grow indefinitely. Even a twofold increase is likely to be perilous for the biosphere. There is no such thing as sustainable growth any more.

The transition to an ecologically sustainable society involves many steps that run counter to present trends; an emphasis on the health of the environment and the health of people instead of an emphasis on economic growth.

That requires reduced consumption of goods, the efficient recycling of materials, a move away from the use of fossil fuels to the use of renewable sources of energy, zero global population growth, a reduced standard of living for the rich, an increased standard of living for the poor and an appeal to quality of life instead of materialism. It is the road not yet taken by the world. To move along that road we need to invent a new economic system that puts the priorities right — people and the environment before growth in material goods. This is the subject of Chapter 4.

# CHAPTER 4
# ORDER AND CHANGE

The art of progress is to preserve order amid change, and to preserve change amid order. Life refuses to be embalmed alive. The more prolonged the halt in some unrelieved system of order, the greater the crash of the dead society.
*A. N. Whitehead (1978, p. 339)*

The crisis of our age is undoubtedly due primarily to the fact that requirements of a technical civilisation have outrun the limited order which national communities have achieved, while the resources of our civilisation have not been adequate for the creation of political instruments of order, wide enough to meet these requirements.
*Reinhold Niebuhr (1944, p. 153)*

The global system will change during the next forty years, because it will be physically forced to change. But if humanity waits until it is physically compelled to change, its options will be few indeed. None of them will be attractive. If it changes before it has to change, while it can still choose to change, it will not avoid suffering and crises, but it can be drawn through them by a realistic hope for a better world.
*Herman E. Daly & John B. Cobb. (1989, p. 21)*

ometimes change to established order forces itself upon society and that society then struggles to find a new sort of order. That happened in Eastern Europe at the end of the 1980s. East European expert Timothy Garton Ash paid a visit to Prague in the mid-80s to a lonesome student of philosophy, an oppositionist reduced by the Husak regime to making his living by stoking the furnace boiler in the basement of the Ministry of Culture. The room in the basement in which Garton Ash was received contained, among the usual bric-a-brac consigned to such premises, a discarded piano. After a two-hour discussion about the future the student of philosophy proceeded to play the piano. He was not really a good player, but his playing had an electric quality, a sort of defiant ferocity. Garton Ash reported that the music seemed to leap out of the basement skylight, like an escaping genie, forced its way up through the pouring rain, up and up high above the sodden city, above the smoke from the boiler's chimney. It seemed to form a salute V for victory before it faded away (Garton Ash 1990).

The student had premonitions of impending change in a situation that was so bad he couldn't believe it could continue for ever. About the same time in 1984 Vaclav Havel attributed to the Czechoslovakian opposition group, the Chartists, the 'knowledge' of 'how suddenly a society that seemed atomised, apathetic, and broken can be transformed into an articulate, united civil society. How private opinion can become public opinion. How a nation can stand on its feet again.' They too had a premonition of what was to happen. There could have scarcely have been a better description of the changes that were to take place in that country in the final weeks of 1989.

Sooner or later it seems that oppressed peoples strike out for freedom. This happened during the collapse of the Soviet Union in 1992, which for seven decades had been a tightly regimented society. There is a Russian story about a sultan who decided to punish one of his wives for some misdeed and ordered her sealed up, with her son, in a barrel. The sultan set them afloat at sea to perish. After several days the son said to the mother, 'I can't bear being so cramped, I want to stretch out'. 'You can't,' she responded, 'you'll push out the bottom, and we'll drown'. Some days later, the son protested again, 'I long for room'. 'For God's sake don't do it', the mother said 'we'll drown'. The son then said, 'So be it, I must stretch out, just this once'. He got his moment of freedom, and perished. The story has been applied to the condition of the Russian people. They were, sooner or later, bound to strike out of their oppressive order for freedom, no matter what came after.

The two hardest tasks of all for humanity seem to be the international political and economic one of managing the world and that of reforming religion. In this chapter I have therefore chosen these two areas in which to explore the relation of order to change.

# THE ECONOMIC ORDER AND CHANGE

In the quotation at the head of this chapter, Daly and Cobb write of the impending change to the present global order necessitated by the deteriorating environment resulting from the dominant economic and political order. They point to the necessity to change before it literally has to come. In both this case and in Eastern Europe, change is coming as a consequence of the realistic hope of a minority for a better world.

Assuming the will of the minority in any particular situation is right and that of the majority wrong, it may still be the duty of the minority to act with the majority, while retaining the freedom to persuade the majority of its point of view. The reason for this is that the principle of order has a greater value than the immediate realisation of the will of the minority. In this situation the minority has the opportunity to be a leaven.

Much of this chapter is about the necessity for change in the economic order and in the political order to the extent to which the political order takes its cues from traditional thinking in economics. Many political decisions are made on the advice of economists. Illustrating the influence of economists, Lord Keynes wrote: 'The ideas of economics and political philosophy, both when they are right and when they are wrong, are more powerful than is commonly understood. Indeed the world is ruled by little else' (quoted by Ehrlich, Ehrlich & Holdren 1977, p. 843). The director of the United Nations Environmental Program reported in 1991 that 'the global economy continued to be one of the major driving forces behind environmental degradation'. Whether it is the sprawl of deserts or the loss of tropical forests as the world's poor cut trees for firewood and clear land for agriculture, or the ineluctable warming of the planet as vehicles and factories deposit millions of tonnes of greenhouse gases into the atmosphere, 'economic pressures lie behind them all' (Tolba 1991, p. 10).

In recent years ecologists have turned their attention to the economy as one of the major influences determining the fate of the earth. The growth of the economy has meant the exponential increase of inputs of raw materials from the environment and outputs of waste into the environment. The charge against economists is that they have ignored the effects of this on the environment. Instead they have encouraged the maximisation of both use of raw materials and production of pollutants. The world requires that both should be kept to a minimum, sufficient to meet human needs.

Daly and Cobb (1989) have examined the charge and find economics guilty. They point out that the key assumption behind traditional economic theory is its understanding of the nature of the human person. Its proposition is that individuals act so as to optimise their own interests. Economists typically identify the pursuit of private gain as rational and imply that other sorts of behaviour are not rational. These other sorts of behaviour include regard for others and actions directed to the public good.

Economists have taught that checks on self-interest are both unnecessary and harmful. It is through self-interested behaviour that all benefit the most. The self-interest includes the assumption that the wants of human beings are insatiable. The luxuries of this generation should become the necessities of the next. The satisfied 'economic man' is the one who procures an unlimited supply of commodities.

What happens to other people is of no importance in this concept of the human. Indeed, economic theory ignores everything to which a monetary value cannot be assigned. So the gifts of nature are of no importance, nor is the morale of the community of which the individual is a part. The operation of self-interest is accomplished through the market. This is the doctrine of consumer sovereignty. Emerson already said 'things are in the saddle and ride mankind'. Walter Bagehot, in his *Economic Studies*, wrote of David Ricardo, one of the founding fathers of economics: 'He thought he was considering actual human nature in its actual circumstances, when he was considering a fictitious nature in fictitious circumstances' (quoted in Daly & Cobb 1989, p. 36).

This understanding of human nature is profoundly erroneous and is diametrically opposed to the understanding of human nature proposed in Chapters 1 and 2. There the emphasis is on concern for others as an ethical ideal that is fulfilling for the individual. Furthermore, I argued in Chapter 3 the necessity to develop strategies to reduce demand rather than strategies to increase consumption.

Concern for others should still leave room for legitimate self-interest as a motivating force in life. A critical issue in rethinking economics is the relation between self-interest and social justice. As a former Archbishop of Canterbury, William Temple said: 'The art of government in fact is the art of so ordering life that self-interest prompts what justice demands'. John Maynard Keynes in 1926 put the issue this way: 'The political problem of mankind is to combine three things: economic efficiency, social justice, and individual liberty'. In quoting this statement Roger Shinn adds that today we might add a fourth, ecological viability (Shinn 1991, p. 722).

In the context of economic development, Paul Ekins (1986) suggests five components of human well-being: being, doing, having, relating and surviving (p. 149):

*Being* is concerned with the physical and mental state of the person.

*Doing* has to do with activities in all spheres of leisure and employment.

*Having* has to do with the person's access to materials to satisfy basic needs such as food, housing, clothing, clean air and water.

*Relating* is about the relationships the person has with others in the community. These are the 'internal relations' discussed in Chapters 1 and 6.

*Surviving* is concerned with freedom from threats to security from other individuals, groups or the state.

The component *relating* is the primary concern of this chapter. It is also the primary concern of Daly and Cobb (1989), who seek to replace the radically individualistic picture of the economic human with an image of the human as a 'person-in-community'.

The basic idea of 'person-in-community' is that human beings are constituted by their relationships. Our dependence upon others is not simply for goods and services. Our sense of well-being and fulfilment has spiritual components such as our innermost relationships with others, with nature and with God. In the real world the self-contained individual does not exist. Our relationships define our identities as persons. We are members one of another.

Much so-called development in the Third World has resulted in villages being replaced by agribusiness and factories, with villagers driven to slums in cities such as Calcutta and Sao Paulo. The overall economic effect may be an increase in production, but at the enormous cost of breaking up the community and relationships dependent upon that community. The application of traditional economic theory weakens existing patterns of social relationships. But these never did enter the assessment of the effects of economic development in the first place. They are not part of the economic equation.

The development of the economy since the Industrial Revolution has, without question, resulted in the provision of more goods and services. The standard of living of many people has risen rapidly. But we are now finding that the standard of living is not a sufficient index of progress. What matters is the quality of life of the inhabitants of the Earth. There is much evidence that the quality of life of many people has fallen in recent decades and is still falling as a result of the economy.

We need a new index of the state of health of the people and the health of the environment. The standard index of Gross National Product (GNP) is a very poor indicator of well-being. It does not take account of the depletion of resources or the pollution of the environment. Indeed, money spent on cleaning up pollution adds to the GNP. This is why the state of Alaska's gross product rose dramatically in the year of the *Exxon Valdez* oil spill! Some analysts actually suggest that rising GNP in industrial countries now means mainly rising costs of pollution, environmental degradation and human suffering (Robertson 1978a). Nor does GNP register the value of work in the informal economy such as household labour (Eckersley 1992). We need better tools for measuring development and human well-being. Aware of this need, Lawrence Summers, chief economist of the World Bank, remarked: 'I would suggest that too often we, as development economists, operate in a kind of statistical Stone Age' (Anon 1991, p. 18).

Daly and Cobb (1989, pp. 401 et seq) have devised an index of sustainable economic welfare (ISEW) as a measure of the well-being of humans and the environment. This index has twenty-three components that include equality in the distribution of income, services such as highways, household labour, expenditure on health and education, cost of commuting, cost of pollution, loss of farm lands, depletion of non-renewable resources and long-term environmental damage.

In the USA the GNP which is used as a measure of economic well-being increased steadily since the Second World War. On the other hand the ISEW increased very slowly until about 1975 when it began to decline and has done so ever since. Despite the increase in GNP the individual welfare of the citizens has fallen by 12 per cent over these years (Brown 1991, p. 10).

Traditional economics has been tied to the idea that the creation of wealth by industry and commerce is necessary before it can be spent on services that enhance human well-being. I asked a thoughtful Dutch economist if we could have increased services for human well-being without increased production of goods from factories and the like. She wisely replied that a society can have what it chooses in this respect. It is not necessary to build and sell more motor cars in order to be able to afford more schools and teachers. It is not necessary to make and sell more cigarettes and sweets in order to be able to afford more doctors and dentists. There is no law of nature that compels us to make more and more things, including many that are harmful and useless, before we can attend to the needs of people.

## THE PRINCIPLE OF 'PERSON IN COMMUNITY'

Daly and Cobb (1989) urge that when economics rethinks its theory of the human person it needs to replace its emphasis on the self-seeking individual, which results in destruction of the community with one that sees the 'person in community', where other-regarding actions are paramount. They quote Victor Furkiss who describes our situation in graphic terms as follows:

> Present-day society is locked into four positive feedback loops which need to be broken: economic growth which feeds on itself, population growth which feeds on itself, technological change which feeds on itself, and a pattern of income inequality which seems to be self-sustaining and which tends to spur growth in the other three areas. Ecological humanity must create an economy in which economic and population growth is halted, technology is controlled, and gross inequalities of income are done away with. (p. 21)

Daly and Cobb add a fifth positive feedback, the arms race which also feeds on itself. Economics for the common good calls for the breaking of these feedback loops.

The statement of the Australian Roman Catholic Bishops on wealth in Australia asserts the principle that a healthy society is not made up of a collection of selfish individuals, each struggling solely for his or her own interests. It is rather a sharing community (Bishops Draft Statement 1992). Their statement makes a strong contrast with the speech of former British Prime Minister Margaret Thatcher to the General Assembly of the Church of Scotland when she told them there was no such thing as 'society', only individuals, families and government. She stated in unambiguous terms the doctrine that wealth is created by maximising the freedom of individuals to exploit economic opportunities.

To preserve the 'person in community' Daly and Cobb (1989, p. 165) favour development that takes the small group, such as the village, rather than the individual or the nation as the unit of development. So does Paul Ekins in his book *The Living Economy* (1986). He points out that whenever a city or enterprise grows beyond a critical size, the people involved become, at best, 'efficient objects' at the expense of losing their possibilities as 'creative subjects'.

The efficiency of a city or enterprise should not be measured simply in terms of its economic productivity, but also, and more importantly, in terms of its ability to contribute to the satisfaction of basic human needs of those affected by the city or enterprise. Ekins adds that implementation of this principle may lead to the conclusion that it may be better to strive for the coexistence of several styles of development in different regions of one country, instead of insisting on one national style which may have proved efficient for one region but at the expense of other regions. National styles of development are generally conceived for the purpose of advancing national unity. But unity does not mean uniformity (Ekins 1986, p. 51).

Daly and Cobb (1989) give examples in Sri Lanka where the village asks of itself what are its basic needs and how can they be better met. The villagers themselves make the decision and so determine their own fate. This usually results in an increase in their productive capacities. It may involve a peasant willing to have a bore put down on his farm provided the water can be pumped to surrounding properties. The initial cost may be covered from a bank loan. Wooden ploughs may be replaced in the whole village by metal ones. Not only is production increased but community is strengthened (Daly & Cobb 1989, p. 165).

The state of Kerala in India provides a model of development for the benefit of the poor under democratic and decentralised rule. Peasants and labourers are exceptionally well organised. Their grassroots organisations have enabled the poor to direct their own development by working together as communities. Kerala's villages have access to basic health care, education and transportation unknown elsewhere in India. A comprehensive program of land-reform, begun in 1969, gave 1.5 million tenants and labourers rights to the land they tilled and to their homes and gardens. Kerala's adult literacy rate is about twice that of the national average and its people live eleven years longer than the Indian average. The infant death rate is one-third of the Indian average.

The ingredients of Kerala's success have much to do with a strong sense of community which has consolidated village communities. Local control over common resources helps to break the cycle of economic and ecological degradation. Credit helps the poor to get access to livestock and tools. Community-based healthcare protects people from debilitating diseases. Family planning gives women control over their fertility, such that the birthrate is one-third lower than the Indian average (Durning 1989). According to Durning the ingredients of Kerala's success are common to all effective efforts to dismantle the poverty trap anywhere in the world.

The promotion of community within an industry or trade not only enhances a sense of worth among the individuals involved but also promotes productivity. Styles of management in factories that give workers greater autonomy, decision-making powers and a sense of belonging have been shown to increase productivity in case after case. Many experiments with worker participation in North America and Europe have been initiated in response to the demands of labour unions for more control over the introduction of new technology.

Japanese companies are well known for giving workers a major voice in the organisation of tasks and the solution of problems of production. Many companies in the US have introduced groups in which employees discuss ways to improve production. Hewlett-Packard, a giant US office equipment and computer firm, had five hundred such groups meeting regularly by mid-1981 (Newland 1982). While the objective of these firms is to increase production, they do so by enhancing community and creativity of employees on the job.

In 1972 the construction industry in St Louis, beset by many damaging problems, formed an organisation called PRIDE. Before PRIDE came on the scene, construction projects were completed behind schedule and above original estimates of cost. A major reason for these problems was that work would stop whenever a jurisdictional dispute arose. Since PRIDE came into existence these disputes are handled without stopping work and work rules are updated as technology changes. As a consequence projects are completed on time and without overruns of cost (Daly & Cobb 1989, p. 183).

The dominant patterns of economic development throughout the world have been quite the reverse of the development of the 'person in community'. They have systematically destroyed existing traditional communities, especially in rural areas. Urban industrial development has been bought at the expense of rural communities.

Daly and Cobb (1989, p. 210) and Eckersley (1992) consider that the theme of individualism versus community emerges nowhere more clearly than in the issue of free trade. The essence of free trade is that governments should not interfere with the price mechanism, which is the so- called 'invisible hand' which is said to ensure that the self-seeking behaviour of firms and individuals will give rise to the most efficient allocation of resources.

The dogma that claims that markets and money can do everything better than governments and the law is known as 'economic rationalism'. Michael Pusey argues that the central policy departments of the Australian Federal government of the 1980s and 1990s have been dominated by economists who think like this. Further, he says, it doesn't work (Pusey 1991).

Eckersley (1992) lists some ten criticisms of the way the free market operates. This is a complex issue which we need not pursue here except for the criticism that free trade operates against community. Daly and Cobb (1989), as well as Eckersley, argue against free trade as it exists in the world today between national economies, because at present free trade destroys existing national and sub-national communities in the name of a mythical world community. Yet often the people in that community are not benefited. The big players in free trade have effectively freed themselves from most community obligations, nationally, sub-nationally and internationally, including obligations to the environment. Preston (1991), who values the economic efficiency of the market, nevertheless acknowledges that left to itself the market leads to great inequalities of wealth and is unable to cope with environmental degradation such as is caused by industrial pollution.

Despite their quite trenchant criticisms of the free market, Daly and Cobb (1989) and Preston (1991) are not against the market as such, provided its decision-making is decentralised and that it operates enterprises on a human scale. Daly and Cobb say there is plenty of room to complain about monopoly profits, but that is a complaint against monopoly, not against profits per se: 'If one dislikes bureaucratic decision making then one must accept the market and the profit motive, if not as a positive good then as the lesser of two evils ... We have no hesitation in opting for the market as the basic institution of resource allocation' (p. 48). But as they operate at present, both the free market and the state fail miserably in maintaining community on a human scale and with a human face. There is good reason to argue for 'person-in-community' on a more local scale, where also the concept of self-reliance is practised as far as possible.

# THE PRINCIPLE OF SELF-RELIANCE

In addition to the principle of 'person-in-community', a second value an alternative economics seeks to promote is self-reliance. Self-reliance does not necessarily mean self-sufficiency, though it might in some situations. Rather it means the revitalising of capabilities and resources through individual effort. It means that what can be produced at the local level should be produced at that level. The same principle holds at the regional and national levels. There will probably always be goods and services that cannot be produced locally, regionally or nationally. Self-reliance then turns into a process of interdependence among equal partners, as contrasted with blind competition (Ekins 1986, pp. 52, 97 et seq.).

The idea of a nationally self-sufficient economy is in principle quite logical. It would involve setting limits to the amount of product a nation needs and then striving to reduce the amount of work required to produce that product. As Ehrlich, Ehrlich and Holdren (1977, p. 846) point out, such an approach is against the conventional wisdom of economic theory. Yet it makes much more sense in a world of finite resources.

The concept of self-reliance is the antithesis of much of the thinking behind the growth economy. The national and international division of labour are part of the backbone of traditional economics. This economy has resulted in overspecialisation, fragmentation and debilitating dependencies of some countries on others.

# THE ECOLOGICAL DILEMMA POSED BY TRADITIONAL ECONOMICS

The dilemma created by traditional economics in its support of the growth-driven economy in the ecological system of the world that does not grow is discussed in Chapter 3. The dilemma leads traditional economists to ignore the limits to growth and the environmental devastation that unlimited growth causes. Somehow a new ecological–economic paradigm must be constructed that unites nature's housekeeping (ecology) and society's housekeeping (economics) with the priority of keeping nature's house in order (Ehrlich 1989). Probably the most significant contribution of the Report of the World Commission on Environment and Development published as Our Common Future (WCED 1987), is the proposition that improvements in material well-being need not come at the expense of the degradation of the environment. Economics and ecology can, and must, work together.

Australian economist and ecological thinker H. C. Coombs (1990) has said: 'There is nothing divinely ordained about the economic system: it is the product of human ingenuity, effort and capacity to organise and, therefore, can be properly questioned, criticised and, if a better alternative exist, rejected' (p. 143). Coombs has himself been instrumental in seeking ways of matching ecological and economic realities, as have the other thinkers in economics referred to in this chapter.

# SOME NECESSARY CHANGES IN DIRECTION TO THE ECONOMIC ORDER

On the basis of this discussion we can now list some of the changes of direction needed in the economic order of rich countries as follows:

◆ from growth in material goods to growth in human well-being.

◆ from increasing dependence on large organisations to increasing self-reliance.

◆ from increasing specialisation to increasing self-sufficiency.

◆ from polarisation of the roles of the sexes to a new balance between them.

◆ from increasing urbanisation to a more dispersed pattern of habitation.

◆ from increasing centralisation to more decentralisation of power.

◆ from increasing dependence on technologies that pollute the environment, waste resources and dominate the people who work with them, to increasing emphasis on technologies appropriate to the environment and the needs of people.

◆ from increasing production of things to increasing production of services for human well-being.

All these items are part and parcel of appropriate development in poor countries as well, with the addition that they still need to produce more things for food, housing, clothing and the other physical necessities of life. Further, these things should be produced to fulfil local needs rather than to provide yet more things to the rich world. One of the tragedies of the present economic order between nations is that the flow of goods is greater from the poor to the rich countries than the other way around.

In a renewed economic order James Robertson sees the international trading and financial systems operated by the multinational companies, international banks and international governmental agencies as still important, but as playing a relatively smaller part than they do today. Managing the superstructure will become relatively less important than activity to meet one's own needs close to where they arise. These international organisations may ask of themselves: 'what can we do to help people to become more self-reliant in their economic activity and less dependent upon us and the services we provide?' (Robertson 1978b).

# HOW BRAVE A NEW WORLD?

The advancement of the human lot has never come on the wings of inevitability. It has always depended upon human choice, that is to say on individual decisions and on public policy. The modern industrial world and the would-be industrial world have made their choices in terms of a human future dependent upon increased economic growth in material goods, despite the warning of ecologists. They have made another choice in that one in every two scientists and technologists is employed in perfecting the instruments of war. This tragic choice brands scientists and technologists as among the most destructive people on earth today. That is one reason for the public disenchantment of science, 'lest', in the words of Winston Churchill 'the stone age return on the gleaming wings of science'.

But there is no scientific or technological imperative that determines things must remain that way. Despite appearances, we are not in the grip of a technological determinism that closes our options for ever. A new way is possible. But that will depend upon a new sort of science and technology and a new sort of human commitment. Such a venture is full of risks. A critical question is how brave can we be as we begin to design a new sort of world order and how brave can we be in casting off our religious and other prejudices that belong to another age in order to remould them in the service of a new world?

Various attitudes to the unknown are captured in the century-old story of the maiden and the tiger. Three men were given the option of opening one of two doors. Behind one there was a hungry tiger. Behind the other was a maiden.

The first man who tried, refused to take the chance. He lived safely and died chaste.

The second man hired a risk-assessment consultant. He collected all the available data on maidens and tigers.

He brought in sophisticated technology to listen for growling and to detect the faintest whiff of perfume. He completed checklists. He developed a utility function and assessed his risk-averseness. Finally, sensing that in a few more years he would be in no condition to enjoy the maiden's company anyway, he opened the optimum door. And was eaten by a 'low-probability' tiger.

The third man took a course in tiger-taming. He opened a door at random and was eaten by the maiden.

To interpret the story: we respond to the unknown by trying to *retreat* from it, by trying to *comprehend* it or by trying to *control* it.

To *retreat* from the future is the Arcadian approach. It is directed backwards to a mythical golden age, to a state of innocence in a pastoral world where peace of mind is not threatened, intellectual aspiration is not called for and virtue is not at risk. Arcadia is a world without strife, without ambition and without material accomplishments. This approach is evident in longings for a return to a simpler risk-free life that never was. But a world without science and technology is not a possible choice for us. Five billion or more people cannot survive without some form of science and technology. We can choose between technologies, but apart from that there is no option open to us.

To attempt to *comprehend* the future these days means a risk/benefit analysis. Measure the probabilities and trade-offs, calculate the social risk/benefit ratio and then the common good will be defined. But it isn't. A risk/benefit analysis was made of a project to remove crossing lights in front of a home for elderly people. The analysis resulted in the crossing lights being removed. What value are old people in a retirement home to the economy?

The choice of methods of risk-assessment are themselves biased by underlying cultural assumptions or those of the analyst. The assessment and management of risk to workers in industry in the US is estimated to cost about $300 billion a year. That is about 10 per cent of the GNP. The underlying question is how to determine how much to spend? How safe is safe enough? And we have to remember that we can always be eaten by a low-probability tiger.

To attempt to *control* the future is the approach of the tiger-tamer. It could be said to be represented by utopian visions that began to be taken seriously from the seventeenth century onwards. One of the writers at the time whose name was Foigny, like Francis Bacon, placed his imaginary utopia on an island in the southern seas which he called *Terra Australe*. Its inhabitants he called Australians! In utopia, humans create the world anew and improve it through their own exertions. They begin as tenants or lodgers in the world and end up as landlords. And as the environment improves from their labours, so, it is alleged, will the inhabitants. Human beings in utopia look forward, never backward and seldom upward.

The utopian approach is the dominant tradition of professional engineers, scientists and technologists. It serves well up to a point. But as some engineers have been the first to point out, it has met its match and more in the complex unmanageable world it is called upon to address. There is, despite its benefits, one long-recognised weakness in utopian speculation — the inadequacies of human beings and therefore the unlikelihood that they can live up to their ambitions in utopia. Utopias that have managed to get to the experimental stage have collapsed. It is for this reason that utopian thinking led some of its modern promoters, such as Arthur Koestler and Carl Sagan, to propose ways of 'improving' human beings by biological manipulation such as surgical removal of certain centres in the brain or by genetic engineering to remove 'bad' genes.

The utopian vision leads to a paradox. We find ourselves with a technical ability to be creators of a material paradise without parallel in all history. We also find ourselves, equally without parallel in history, with a technical capacity to destroy that paradise. Caught in the middle we face a spiritual perplexity without parallel in all history. Utopian man who trained himself to become a tiger-tamer finds himself confronted with a carnivorous lady. Why?

The maiden the young man thought was behind the door is quite different from what he anticipated. The unknown is not a wrinkle to be ironed out of the social fabric. We not only face the inadequacy of human nature but, in addition, as knowledge grows so does the unknown and our ability to control it.

There is a law that says, as knowledge increases arithmetically ignorance increases geometrically. As our knowledge of nuclear power, for example, increased and we built more and more nuclear power plants, we discovered how little we really knew about the new world of technology we ushered ourselves into, with risks previously unknown and unanticipated.

There is an alternative to these three approaches to the future. It accepts the inevitability of incomplete knowledge. It accepts the challenge of the surprising world around us. It accepts the imperfections of human beings. The fundamental question is not how to calculate, control or even reduce risk, important as they are in many situations. It is how to increase our risk-taking abilities. How can we attain the intellectual and moral maturity to live fully and safely in a complex world? How brave is our world to be?

Every creative step forward in civilisation has involved an increase in risk-taking. Whitehead (1926) believed the major advances of civilisation are processes that all but wreck the societies in which they occur: 'It is the business of the future to be dangerous' (p. 259). Advances in civilisation were never throwbacks to some garden of Eden with a restoration of primitive innocence. They have always brought a maturer fulfilment of life, but with a cost. The price paid for Neolithic culture was enormous, so too was the cost of the Agricultural Revolution and urbanisation, and later the Industrial Revolution with its dark satanic mills. Every new liberation in technology, politics, education and sex produces as well new forms of enslavement. The new brings creative possibilities that did not exist before and with them new possibilities of evil and suffering.

The prosperous middle classes in Britain who ruled the nineteenth century placed an excessive value upon a placid existence. They refused to face the necessities for social reform imposed by the new industrial system and later they refused to face the necessity for intellectual reform imposed by the new knowledge. In the immediate future there will be less security than in the immediate past, and less stability. We live in exciting times. There is, of course, a degree of instability which is so great as to be incompatible with civilisation. Yet, on the whole, great ages of the past have been unstable ones.

The question for us is whether we have the capacity for change to enable us to live fully in a risky future? The ecologically sustainable and just society of the future will be a changed society full of risks. But the risks taken won't be the sort of foolhardy ones of the present that could, if continued, lead to our extinction. The fate of the dinosaurs was their inability to adjust to a changed environment. That could be our fate also.

If we were able to put ourselves back at the edge of history, say at the brink of the Industrial Revolution, how would we with hindsight have steered its course? Would we have feared the risks involved in forging ahead? How could we have accepted the challenge and taken the increased risks while at the same time refusing to accept the enormous cost that history claimed? Perhaps we would have decided to skip some of it, as was suggested in a cartoon depicting a group of tribesmen who were consulting the future together: the caption read, 'So by a vote of 8 to 2 we have decided to skip the Industrial Revolution and go right into the electronic age'. It is a nice utopian idea but not a possible one. Each age with its promises and risks becomes a preparation for the one that follows. There are probably few short-cuts in civilisation, just as there are few in growing up.

# RELIGION AND CHANGE

Although our age is often described as a secular one, nevertheless religion remains a potent force for good and for evil. Many, if not most, of the armed conflicts in the world today pit one religion against another, be it Protestants and

Catholics in Northern Ireland or sects of Islam in the Middle East. This is the unhappy side of religion.

Yet there is another side to religion which is the positive effort of religion to transform itself in a changing world. If that were not so, religion would become a fossil in the modern world, appropriate only as a museum piece. Some religions doubtless come into that category. Christians, on the whole, have little sense of history and are unaware of the sources of the tradition from which they come. Many committed Christians sincerely and unabashedly propound their faith as if the past three centuries had not occurred.

What then are some of the ways in which a changing religion has helped to mould both the present and our attitude to the future? In the 1960s a number of theologians proclaimed that God is dead. They presumed that with the death of God there would follow the death of the church, at least as it was then known. Religion would have no future. Man come of age would get on without it. For many people news of this radical thinking in Christian theology broke with an article in the London *Observer* of 17 March 1963, headed *Our Image of God Must Go*. The article drew widespread attention for its author was a bishop, John A. T. Robinson, Bishop of Woolwich in London. The article was a forerunner to his book *Honest to God* which became a bestseller. More dramatically *Time* magazine of 8 April 1966 took up the topic in its characteristic way. Against a black cover background was printed in blood red the question, 'Is God dead?' The topic was now good 'copy'. But it was more than this. It demonstrated to the ordinary reader the extent to which profound dissatisfaction with the traditional image of God in the Christian world was being voiced.

This was not an exercise in academic theology, but a case of theologians addressing themselves to the worldly fact that religious beliefs had not kept pace with the radical transformation of society by science and the rest of modern culture. Bishop Robinson had brought to his argument the thinking of two theologians in particular, Dietrich Bonhoeffer, a young German pastor executed by the Nazis, and

Paul Tillich, an elder statesman of theology who had earlier escaped the Nazi tyranny.

To a group of other theologians, these three did not go far enough. For them, not only had the traditional image of God died in the secular world, there was no clear alternative image to replace the one that had died. Thomas J. J. Altizer and William Hamilton were amongst the most vocal and radical of this group. There were others with a different emphasis, such as Harvey Cox and Paul van Buren.

In a sense there was nothing new about this. The phrase 'God is dead' came from Friedrich Nietzsche some eighty years earlier in *The Joyful Wisdom*. It is generally thought that, for Nietzsche, God had been slain by the prevailing spirit-deadening ethos of the nineteenth century. Its spiritual aspirations were embodied in the utilitarianism of Jeremy Bentham and J. S. Mill. This doctrine rendered meaningless the traditional God of justice, compassion and salvation, replacing it with an ethics fit only for a society of unimaginative shopkeepers.

Robinson, Bonhoeffer and Tillich spoke to many in my generation. We were profoundly influenced by them. They had a word for our time that broke through the established order of religion and brought to it a new vitality. But how long did this new thinking have an influence? I do not really know. There is the famous remark made by Tillich, in his Germanic English, to fellow theologian Langdon Gilkey towards the end of Tillich's life, 'Vy, Langdon, am I so soon on ze dust heap of history?' (Ved Mehta 1965, p. 59). Much the same could be said about an equally famous theologian of that period, Reinhold Niebuhr, who brought new critical thinking in politics and social justice to the Christian church. His contribution stands in strong contrast to the politics of fundamentalism that later produced the 'moral majority' so influential in the election of Ronald Reagan to the presidency of the US.

Today religious fundamentalism dominates the religious scene in the US and to a lesser extent elsewhere, leaving the main-line churches with depleted membership and waning influence. This is a very tight form of order which had its origin earlier in the century. The name fundamentalism derives from a series of books on *The Fundamentals: A testimony to the truth*, launched in 1909. The World's Christian Fundamentals Association founded ten years later prepared the way for attacks on many 'liberal' or 'modernist' preachers. A climax came with the prosecution in 1925 of a schoolteacher, John Scopes, in Dayton, Tennessee, for teaching that humans had evolved from non-human animals. In the 'monkey trial' William Jennings Bryan, a former Secretary of State and presidential candidate, secured the condemnation of the teacher by arguing that American society would be in danger if the literal authority of Genesis were to be overthrown.

Although Scopes was convicted, the cause that Bryan championed was popularly discredited in the nationwide press coverage the case received. However, the upheaval of the '20s has received renewed public concern in recent years because of the revival of fundamentalism in the US and the sponsorship of creationism in schools as opposed to the teaching of evolution.

Central to the fundamentalist position is belief in the inerrancy and centrality of the Bible and in a pietistic morality. In both these emphases fundamentalism, despite its much reading of the Bible, betrays a profound ignorance of the Bible, including the way in which it was written and came into existence. Biblical scholars claim that the Bible does not support the views fundamentalists so zealously proclaim in its name (Barr 1975, 1984; Spong 1991). They rebuff intellectual relativity and uncertainty by claiming unquestionable and unchanging truth. This also means a rejection of those who do not give unquestioned submission to the prevailing teachings (Ruether 1992).

Two obvious questions to ask of fundamentalism are: what is its appeal to the millions of its followers? and secondly, to what extent does it provide a real answer to human needs? Both questions are difficult to answer. One appeal is its simplicity and apparent certainty. Fundamentalism seems to be a way of coping with the loss of identity, meaning and security in a society which is changing rapidly socially, politically, technologically, economically and in its religious values. In a rapidly changing and chaotic society, fundamentalism provides identity, certainty and some social security. People seem to want simple answers to life's complex questions. Secondly, it provides a fellowship that is deeply appealing, especially to lonely people, even though this is sometimes a fanatical sort of fellowship. As to the long-term consequences, it is well known that many fundamentalists fall by the wayside in what is referred to as 'backsliding'. It is not at all clear that fundamentalism provides an answer to the need for personal well-being of large numbers of people over a long period of time. It can be quite damaging, unless it happens to be a stepping-stone to a more mature faith. That it can also be. It was so for Bishop Spong (1991) and for myself also.

In my schooldays I craved for meaning, for something to make sense of life. I thought I had found it in a fundamentalist faith. I accepted a very simple set of affirmations about God, the world and myself. As my understanding of the world, and particularly science, grew, I found I was unable to reconcile my faith with facts. It was through a liberal Christian movement, the Student Christian Movement, that I discovered an alternative faith. The effect was to re-establish a fundamental trust with respect to the meaningfulness of life as I indicated in more detail in Chapter 1.

The term fundamentalism now has a much broader connotation than its origin in the Christian churches. Fundamentalism in a variety of forms exists in Judaism and Islam, in militant forms of Hinduism and Sikhism in India and in Confucian renewal in Japan, Taiwan and Korea (Marty & Appleby 1991). Wherever there is some book, document, principle or institution to which absolute authority is ascribed, the term is used by analogy with its original use.

A contrast is sometimes drawn between religion and science by saying that science thrives on change whereas religion clings to the past. A clash of doctrines in science is not a disaster but an opportunity. Newtonian science was succeeded by Einstein's relativity which, in its turn, was succeeded by quantum physics. Neither one successively overthrew the other, but modified it substantially. The biological doctrine of evolution has also evolved since Darwin's day, being first transformed by classical genetics and later by molecular biology, with plenty of controversy still associated with the contemporary understanding of how evolution occurs.

'Religion', says Whitehead (1926), 'will not regain its old power until it can face change in the same spirit as does science. Its principles may be eternal, but the expression of those principles requires continual development' (p. 234). Whitehead preceded this statement with the proposition that in the evolution of real knowledge a contradiction is not the signal of defeat but the first step in progress towards a victory. This is one good reason for toleration of a variety of opinions. He makes his point by referring to the parable of the tares (the weeds that look like wheat in a field of wheat) with its moral, 'Let both grow together until the harvest'. Why, he asks, have Christians not acted up to this precept from their highest authority?

A living vital religion cannot remain static as the world around it changes dramatically day by day. To be vital, religion, like science, has to grow. Christian doctrines may be good signposts, but they are bad hitching posts.

Over time religion does exhibit a gradual change and development, though it is much less changeable than science. Recent examples of this have already been given. Some things which were once regarded as vital have, after struggle and distress, been modified and otherwise interpreted. We witness this in the clash of religion with Galileo and with Darwinism. Now the main-line churches have accepted an understanding to each of these former conflicts.

The broad development of Protestantism since the Reformation illustrates adaptation of an existing order of understanding to changing needs of the world. The name Protestant derives from the written 'protest' made against the acts of the Diet of Speyer in 1529 by the princes supporting Luther (1483–1546). The Reformation itself was born with diversity. The German Reformation under Luther differed substantially from the Swiss Reformation under Zwingli (1484–1531) in Zurich and Calvin (1509–1564) in Geneva. The Reformation in France came from Calvinists who took the name Huguenots. In England the Anglican Church was the product of the Reformation. John Knox brought the Reformation, in the form of Calvinism, to Scotland to establish the Scottish Church.

The immediate wave which followed the Reformation was a period of orthodoxy known as classical orthodoxy or Protestant scholasticism (Tillich 1968, p. 276). Elements of this orthodoxy were retained in subsequent changes such as in the next big movement, known as pietism, which emphasised the subjective aspect of individual salvation as contrasted with intellectual acceptance of doctrines. This happened first in Germany with men like Spener and Zizendorf in the seventeenth century. Then it happened in British Methodism with the Wesley brothers. Anglicans who had pietistic views existed before this, such as the Puritans who were first given this name in the sixteenth century.

The pietists of the seventeenth century became deeply concerned with social ethics, founding the first orphanages in Europe and starting the first missionary enterprises. John Wesley looked to America to extend his missionary activity. He said his field was the world. Pietism had a deep concern for morals. Life in Europe was brutal and unrefined. The orthodox theologians did not do much about it. The pietists stressed the idea of individual sanctification and rejected love of 'worldy' things. Anything that could be labelled 'worldy' was, and still is today, anathema in pietistic circles. In general they resembled the Puritans in their strict moral attitude. But the pietists failed to recognise that the structures of society are unchristian. They failed to appreciate the need to replace existing social structures with more just and liberating ones. The subjectivity of the pietists became the doctrine of the 'inner light' of the Quakers, which was an ecstatic movement in the time of George Fox in the seventeenth century.

The Enlightenment criticised both orthodoxy and

pietism. Yet the church was not only greatly influenced by the Enlightenment, but contributed to it through Faustus Socinus and the Socinian movement. They declared that nothing can be a revelation of God in the Bible that is against reason and common sense. They brought a strong element of rationalism into theology which contrasted strongly with pietism.

English deism is another movement which used philosophy to solve theological problems. Deists attacked traditional orthodoxy as Socinus had done. This critical line of development was continued in theology in other contexts by Strauss, Schleiermacher and Johannes Weiss (Tillich 1968). Their thinking led to modern demythologisers of the Bible such as Bultmann. The deists did not look to theology for evidence of God but to nature. Nature was the great alternative background to the confusion in theology of preceding centuries. Hence their so-called natural theology which culminated in William Paley's *Natural Theology*. This book remained an alternative to logic in the entrance examination for Cambridge University until 1920.

The emphasis of deism was on evidence for the existence of God from design in nature. Furthermore, Paley's utilitarian ethics portrayed all living beings as having been designed for human benefit. Paley was the theologian of deism as Locke was its philosopher.

Deism received its death warrant from two events. The first was the Lisbon earthquake in the middle of the eighteenth century which killed 60,000 people. This was, in the world of that day, a catastrophe of monumental proportions. After all, God was supposed to have created the world for the purpose of serving human beings. It shook philosophers such as Goethe and Voltaire. A second blow to deism came in the middle of the nineteenth century with Darwin's alternative explanation of the design of nature with its emphasis on chance and struggle rather than on beneficent design.

The middle of the eighteenth century saw the first serious historical criticism of the synoptic gospels. People were shocked, as they were in our time, with the discovery of the Dead Sea Scrolls. Later in the nineteenth century, historical criticism gave a whole new perspective to the Hebrew scriptures and how they came to be. This analysis, particularly of the first five books of the Bible, continues today with the emphasis on the so-called four-document theory which replaced the belief that one writer such as Moses was the author of these books. The four documents, each with different authorship, are referred to as J (Y) for Yahwist, E for Elohist, D for Deuteronomic and P for Priestly.

In the religious movements within Christendom this century we find strands of many of the changes that took place through the centuries, while other strands have been ignored. The ethics of fundamentalism, for example, are based on pietism. The 'social gospel', transmitted to American theology by Walter Rausenbusch earlier in this century, drew much from Enlightenment theology but little, if anything, from pietism. It was quite a powerful movement up to the years before the Second World War when Reinhold Niebuhr attacked it vigorously.

Neo-orthodoxy in the 1930s and 1940s was a return to many elements of classical orthodoxy and a rejection of the natural theology of deism. It had a strong prophetic element based on the Bible. We live in the aftermath of the collapse of much of neo-orthodoxy. Process theology, or what Charles Hartshorne prefers to call neo-classical theology, has links with the theology of the early church fathers who were influenced by Greek thought, Socinus in the sixteenth century and the philosopher A. N. Whitehead of this century, who took science more seriously than his contemporary philosophers and theologians.

The point I want to make in this brief and incomplete survey is that history shows that religion takes change seriously and modifies its concepts as knowledge grows, though it could learn a lot more of this from ever-changing science. It is a misinterpretation of history to suppose that religion is transmitted unchanged from one generation to the next. It too develops, or else it dies, though the death pangs may be somewhat drawn out.

# A NEW SHARED ORDER OF THE MEANING OF LIFE

We live in a tower of Babel in which the disciplines, located on different floors, have little communication with one another. Economics, ecology, science, politics, religion and the arts live their separate existences unaware of the importance of some overall meaning and understanding. Yet somehow the disciplines have to come together in a shared vision of the meaning of life.

The common response to problems is to say, leave it to the experts. But that creates more problems because experts are more often wrong than right. They have tunnel vision when what we need is a wide-angled view of the world.

To do something about that is to ask for the greatest change of all to the order of present society. It is to ask that economists learn ecology and that ecologists learn economics; that science meets religion and both learn from each other; that our innermost human problems are seen, not simply as some personal aberration, but as intimately linked with the sort of society we create for ourselves. It is significant that when Daly and Cobb wrote about needed changes to the economic order, they concluded with criticism of the disciplinary organisation of knowledge and its domination of educational institutions, particularly the university (Daly & Cobb 1989, p. 357–60).

The basic reason for organising knowledge in separate disciplines is the idea that things are related to each other only externally. I have already discussed the effects of regarding the human person in traditional economics as an isolated ego instead of a 'person in community'. The person is regarded as a substance rather than as having internal relations with other persons.

Classical physics carved the universe up into bits of substances called particles, each one independent of its neighbours. The new physics no longer has a substance view of the universe. A substance is something that exists in its own right independent of any other things. But there are no such things! Our society is dominated by a substance view of the world from protons to people. So our society was consistent when it looked at all knowledge that way. Knowledge too, it supposed, could be divided into separate bits like the pieces in a jigsaw puzzle. But knowledge is not like that. To treat knowledge as if it were a substance is to miss out profoundly on the meaning of knowledge. (Birch 1990, Ch. 6).

The book of Genesis contains a revealing mythology of the human treatment of knowledge. In the garden of Eden everything in the garden was lovely until the occupants partook of the fruit of the tree of knowledge. Right from the beginning they got into trouble. Eating of the fruit gave them a knowledge of the difference between good and evil. It is presumed that if they had not eaten there would be no evil. But now that they had eaten, the knowledge they had and everything else was contaminated by evil. Well, you might say, as some do, let's go back to a state of innocence. Let's ban any further investigation into nuclear energy or genetic engineering. The possible fruits of that knowledge are awesome and even terrible to contemplate. Chernobyl is one consequence. And there will be others. But there is no possibility of going back to an Arcadian state of innocence.

An angel with a flaming sword bars the way! There is no turning back. So we are told in Genesis 3:24. The world we live in is full of ambiguity. That is how it is. The knowledge that is needed to put a world in tatters together again is itself in tatters. Yet there is hope.

Realising the ambiguity of human choices, we nevertheless can work to transcend the sorry state at every turn of the road. It is a task for every generation to be wary of false understanding and to seek to widen the picture we have of the world. We shall not find a blueprint for the world of the distant future. We may find some sort of blueprint for today. But it has to be subject to careful scrutiny tomorrow and again tomorrow after that. The wise virgins keep their lamps trimmed.

A major problem of world order is world management. Yet the approach to solving that problem is to bring in experts in economics, in technology and so on to seek solutions to each problem as it arises separately. The problems to do with management of the world order are all interconnected and indeed have a common source. The postmodern worldview affirms that knowledge is one and indivisible. When knowledge is divided into separate disciplines whose experts hardly talk to one another, we no longer find the vision that real understanding brings. The modern university can be compared to an encyclopaedia. The encyclopaedia contains many facts. It may contain nothing else. Its only unity is to be found in its alphabetical arrangement. The university is much the same. It has departments running from arts to zoology, but neither the students nor the professors know what is the relation of one department of truth to another.

Daly and Cobb (1989) make some practical suggestions as to how a university can begin to overcome the problem of the fragmentation of knowledge and understanding. In addition, each one of us can be part of a new consciousness of shared meaning.

One of the most exciting things happening in the lives of some people today is their own search for meaning beyond the horizons of meaning they were bequeathed by an older generation. They see the old order collapsing around them. The religion they acquired is dry bones. It failed to provide the necessary understanding and courage in the midst of the ambiguity of life. Then life was jolted into a new and larger circle. They experienced a heightened consciousness. The bones of an old understanding put on flesh. These people become committed to changing the world, or at least that part of it where they live. One of the most successful radio programs ever broadcast in Australia which has continued for many years is called *The search for meaning*. Its famous interviewer Caroline Jones speaks with subtle intimacy to someone each week about meaning in their life. The response has shown how deep is the need people feel to make sense of their lives. Something of these programs is captured in a published selection (Jones 1989, 1990).

I have seen conversion to a wider meaning come to

young people who were trying to save a tree in a forest threatened by timber merchants. To others it comes in finding there are values that come into life to sustain it in the most tragic circumstances. There are emotional conversions. There are intellectual conversions. It means our direction is changed. It does not mean we have all the answers. It could mean we are better fitted to live in the real world beyond the utopian garden where an angel blocks the way to our return to innocence.

## CONCLUSION

This chapter deals with the relation of order and change in two areas of life, the economic order and the religious order. I selected these two areas because they illustrate the need to preserve order amid change and to preserve change amid order. If I were to have selected an area where change successfully builds on order, I would have chosen science. It has been far more successful than either politics or religion in holding order and change together. However, the urgent necessity of today is that the sort of principles science has worked with so successfully in relating established order to changed knowledge may be applied in these other areas.

The changes needed in the economic order are profound. The 'object' called economic man needs to be replaced with the 'subject' called 'person in community'. The understanding of human nature in traditional economics is profoundly erroneous. It is diametrically opposed to the view of human nature developed in this book, where humans are understood to be constituted by their relations.

It is the business of the future to be dangerous and to take risks. But the sort of risks to be faced are not the foolhardy ones that are destroying the biosphere right now. A mature approach accepts the inevitability of incomplete knowledge and the imperfections of human beings. How can we, within these restrictions, attain the intellectual and moral maturity to live fully and safely in the complex world of economics and politics?

Religion is a potent force both for good and for evil in society. If it is to work for good, it is necessary that religion face change in much the same spirit as does science. Its principles may be eternal but the working out of these principles has to be done in the context of the world of science and change.

Christians tend to have little sense of history and many of them behave as though the truths of their religion have been handed down unchanged from generation to generation on a platter. A review of the history of Protestantism in particular shows how the Christian religion has undergone profound changes in the last 300 years and will continue to do so. It just needs to speed up the process a bit, else it shall become fossilised and be fit only as a museum piece.

We live in a collapsing tower of Babel at a time when we need an integrating view of all knowledge and understanding. There is, nevertheless, the possibility that each one of us may discover a new shared order of the meaning of life. It is the task of each generation to be wary of false understanding and to seek to widen the picture we have of the world. The wise virgins keep their lamps trimmed, that they be ready to usher in the approaching new order.

# CHAPTER 5
# HUMAN RE-SPONSE TO CHANGE

To constitute a socially significant change, the new must be not only adopted by a sufficient number of the members of a social population to give it currency, but so integrated into the social system that it will endure.
*La Piere (1965, p. 66)*

n 23 May 1946 Albert Einstein sent a telegram to President Roosevelt on behalf of the Emergency Committee of Atomic Scientists, saying in reference to nuclear explosions, 'The unleashed power of the atom has changed everything save our modes of thinking, and thus we drift towards unparalleled catastrophe'. Everything had changed because of our ability to destroy the world by pressing a few buttons. Science and technology had harnessed the power of the atom to destroy, on a global scale, as was never possible before. Einstein's implication was that humanity was quite unprepared to cope with this new power. The only possibility of a viable world in the future was if people changed in response to the new power at their disposal.

A most dramatic change of heart did, in fact, come from a most unexpected quarter, with a delay of some four decades after Einstein's telegram. It didn't come from the president of the United States, but from the president of the then Soviet Union, Mickhail Gorbachev. He reversed the policy of the Soviet Union and took immediate steps to reduce the mass of nuclear weapons both in his country and in the US.

This change in policy was not, of course, simply a change in heart of one man. Much had been going on at a grassroots level that was indicating to the world the nature of a global nuclear war. Up until the early 1980s the international community of statesmen, diplomats and military analysts had tended to regard the prospect of a nuclear war as a problem only for the adversaries in possession of the weapons. Endless negotiations aimed at the reduction of nuclear explosives had been viewed as the responsibility of those few nations in actual confrontation.

Then everything changed. Computer models being investigated both in the US and in the Soviet Union were demonstrating that a nuclear war involving the exchange of a small fraction of the total American and Russian bombs could change the climate of the entire Northern Hemisphere, shifting it abruptly from its present seasonal state to a long, sunless, frozen night. Nor would the Southern Hemisphere escape profound climatic changes. Subsequent studies by a group of twenty biologists, headed by Paul Ehrlich, showed that the predictions meant nothing less than the extinction of much of the Earth's biosphere. Taken together, these two discoveries changed everything in the world about the prospect of thermonuclear war. It is a new world, demanding a new kind of diplomacy and a new logic.

Up to then the risks of a thermonuclear war had been conventionally calculated by the number of human beings who would be dead on either side at the end of the battle. The terms 'acceptable' and 'unacceptable' signified so many millions of human casualties on which cool judgments could be made about the need for new and more weapons. But now something else was predicted to happen as well. The organised ecological systems of the Earth would have been dealt a mortal or near mortal blow, perhaps putting the Earth's future toward a state comparable to what was here a billion years ago. Here was a global dilemma involving all humanity.

For the first time satellite communications were used to bring together a group of scientists in Moscow and a group in Washington for an extensive exchange of scientific information in what became known as 'the Moscow link'. The principal secretary of the USSR Academy of Sciences expressed the view that scientists on both sides of the Atlantic had reached a consensus and were unified in their view that nuclear war would spell disaster for the world. This television program was widely seen throughout the world.

There is little doubt now of the huge impact of these deliberations on politicians, scientists and the general public. It stands as a star example of how new information about our world can become widely appreciated across the world. The story, which is only briefly told here, is fully documented by Ehrlich and Sagan (1984) in *The Cold and the Dark* and more recently by Sagan and Turco (1991).

This particular response to change is unfortunately not typical. Ornstein and Ehrlich have written a book which aims to tell us that the human mind is largely failing

to comprehend the world we live in and that we need a
new mind for the new world (Ornstein & Ehrlich 1989).

# THE MISMATCH BETWEEN OUR MINDS AND THE WORLD

Ornstein and Ehrlich (1989) argue that the human mind
has evolved through countless ages to cope with sudden
and dramatic changes that threaten survival such, for example, as the threat of a predator, fire or flood. We are genetically programmed to deal with these emergencies. That was
about all we had until perhaps a million years ago. Cultural
evolution then outpaced genetical evolution of humans.
That simply means that information learned from experience was passed on to subsequent generations through
teaching and learning. This was a much more rapid way of
adaptation to a changing environment. The difference between humans who lived in caves and us is primarily cultural, not genetical. Science and its transformation of the
world is an outstanding example of cultural evolution.

However, Ornstein and Ehrlich argue that even our
capacity for cultural evolution has not matched the changing circumstances of our life on earth. We have learned to
react to sudden and dramatic changes such as the highjack-
ing of aircraft or drunken drivers on the road. But we have
not learned to respond to slow changes with long-term effects such as the population explosion, the increasing extinction of species and the deterioration of the environment. These are far more critical to the human future.

What can we do about this dilemma? There must be
more public awareness, public debate and decisions to take
action as a society. Ehrlich and Ornstein see this as involving a much more conscious cultural evolution of the mind
and a rethinking of education. There are those who pes-
simistically say, 'You can't change human nature'. Yet we
do change human nature daily in our schools and over
time in societies. We need now to consciously manage that
change. It can be done and it is being done. Here are some
examples:

◆ Social scientists in the 1960s believed it would take decades of consistent government pressure to persuade Americans to change their reproductive habits and have small families. The habit of having as many children as one could afford was considered a fundamental part of human nature. Yet the shift to small families took about three years in the early 1970s. This was due in no small measure to the way in which the campaign for 'zero population growth' spread across the nation.

◆ Until the United Nations' first major conference on the global environment in 1972 in Stockholm, few national governments had departments of environment. Now most of them do, with a few notable exceptions such as Japan.

◆ Many countries are recognising the seriousness of the population problem and some have had success in deliberately curbing population growth, notably the richer countries of South-East Asia and also China.

◆ More people are becoming sympathetic to the other organisms that also inhabit the Earth. They are trying to save endangered species and protect domestic and laboratory animals from abuse.

◆ Millions of people realise that nuclear weapons threaten everyone together with the biosphere and are trying to find ways of eliminating them.

◆ Winds of change have blown through all countries of Eastern Europe in a way not dreamed of less than a decade ago.

◆ Some ecologists believe that we cannot convert to an ecologically sustainable society with a new economics quickly enough to prevent ecological collapse. Yet our economy was transformed to a wartime basis in a matter of a year or so at the beginning of the Second World War and changed back to a peacetime basis in a similar period at the end of that war. What we need is a change of heart such that ecological issues have for us 'the moral equivalent of war'.

Human beings changed from cave people, to Neolithic people, to Agricultural people to Industrial people. If we can increase global consciousness and people become sufficiently motivated, we could change to a postmodern people with an ecologically sustainable society. It is to promote such a consciousness and to induce such a motivation that some of us write books.

# THE JOHARI WINDOW

The response people make to change is varied and the nature of that variation can be understood with the help of a model. Figure 5.1 is a modification of the so-called Johari window described by Luft (1984). The vertical axis of the diagram represents different degrees of awareness of benefit brought by a particular change. This ranges on a scale from 0 to 10. The horizontal axis of the diagram represents different degrees of awareness of detrimental aspects of the change. Again the scale goes from 0 to 10. The detrimental aspects may have to do with the costs, losses and fears of change. Any point within the diagram represents some combination of the two elements of awareness and so represents the reaction of a particular person to a particular change. Here are five typical responses within the total field with the names given them by Wasdell (1986).

*Blissful ignorance* (1.1). There is virtually no awareness of either the good or the bad aspects of the change. It is an attitude of apathy.

*Idealised endorsement* (1.9). This position at the left-hand top of the diagram represents maximal awareness of the benefits of change with no objections at all. It is a utopian attitude.

*Unrelieved opposition* (9.1). This position at the right-hand corner of the diagram represents change as perceived to be completely bad. Change represents a serious threat. This person is all for maintaining the status quo. It is an attitude of bias that can become fanatical.

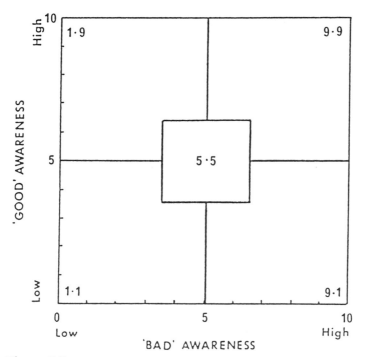

**Figure 5.1**
*Johari window of response to change (After Wasdell 1986)*

*Conflicted ambivalence* (5.5). There is some awareness of the advantages of change but this is balanced by an equal and opposite awareness of the disadvantages. It is a position of ambivalence and indecision.

*Realistic integration* (9.9). This position at the top right-hand corner of the diagram represents a high awareness of the advantages of change together with a high awareness of the disadvantages. There is commitment to accept change, despite an awareness of many disadvantages, and to work realistically for change in an ambiguous world. The reformer hopes that society will move from positions around 1.1 to those around 9.9.

For the most part, the ideas that people hold as valid reflect the activities they accept as normal, rather than the other way around. A movement for change reverses this order. Those who join the movement are encouraged by the new idea to act in new ways.

The future is helped only by people in the second and the last categories above. Those in the other groups are part of the problem and not part of the answer. The utopians have their hearts in the right place but they have their problems because they are unrealistic. They can easily be put off by finding the world is not such a dream world after all. However, once started on that road they might hopefully make their pilgrimage toward realism more readily than the others and accept that we do not live in a garden of Eden after all. They may make the pilgrimage from the garden of blissful contentment to one that is full of weeds and entanglements. Even so, they may come to realise at position 9.1 the lot of a realist and press on in hope.

Possibly no other social ethicist was as committed to realism as Reinhold Niebuhr. He was a prophet of change. Nevertheless he strongly believed

> ... that no matter how wide the perspectives which the human mind may reach, how broad the loyalties which the human imagination may conceive, how universal the community which human statecraft may organise or how pure the aspirations of the saintliest idealist may be, there is no level of human moral or social achievement in which there is not some corruption of inordinate self-love. (Niebuhr 1944, p. 17).

For Niebuhr, every civilisation and culture, every empire and nation, has destructive elements in its period of creativity, and even creative elements in its period of decline. One of Niebuhr's most quoted statements is: 'Man's capacity for justice makes democracy possible; but man's inclination to injustice makes democracy necessary' (p. xiii). Niebuhr saw democracy as steering a road between the Scylla of anarchy and the Charybdis of tyranny. He countered the naivete of activist utopian liberals, who regarded humanity as good by nature, awaiting perfection through social reform and education. He saw in the real world the search for moral righteousness as filled with ambiguity. The choices are not between pure virtue and absolute vice, but between differing combinations of vice and virtue. His approach became known as Christian realism.

# CAN JACK GET OUT OF HIS BOX?

This is the title of a lecture I heard Theodore Roszak (1971) give on the counter-cultural image of the future. He made three propositions. Jack is in the box. Jack does not know he is in the box. Jack must get out of the box. The box imprisons Jack within a view that depends almost exclusively on the perception of the eye and the ear and upon things that can be spoken. Roszak was calling for a change in consciousness not dissimilar to the change to a new consciousness proposed in this book. It is a major change that requires Jack to get out of his box. In the context of this book it is a change from the dominant modern worldview to a postmodern worldview to use the terminology of my earlier book, *On Purpose* (Birch 1990).

The modern worldview is derived from the Scientific Revolution, the Enlightenment and the Industrial Revolution. The postmodern worldview is more concerned with the subjective, feelings, values, consciousness and internal relations. It is an organic or holistic view contrasted with a mechanical or substance view of things. To embrace it involves a paradigm (*paradeigma* = pattern) shift in thinking and in behaviour.

The box that Jack is imprisoned in is the modern worldview. He was put into it early in his schooling and in further education at college or university, with the result that all else has nothing to do with the real world or at best is of marginal value. The beginning of wisdom is the awareness that what Jack knows in his box is not the world, but only a small box within the world, a very small box indeed.

Roszak ended his lecture with a prediction of what was going to happen to some Jacks in the box. It was something like this. This is Jack speaking and going through some stages of development. What do you mean, I am in the box? So what? I like the box. The box is the best place to be. God only knows what is outside of this box. Good old box. True, it is somewhat stuffy and cramped in this box, but that makes me feel responsible.

It is good to be miserable, it brings out the best in us. Besides, the box does not have to be that uncomfortable. I can put in some air-conditioning and wall-to-wall carpeting. And listen, I have got some swell new stereophonic sound equipment. I could turn this box into a real pleasure palace. If I don't get out of this box soon I am going to go crazy. I am crazy. Everybody in the box is crazy. Crazy is normal. No I cannot help it. I've got to get out of this box, maybe just for weekends. There are people living outside the box. And they seem happy. But I don't really know what happy means anymore. Maybe if I left the box just for a while I could see what it is like outside.

And finally, what a tiny little box right there in the middle of the universe. People used to live in that box, they say. But that's very hard to believe. Jack made his choice.

## CONCLUSION

Human beings can change, though their response to change varies greatly from one person to another. On a grand scale societies have responded to change in major ways. A recent example is the changed attitude to nuclear war as compared with attitudes less than a decade ago. Changes of this sort require a deliberate reorientation in consciousness at the grassroots level.

We are genetically programmed to deal with immediate emergencies and not long-term threats. To cope with the latter involves a cultural change. Our capacity for such cultural change has not matched the changing circumstances on Earth today. Yet there is hope as we contemplate examples of major cultural changes that have taken place in our own time.

The individual person may respond to change in one of five ways: blissful ignorance, idealised endorsement, unrelieved opposition, conflicting ambivalence or realistic integration of the advantages and disadvantages of change.

The future is helped by people in the second and the last categories. But it is possible for people who find themselves in one of the other negative categories to jump out of their confinement to take a more hopeful and creative attitude.

# CHAPTER 6
# AT-ONE-
# MENT

Why is there not nothing?
*Parmenides*


O God, who himself fashioned himself,
The world subsists in thy hand.
Men live through thee.
*Ikhnaton*


I choose the term 'Peace' for that Harmony of Harmonies ...
It is a broadening of feeling due to the emergence of some
deep metaphysical insight, unverbalised and yet momentous in its co-ordination of values. There is thus involved a
grasp of infinitude, an appeal beyond boundaries ... The experience of 'Peace' is largely beyond the control of purpose.
It comes as a gift.
*A.N. Whitehead (1942, p. 327)*

The first Greek philosopher, Parmenides, asks that most difficult of all questions. Why is there not nothing? I respond to that question when I gaze at a beautifully made rainbow lorikeet feeding on my balcony. There could have been a world without birds, without anything living at all. The universe could have been just empty space stretching out for ever. But it isn't. The modern philosopher Ludwig Wittgenstein expressed the same thought when he wrote: 'Not *how* the world is, is the mystical, but *that* it is'.

More than 3000 years ago the first monotheist, Ikhnaton, in his poems to the one God, wrote of all things, including the birds he was familiar with on the Nile, subsisting in God's hand. God gave unity to the creation. And the greatest metaphysical philosopher of our time, A.N. Whitehead, speaks of experiencing this unity as a momentous harmony with the universe.

Human life is infinitely complex and inexhaustible in its possibilities. More than in any other being we experience diverse and divergent trends that need be continuously kept in some sort of harmony. 'Health', said Paul Tillich (1963) 'is not the lack of divergent trends in our bodily or mental or spiritual life, but the power to keep them united' (p. 50). The word that describes the state of being disunited is estrangement, meaning a stranger to any unitary meaning to life. As a philosophical term it was given meaning by Hegel. Alienation has a similar meaning.

Estrangement and alienation are not biblical terms, but they are implied in the biblical description of the human predicament; the expulsion from paradise, the hostility between humanity and nature, the hostility of person against person, of nation against nation, and of the continuous complaint of the prophets against the rulers. Estrangement is implied in Paul's classical description of the human predicament of 'man against himself' because of his conflicting desires. 'For I do not do the good I want, but the evil I do not want is what I do' (Romans 7:19–20).

# ESTRANGEMENT AND 'PEACE'

Estrangement presupposes the possibility of an ultimate harmony. Human beings strive to unite themselves with that to which they belong and from which they are separated. Life is separation and reunion. And it is true not only for humans but for every living creature. They desire food, warmth, play, participation in groups, sexual union and so on. The fulfilment of these desires is accompanied by pleasure. But it is not the pleasure as such which is desired, but the union with that which fulfils desire.

It is a distortion of life if one supposes from these facts that life consists essentially in fleeing from pain and striving for pleasure. Whenever that happens, life is corrupted. Authentic life strives for that which it lacks. It strives for union with that from which it is separated, because it belongs to it. All people, since they are separated from the whole, desire union with the whole. One's poverty makes one seek for abundance.

There is a word that speaks to this harmony which is the opposite of estrangement and alienation. It is at-one-ment (or atonement), being at one with. The word salvation also means being made whole or being healed. Paul Tillich's 'New Being' speaks to a similar new creation. Whitehead's 'Peace', as the harmony of harmonies, expresses these meanings. Peace is not the absence of strife but the presence of something extraordinarily positive and uniting. Peace is the lure in existence that includes all values. It is forever transforming. But it is more. The ultimate hunger of the human soul is not satisfied with purely personal enjoyment. The value one seeks must be more than the sum of human attainments. 'Otherwise', says John Cobb (1965):

> the restlessness of the soul is not quenched. Peace is the sense that indeed there are aims in the universe beyond our own and that our aims can be harmonious with them and contribute to them. It is the sense that what we attain is taken up into the larger whole and preserved in harmony with all the other achievements of value. (p. 132)

How can it be meaningful to take a single step, if the whole journey is meaningless?

The discussion of Whitehead's 'Peace' cannot be separated from the discussion of God. 'Peace ... is a direct apprehension of one's relatedness with that factor in the universe which is divine' (Cobb 1965, p. 133). God is the ultimate source of that peace. It is the peace that passes understanding, yet is known in experience. According to Whitehead (1926):

> It is the vision of something which stands beyond, behind, and within, the passing flux of immediate things; something which is real, and yet waiting to be realized; something which is a remote possibility, and yet the greatest of present facts; something that gives meaning to all that passes, and yet eludes apprehension; something whose possession is the final good, and yet is beyond all reach; something which is the ultimate ideal, and the hopeless quest. (p. 238)

'Peace' is experienced as ineffable unity and harmony, yet is only partially grasped and understood. It is the endless quest, yet the ultimate attainment. It is like fulfilled love; at the same time extreme happiness because separation is overcome, yet also a restlessness because unity is never complete. But without the separation there is no life, no motivation for further exploration of the human spirit. We live in tension between contentedness and discontentedness. I discussed this tension in discussing love between oneself and another in Chapter 1. Relationships between some people, perhaps a very few, are suffocatingly close. But genuine love preserves the separation of the individuality of each self, making real their interdependence in love.

Real knowing is not simply cognition, but a possessing that transforms the one who knows. Perfect knowledge is perfect possession. When Socrates asserted that out of knowing the good the doing of the good follows, he knew that real knowing includes union and therefore openness to receive that with which one unites. He knew as well that one may know the good in another sense without doing it. Such a person is not grasped by the good as something that possesses him or her in such a way as to transform life.

I shall return to this harmony of harmonies. But first we need to identify the realities of our disharmonies. The preceding chapters are replete with examples of our estrangement in the world of today. It is no exaggeration to say that human beings today experience life in terms of disruption, conflict, self-destruction, meaninglessness and despair in all realms of life. This is expressed in literature, the arts, in existential and positivist philosophy and it is actualised in social and political life of all kinds.

We are estranged in four ways: from ourselves, from other human beings, from nature and from God. Our estrangement from ourselves, from humanity and from nature can all be regarded as alienation from 'Peace' in the sense discussed in the previous paragraphs. The question for us is how can the self-estrangement of our existence be overcome in a new reconciliation of meaning and hope?

# ESTRANGEMENT FROM OURSELVES AND FROM HUMANITY

We experience estrangement from ourselves when we are other than what we could be as fulfilled human beings, experiencing life to the full. During the Second World War a special psychological clinic was established in the United States for people who had, through exigencies of war, lost a sense of a central control over their lives. They were very confused. The psychologist Erik Erikson referred to their condition as a loss of 'ego identity'.

Later Erikson recognised a similar disturbance in young people who were confused because of a 'war within themselves'. He referred to this condition as 'identity confusion'. Later still this became known as an 'identity crisis' (Erikson 1968). A young person passing from childhood to adolescence changes from that which he has come to be as a child toward the promise of a changed future. Youth begins to realise a certain perception of the changing self and perceives others to have certain expectations of that same youth which might be quite different. A youth who is not sure of his or her identity, perhaps his or her sexual orientation or what his or her main commitments are to be, may find life anything but fulfilling. One may, for example, shy away from intimacy and become lonely and isolated. Youth can be a time of frustration and confusion when various options have to be sorted out and only some paths chosen.

William James had a prolonged identity crisis during which he experienced his world as stagnant and he became very depressed. At the age of twenty-six he wrote to Oliver Wendell Holmes: 'Much would I give for a constructive passion of some kind' (Erikson 1968, p. 151). By dint of sheer will he persuaded himself that he had to find a work that would interest him and at the same time allow him 'to feel that through it he takes hold of the reality of things'. (Dean 1990, p. 89). James said he was entirely broken down before he was thirty. Yet in middle age he wrote his acclaimed *Varieties of Religious Experience,* in which he says that if he had not, in his state of despair, clung to two biblical verses he had learned in his youth — 'God is my refuge' and 'Come unto me all you that labour and are heavy laden' — he would have gone mad. Later William James was able to write to his wife:

> A man's character is discernable in the mental or moral attitude in which, when it came upon him, he felt himself most deeply and intensely active and alive. At such moments there is a voice inside which speaks and says: This is the real me! (Erikson 1968, p. 21)

Erikson suggests that the word 'character' which James uses in this letter means a sense of identity. He writes in a way to suggest that a sense of identity can be experienced by anyone. He acknowledges that the real me is not the stagnant me in a state of depression but the me who has found a deep sense of life as fulfilling to overflowing.

Tolstoy seemed forever in an identity crisis in three areas of his life; his attitudes to Russian nationalism, to religion and to sex. Many of his novels are thinly disguised accounts of his struggles with each. One wonders if he ever really came to terms with any of them (Wilson 1988).

According to psychiatrist Scott Peck (1990), most people who come to see a psychiatrist are suffering from

either a 'neurosis' or a 'character disorder'. These are opposite ways of relating to the world and its problems. When
neurotic people are in conflict with the world they assume
that they are at fault. When those with 'character disorders'
are in conflict with the world they assume that the world is
at fault. People don't like me and I don't like myself, says
the neurotic. On the other hand, people with a 'character
disorder' don't see themselves as the source of their problems. Other people are. Both conditions are disorders of responsibility. Both give a sense of deep estrangement, one
from self, the other from the world.

We can hide from ourselves our real motives that can
lead to a sense of alienation. But we cannot hide from ourselves for ever. A man works with dedication to his business or profession, feeling assured of the good he is doing.
Yet his commitment to his work may be a way of escaping
genuine human commitments and of escaping from himself. A mother who lives for her children passionately feels
only love for them. Yet her anxiety concerning them may
be an expression of her will to dominate them. We cannot
applaud our every act of moral self-restraint. Its cause may
be cowardice, preventing us from making a revolution
against inherited rules of behaviour.

The evil I do not want to do is what I do, because I kid
myself that what I am doing is good. In countless ways we
experience a power that dwells within us and directs our
will in ways we seem unable to control. We are a battlefield
of influences where decisive choices are made. This is our
despair. It is also our glory.

The decisive aspect of estrangement, be it in youth or
adulthood, comes from choosing to make ultimate that
which is not of ultimate concern for our lives. The classical
name of this distortion is idolatry.

Idolatry is the worshipping of false values. It leads to
the estrangement of self. This was clearly recognised in the
Old Testament: 'those who make them [idols] will be like
them, and so will all who trust in them' (Psalm 115:8). Idolatry is the basic distortion in life. One way people try to overcome an identity crisis is to idolise themselves. They per-

suade themselves that what is evil and divisive is good.

Idolatry leads to pride, which is very destructive and terrible in perverting relations between human beings. This is the theme of the story of the fall and the tower of Babel in the Old Testament. Pride is the main subject of Greek tragedy, where it is called *hubris*. Hubris is the self-elevation of a person into the sphere of the divine. The individual, who is usually a hero in Greek drama, becomes a god to himself. It is a turning inward to oneself and away from at-one-ment with others and the world.

The Pharisees, at the time of Jesus, identified their supposed goodness with an absoluteness that made them see themselves as local gods. They deeply resented the possibility that anyone else could be more virtuous than they.

The Emperor Nero is a classic embodiment of a man who draws everything into himself to use it for himself in whatever way he wants.

Goethe's Faust has an unlimited passion for knowledge, therefore in order to know everything he accepts a pact with the devil. It is the 'everything', not the knowledge as such, that produces his demonic temptation. The modern Faust is the technocrat who puts his complete trust in yet more technical knowledge with which to control the world. So it was appropriate that those who put their utmost faith in nuclear power in the 1970s and 1980s were said by their opponents to have made a Faustian pact.

Pride, with its overweening self-interest, becomes transmuted into the will to power. There is a legitimate role for power in maintaining order in society. Just what that role is has always been a problem for ethics, particularly one that has love as its guiding principle. How can power be united with love?

This was a problem that perplexed Luther. He resolved the dilemma for himself with the statement that power is the 'strange work of love'. Tillich (1954) interprets that to mean, 'It is the strange work of love to destroy that which is against love' (p. 49). The strange work of love has to do with judgment and punishment. It is to destroy that which is against love, but not the one who acts against love. But, as Tillich points out, Luther did not appreciate sufficiently that love's strange work can be used by those in power as a means for keeping themselves in power.

John Calvin was guilty of that. He said the state must use its power to punish the impious, otherwise how could he maintain the sort of theocratic society he was creating in Geneva. He was true to his word. The Spanish biologist Servetus, who had discovered the pulmonary circulation of the blood before William Harvey, was deeply religious. In a book published in Vienna he made a vigorous attack on Calvin. Calvin was furious and had Servetus brought before the Inquisition in Vienna. Servetus was cast into prison, but escaped. He sought refuge in Geneva, probably to co-operate with the anti-Calvinistic party which was planning to attack the despotic reformer. However, Calvin was on his guard. Servetus was arrested, tried in Geneva and condemned to be burnt at the stake. The verdict was carried out on 27 October 1553 to the eternal shame of Calvin. Many others in Geneva suffered lesser fates under the rule of Calvin for their 'impiety'. Those who objected to the conditions he laid down for being a citizen of Geneva simply left, or were goaled or executed. Such was the moral, legal and political power Calvin gave to himself, though he never held a post higher than that of pastor.

I have discussed estrangement of the individual person from self; how self-centredness leads to pride which leads to the will to power. Power becomes an idol. Estrangement can also be corporate. The problem of power becomes the central problem of any movement that attempts to change the social order. The Hebrew prophets spent more time denouncing the nation than individuals. The individual in society may be alienated because of an unjust economic system that devalues the personal. The sources of corporate estrangement are the same as those that produce the estrangement of the individual; egoism, pride and the desire for power and domination by a group or groups of people. Such groups work against achieving a true human community.

Initially such groups may be deceptive, because of

what they promise. Hitler and his gang initially promised, and gave, employment and a sense of belonging to the nation. Many people were deceived. They did not realise what was in store for them in terms of genocide and mass destruction. The promised paradise became a living hell. Gerhard Linn was a pastor who lived through both the Fascist and the socialist regimes in Germany. He says it was easier, though more dangerous, to discern the truth when confronting the crimes of Fascist groups, than to cope with the ambiguity of the Communists in East Germany during the first years after the war. In the beginning they made some good moves, such as land-reform, but soon after that people began to disappear mysteriously. The official party claimed they were promoting a democratic renewal of Germany. The first constitution of the German Democratic Republic was an acceptable one. But what was good in it was meant to deceive the reality that was planned for the Communist state (Linn 1991).

It was the abuse of power that shipwrecked the socialist states in Eastern Europe and not the many mistakes that could have been corrected. According to one who has lived through the rise and fall of the socialist state in Czechoslovakia, the real and irreconcilable antagonism between social systems is between restrained and unrestrained power (Macek 1991).

The USSR was established on principles of egalitarianism that seemed noble enough at the time. How was it that what commenced as a reforming movement so quickly became a nightmare for seventy-four years, particularly under Stalin, finally to collapse in August 1991? Of course there are all sorts of reasons. A critical one was the abuse of power when problems in economics, agriculture and other areas became intractable.

When the state dehumanises people for the enforcement of its laws it loses its legitimacy to govern. The totalitarian state of Nazi Germany did this as did the totalitarian socialist regimes in Eastern Europe. They knew no criteria against the tyranny they used to preserve power. Power is a limited good. When power dehumanises people it becomes evil.

We see this evil around the world in the abuse of human rights. The United Nations Development Program made a study of freedom and lack of it in eighty-eight countries in the United Nations General Assembly. They estimated a 'human freedom index' for each country based on 1985 figures for forty different indicators, among them the right to travel, freedom of religion, freedom from unlawful detention, independent press, homosexual activities between consenting adults. All the forty freedoms are endorsed by international accords such as the Universal Declaration of Human Rights. Sweden, Denmark, the Netherlands and Finland were at the top. Sweden had thirty-eight freedoms out of forty; Finland had thirty-six freedoms. At the bottom were Iraq with zero freedoms, Libya with one freedom, Ethiopia and China with two freedoms, and South Africa and the USSR each with three. Countries with a low level of freedom also had a low level of human development (Human Development Report 1991). The achievement of the right balance between power and justice is obviously a major problem in the world today.

It is the genius of democracy to recognise the necessity of restraints on power. One is reminded again of Niebuhr's perceptive statement that it is our human capacity for justice that makes democracy possible, but the human inclination to injustice that makes democracy necessary (Niebuhr 1944, p. xiii).

Pastor Gerhard Linn was active in the Christian church in East Germany. They were a people, he said, who had no power and who did not long for power. They longed for change and they indeed helped to bring it about. His fear is that the church, having now won a certain reputation and role in society, may fall to the temptation to become a master rather than a servant of society (Linn 1991). History suggests his fears are warranted.

For example, Christianity began as a fringe group in society. For the first three hundred years of its existence the church was an alienated minority. Christians felt themselves alienated from the world they lived in. They were discriminated against and persecuted by their rulers. But while there was alienation between the church and society at large, ancient alienations were being overcome within the church. In particular, differences of race, social position and of sex were being reduced by a new spirit of reconciliation. But with Emperor Constantine and the fourth century the picture changed. The one-time alienated minority becomes, first, a tolerated religion and then the religion of the state. The church became identified with society and some of its members engaged in persecution of the remaining pockets of paganism. The Emperor Constantine was not averse to the ruthless despatch of those he regarded as conspiring against him. He murdered his wife and son for this reason in AD 326 while he was actually presiding at the First Ecumenical Council of Nicea! (Chryssavgis 1991).

The close identification of church and state was full of dangers. For something like fifteen centuries, Christianity remained the dominant religious force in Europe, being closely identified with the social and political fabric. This was the phenomenon which we now call 'Christendom'. It was full of ambiguities. So long as the church was an alienated sect, it kept alive a vision of a new humanity but had no power to influence the wider society other than to be a leaven in the loaf. When it attained power and influence its ideal faded and, in large measure, it conformed to the values of the society in which it had power. The same seems to be happening to Islam today in some countries. The power of the corporate group that alienates itself from the society it claims to serve is a corrupting power.

Another sort of estrangement is that of groups within society who are alienated by the prejudice of others. Until recently black people have been excluded from the mainstream of American society. They have lived in separate neighbourhoods and gone to separate schools and churches. They still suffer from alienation. The Aborigines of Australia suffered hideous crimes when European settlement took over. Only in recent decades have serious attempts been made to bring the Aborigines into full community with whites. Yet many of them still live in shanty settlements on the periphery of country towns or in the slums of big cities.

Throughout the world, especially in Europe, the Jews have been an alienated people. They were compelled to live in ghettos and have been excluded from many aspects of public life. The call to inclusiveness has been part of the heritage of the Christian church, yet the church has also been anti-Semitic in much of its history (Cobb 1991b).

A third group who suffer alienation from society at large are homosexuals. At worst they have been persecuted and at best tolerated. Gay men and lesbian women are physically and psychologically abused, they are excluded from families, frozen out of churches and discriminated against in a variety of legal ways. Most people in our society are homophobic. Their self-understanding as sexual beings is disturbed by encounters with homosexuality, both in themselves and in others. This is true of many parents.

Just as the 'woman problem' is really a problem of male chauvinism, the 'homosexual problem', is really a problem of the homophobia of heterosexuals. Christians who claim to be loving, yet who brand homosexuals as sinful and wicked, are themselves full of prejudice. They accuse homosexuals of choosing their sexual orientation when the evidence points to sexual orientation, at least in most cases, as being something we do not choose but are born with. If a homosexual person is so made that an intimate loving relationship is possible only with a member of the same sex, on what basis can this experience of love be declared sinful? Are such people to be celibate for their whole lives? Is not the law of love more important than the laws of biology?

Members of the dominant sexual orientation reason that what is normal for them is also natural. If something is not normal for them it is unnatural. So they argue that homosexual behaviour is unnatural. But as Bishop Spong (1990) says: 'Behind this pronouncement are stereotypic definitions of masculinity and femininity that reflect the rigid gender categories that arise out of a patriarchal society ... Can a religious tradition that has long practiced circumcision and institutionalised celibacy ever dismiss any other practice on the basis of its unnaturalness?' (pp. 70, 71). Homosexuals are not inferior or superior to other people. They are simply different, just as blue-eyed people are neither superior nor inferior to brown-eyed people. They are different.

As Cobb points out, the Christ of the churches today is bad news for homosexual persons. Today churches have conceded to women a place in the sun. There is some measure of repentance for millennia-long oppression sanctioned by the teaching of the church in its appeal to patriarchal morality. Some concession is also made now to the effect that having desire for persons of the same sex may not in itself be sinful. But it is still asserted that to act on that desire is immoral. Hence a homosexual, to satisfy the demands of the patriarchal church, must either abstain from sexual activity or 'convert' to heterosexual behaviour. Whether the latter is a feasible alternative is very questionable. The Christ of the churches is certainly bad news for homosexual persons. But as Cobb makes clear, the Christ who is bad news is not Christ at all (Cobb 1991b). The church has been good at helping homosexuals (with AIDS) to die but has not been good at helping homosexuals to live.

If the church is to make Christ good news for the homosexual person its task will be to help that person envision positive scenarios for a fulfilled and happy future. These will be scenarios that order the sexual life to wider purposes without simply denying it or repressing it. Cobb sees the best choice for most to be a pair bonding that involves mutual responsibility for each other in a possible lifelong commitment. But, of course, it is no more certain that such a partnership can endure for life than in the case of heterosexual pairing. Many homosexual couples have maintained a commitment to each other that has been fulfilling over time. The agony of many a gay man dying of AIDS is eased by the faithful ministrations of a partner who stays with him and ministers to him until death does them part. If the church threw the full weight of its moral support behind this ideal, more of these partnerships would succeed. Cobb argues that temporary and permanent bonding could be distinguished and the latter should be celebrated by the church. It could have the same legal, moral and religious status as heterosexual marriage, whatever name be given to it (Cobb 1991a, 1991b).

A remarkable statement by the House of Bishops of the Church of England in 1991 shows them moving for the first time in this direction. The statement accepts the fact that there are Christians who can find fulfilment only with the help of a loving and faithful homosexual partner, involving a sexually active relationship with that partner. The statement says that Christian tradition contains an emphasis on respect for free conscientious judgment where the individual has seriously weighed the issues involved. The bishops do not reject those who sincerely choose this way. It is important, they say, that in every congregation such homosexual persons should find fellow-Christians who sensitively provide friendship and understanding. If this does not happen, the statement goes on to say, any profession on the part of the church that it is committed to openness and learning about the homosexual situation can be no more than empty words (House of Bishops 1991).

The Methodist church of the US gives a measure of concern in this direction in its concept of the 'reconciling congregation'. Any congregation of the church is free to openly accept and minister to homosexual persons, without distinction and so become a reconciling congregation.

David Oliphant, an archdeacon in the Anglican diocese of Canberra and Goulburn, has perceptively remarked that those who condemn homosexuals have very little appreciation of what goes on within the youth who comes to feel the pain and pleasure of sexual feelings and desire for comfort from someone of their own sex. What is needed at this time of crisis, he says, is someone who can see where I am within myself and relate to me in a non-judging way, without taking advantage of my vulnerability. He went on to suggest that God's acceptance and pleasure in me would be none the less if at this turning point along the way I had accepted sexual comfort from a person of my own sex, even to the point of an identity shift and an adoption of a homosexual lifestyle. It is not a question of rights and wrongs but a question of authenticity in the face of what life presents (Oliphant 1991). Archdeacon Oliphant's statement and that of the House of Bishops of the Church of England stand in strong contrast to the excommunication meted out to practising homosexuals by the Anglican diocese of Sydney (Williams 1992). A practising homosexual in this diocese is to be refused the sacrament of communion by his rector. Yet Jesus at the last supper, when he instituted this sacrament, did not refuse Judas the bread and the wine, despite the fact that he knew Judas was his betrayer. Is the practising homosexual more wicked than Judas who led Jesus into the hands of his crucifiers?

The Archbishop of York, John Habgood, offered the following reflection at a conference of the World Council on Churches on AIDS and the churches:

> The AIDS virus is fragile. For its transmission it depends upon intimate contact. And there is an interesting connection between intimacy and vulnerability. Every intimate contact makes us vulnerable in all sorts of ways not only through transmission of infection but also psychologically and in our personal identity. And this is why every civilisation has in various ways surrounded intimate relationships with rules, with structures, with ceremonies, with taboos. These have as it were protected the relationships. And what I see the AIDS epidemic as teaching us is that we cannot lightly treat these intimate relations any longer. And that is where the world has lost its sense that close contact between human beings needs to be within an ordered framework. Then it is sure to recover that perspective. And this it seems to me is a moral and theological understanding which can be expressed in ways which are accessible not only to those with Christian commitment but to all those who think seriously about our human nature and our contacts with one another. (quoted in Gosling 1992, pp. 45–6)

To be estranged from others means to deprive ourselves and others. To have some sort of at-one-ment with others is to weave our own lives with strands taken from the lives of others and to furnish our own lives as strands to be woven into their lives. It is giving and receiving.

This section has been about estrangement of ourselves from ourselves and from others through idolising false values. The examples so far have been concerned with the idolising of a false view of self and of others which leads to pride or to prejudice.

There is another form of idolising that leads to estrangement. It is the idolising of things. This results in indulgence and greed. We see this in the plethora of devices in our technological age which becomes turned into a multiplication of artificial needs and appetites. In the end these appetites are dehumanising. They are misplaced commitment. They lead to the abuse of power which is clearly seen, for example, in the abuse of the free market principle as discussed in Chapter 4. The free market has to do with freedom of marketing commodities without undue interference from outside powers that may seek to control it. It works well on a small scale, for example in local markets. At the international level it becomes abused. Aggressive competition becomes the rule and human well-being is ignored. The free market becomes sacralised as an idol, a contemporary Baal. What centrally planned economies never understood was that what is needed is not to suppress the market, but to humanise it (de Santa Ana 1991).

## ESTRANGEMENT FROM NATURE

If we are to survive the global crisis that is discussed in Chapter 3 we need to develop a new consciousness about nature which includes those creatures who share the Earth with us. It will have to show us how to bridge the gap between our illusions of separateness from nature and our urge to dominate nature. In Chapter 2 we discussed a twofold responsibility to nature. One is to maintain the life-support systems of nature on which all life depends. We spoke of these systems as having instrumental value to us and to other living creatures. We recognised a second responsibility and that was to respect other living creatures, not because they might be of use to us, but because of their intrinsic value in themselves to themselves.

In so far as we use nature to supply our needs of food, shelter and many other resources, an environmental ethic has to strike a balance between our use of nature for its instrumental value and our respect of nature for the intrinsic value of the organisms in it. Such an ethic would help establish a relationship with nature that would also be fulfilling for ourselves. To break our illusions of separateness from nature and to develop instead a sense of oneness with nature is to be an inclusionist. It is to extend our concern to the whole of life. By contrast, exclusionists see themselves outside nature and in opposition to it.

Indians in the Americas and indigenous peoples of Africa, Asia and Australia seem to have been inclusionists. The indigenous people of Africa, for example, felt the presence of what they called *modimo,* the source and presence of life which penetrated through plants, humans and other animals, dark caverns and tall mountains. For 4000 years the people of the Korean peninsula had been a homogenous people united with the land. They spoke of their home as 'the land of morning calm'. That disappeared with colonisation by foreign powers (Birch, Eakin & McDaniel 1990). The religion of Taoism in China sought the recovery of the primordial harmony of humans and nature, as did other Asian religions.

In Israel, humans tended to distinguish themselves from the rest of nature, as did many interpretations of the book of Genesis by Christians. I have indicated in Chapter 2 that this division has been exaggerated beyond what the text warrants. I also argued that to be an inclusionist does not mean to accept the equal value of all creatures. On the contrary, the uniqueness of the human quality is to be preserved together with an evaluation of all creatures. Jesus had a valuation of nature of this sort which is evident in his parables of nature and his valuation of the sparrows and lilies of the field. They were one with the creation, yet each unique in its own right.

How are we to discover a greater oneness with nature

than the way of the modern world? Here are five principles to that end.

**1.** Biology teaches that all species that live today and that ever have been stem from one, or at most a few, original source of life. Every species is a branch on the tree of life. On that tree human beings are on a direct line of descent from beings called Australopithecenes who have human and ape features. They are sometimes called ape-men. They in turn stem from creatures who were much more like apes, who in turn seem to have come from monkey-like beings. The theory does not say that humans are descended from apes but from ape-like creatures. The apes and monkeys on Earth today were not progenitors of humans.

It is possible that if we were able to arrange all creatures on the direct ancestory of humans in line we would find it difficult, if not impossible, to draw a line and say from that point human beings began. On the other hand, there may be a feature or two that seems to appear without much sharing with the past. On our present information, for example, no creature other than humans provide evidence, anatomical or otherwise, of the capacity for speech. But who knows what anatomical structures were involved in the beginning of speech? At present no-one knows.

The point is that evolution shows we have a common origin with the rest of the animal kingdom. That fact has nothing to do with any valuation of humans we might care to make in relation to other animals. Much opposition to the concept of evolution in the nineteenth century derived from a revulsion against the idea that humans were descended from ape-like animals long ago. This way of thinking is the genetic fallacy of supposing that the origin of something settles the question of its falsehood or truth. It does not.

**2.** Biology reveals an extraordinary similarity between the biochemistry and physiology of all animals. The closer the evolutionary kinship the more similar the biochemistry and physiology. Even complex biochemical compounds, such as the red respiratory pigment haemoglobin, are found in simple single-celled animals and in some plants. Amongst apes on the Earth now, chimpanzees share more similarities with humans than the other apes. The difference between the DNA of chimpanzees and humans is very small; a mere 1.6 per cent of the DNA is different. That indicates not only a close evolutionary relationship, but also that relatively few genes must produce large differences (Diamond 1991).

The nervous system of all mammals is very similar. From that I infer that their feelings are similar to mine. This helps me to have a greater rapport with the feelings of joy and pain of fellow creatures. To have rapport with them means to enter into their feelings and have a degree of oneness with them.

**3.** To get to know the inner life of a pet is a step toward having a feeling for other creatures. We come to appreciate their need for companionship and trust, because they adopt us as their kin. We then come to experience ourselves as part of a wider community of living beings.

**4.** To have a vision of reality that is inclusive of all creatures, indeed of all individual entities of creation from protons to people, is to appreciate more the whole gamut of the creation.

Materialism does not have this vision. Nor does the dominant scientific–technological worldview of mechanism. We have to go beyond these models in imaginative leaps that stretch all our capacities for inclusive thinking. It should include the information that science gives and the more subjective information that comes directly through our intuition and feeling for the world. The great seers such as Buddha, Plato and Jesus had such an inclusive vision as was possible in their day. We need to interpret it for our day. This book is based on one such vision developed in more philosophical ways in its predecessor, *On Purpose* (Birch 1990).

An essential concept of an inclusive vision is the idea of the 'within of things'. Classical physics and traditional biology study the outer aspects of things. The new physics no longer pictures the universe in terms of bits and pieces called particles. It points to mystery at the heart of what classical physics called particles. There is an inner aspect of these entities that the new physics seeks to penetrate. Likewise, a new biology seeks to explore the inner life of creatures such as chimpanzees. We know for ourselves that each of us has a within which we refer to as consciousness, mind, feeling or experience. This is the private part of our lives that only we know. The outsider can only infer what our inner life is like. We have our times of ecstasy, elation, grief and despondency. Our inner life, which is not a matter of outward observation, has been called our internal relations with the world, in contrast to our external relations, such as being hit by a motor car.

There is every reason to suppose that all living creatures have an inner life and internal relations. We are not alone in the universe in having an inner life. The proposition of this book, and of process thought in general, is that the concept of internal relations extends right down to entities such as protons. Of course, we don't talk about conscious feelings at that level, but we do suppose that something analogous to mind is present there. They are not just bits and pieces unrelated to their environment. They too take account of their environment in the inner aspect of their existence. We can put this another way by saying that each individual entity from protons to people has an inner reality, a within of things, which makes them what they are to themselves. Just as my internal relations with my world, which constitute all my feelings, are what I am in myself to myself, so too something analogous applies to the proton and other such entities.

Teilhard de Chardin (1965), palaeontologist and priest, expresses this view quite precisely and poetically when he writes:

> It is a fact beyond question that deep within ourselves we can discern, as though through a rent, an 'interior'' at the heart of things; and this glimpse is sufficient to force upon us the conviction that in one degree or another this 'interior'

exists and has always existed everywhere in nature. Since at one particular point in itself, the stuff of the universe has an inner face, we are forced to conclude that in its very structure — that is, in every region of space and time — it has this double aspect, just as, for instance, in its very structure it is granular. In all things there is a Within, co-extensive with their Without. (p. 83)

We can probably all make sense of the idea that our inner life has reality for us. It is the richness of experience which we know for ourselves. It is the most real thing for us. The view I am propounding and which is expressed in the quotation from Teilhard de Chardin is that this is a characteristic of all entities from protons to cells to humans. This is an experiental view of the world. This view is rejected by materialism which admits no inner reality to non-human entities. The non-human universe is nuts and bolts. The alternative proposition is that there is a 'within of things' in all things from protons to people. It is to think of entities from protons to people as what they are *in themselves to themselves.*

We then view the individual entities from protons to people, and all things in between, as much more alive than we ever did before. The appearance of human beings on earth is not to be seen as an abrupt intervention in which something totally novel and different was created. What existed before humans, even before any living creature, were things which had significance in themselves for themselves and for God. Such a vision inspired Teilhard de Chardin to write his *Hymn of the Universe* which begins as a meditation of *Mon Universe* in a desert in Asia (Teilhard de Chardin 1965).

The world had intrinsic value at every stage of its cosmic evolution. We have kinship not only with the creatures who are closest to us, but to the entities that were there from the foundations of the universe. This extends the idea of evolutionary continuity of an inner being backwards from all living creatures to that in matter as it existed before living beings appeared. Each individual entity from protons to people takes account of its environment in its inner or subjective being. We have maintained that the inner life of humans is richer than that of mice or amoebae, nevertheless there is a continuity that can be recognised. To appreciate that is to find the universe a much more friendly place than materialism allows.

**5.** A vision and understanding of the inclusiveness of humanity and nature leads to commitment. The aspect of life which most stirs my soul is the ability to share in an undertaking and in a reality more enduring than myself. Commitment is not a matter of choice. It is a matter of being grasped by something of ultimate importance. It is the experience of Whitehead's 'Peace', discussed at the beginning of this chapter. The within of things we experience as humans is richness of conscious experience. We do not manufacture the experience so much as appropriate it. Its source for all humans is the same, call that source what you will — ultimate concern or God. Within ourselves an inner life is a part of the life of the cells that constitute our bodies. They too take account of their environment. What they take account of includes the source of all experience, namely God. So too molecules, atoms and protons take account of that same source in so far as it is relevant to their being.

The God whom we meet in our conscious lives is the same God who meets all individual entities of creation. Faith of the profoundest kind has this inclusive meaning to God. In traditional terms the concept is expressed as a faith that the God of redemption is the God of creation of the whole world. Traditional theologies have had great difficulty in bringing these two aspects of the divine together. Today, as never before, we have the opportunity to discover a deeper meaning to that faith and therefore a deeper commitment. As Sallie McFague (1987) writes: 'Only a sensibility that accepts our intrinsic interdependence not only with all other people but also with the Earth will be able to create the conditions necessary to help bring about the fulfilment of all as salvation for our time' (p. 52).

# ESTRANGEMENT FROM THE WHOLE SCHEME OF THINGS

Sartre, Beckett and others contend that we must give ourselves to a universe that is itself devoid of meaning. They express a sense of total alienation from the universe. If there is a whole scheme of things, they know nothing of it. Human life is an isolated phenomenon unable to find any kinship in the surrounding world. This is perhaps the most profound alienation of all.

To the Gnostics the world was utterly alien and demonic. It was created by an evil God whom they equated with the God of the Old Testament. Men and women are lost and alone in an alien world. Therefore salvation is liberation from the world. It was accomplished through direct access to the divine, through ethical values of community and asceticism. The Gnostics were helped in this through their Gnostic gospels which record many sayings attributed to Jesus, whom they regarded as saviour from demonic powers (Pagels 1979). Gnosticism flourished over a wide area of the Middle East about the time of the rise of Christianity. In some of its forms it merged with Christian elements. Indeed at one stage it was regarded as a competitor with Christianity and was severely persecuted.

In the West a parallel to the cosmic nihilism of the Gnostics is found in Nietzsche. For him God had died and everything was growing darker and colder. No way into the future is to be found. This is the ultimate estrangement of despair, whose meaning is indicated in the etymology of the word — without hope.

A basic proposition of this book is that the universe is neither indifferent nor malevolent, but that it is on the side of life and its fulfilment. John Cobb (1972) puts hope in an evolutionary context. He asks, is there a basis for realistic hope? He answers that the fact that chemical conditions make it possible for life to appear, with growth and reproduction, means that there is that in reality that calls forth life and strives against the forces of inertia.

The fact that the human psyche is capable of being

claimed by truth and touched by concern for others means there is a reality that calls forth love and strives against the retreat into security and narrow interests. This power works slowly and quietly by persuasion. It does not present itself for observation by the biologist or the psychologist says Cobb (1972):

> It is not to be found somewhere outside the organisms in which it is at work, but it is not to be identified with them either. We can conceive it best as Spirit. In spite of all the destructive forces man lets loose against life on this planet, the Spirit of Life is at work in ever new and unforeseeable ways, countering and circumventing the obstacles man puts in its path. (p. 143)

Cobb goes on to say that in spite of one's tendencies to complacency and despair, it is possible to experience the Spirit in one's life, calling forth realistic hope. What makes for life and love and hope is not simply the decision of one individual or another, but a Spirit that moves us all. This Spirit is God. Men and women strive to unite themselves with that to which they belong and from which they are separated. This is true not only for us but for all creatures. Life is separation and reunion.

In this way of thinking, God is internally related to all that is. To be internally related is to know by acquaintance. Nothing can be closer. God is to the world as self is to the body. So it is appropriate that Sallie McFague (1987) refers to the world as God's body: 'As the body of the world, God is forever 'nailed to the cross' for as this body suffers, so God suffers' (1987, p. 75). By destroying life-support systems of this planet we are impoverishing the life of God. That is the nature of internal relationships. They are what constitute the participation of one being within another.

Christians find clues for this way of looking at the world in the life of Jesus. The devotion of Jesus to his fellows involved a feeling of sympathetic identity with them in their troubles and sufferings, as well as in their joys. So their cause and their tragedy became his. He paid the price of a bitter death, rather than weaken the intimacy of his relationship with the human lot, with all its suffering and failure. Jesus, to his fellows, was the persuasive love of God in action in their lives.

Paul's letter to the Colossians (1:15–20) has as its theme the persuasive love of God as extended not only to all humanity but to the whole of creation. He identifies the love of God that is manifest in the life of Jesus as the same love that is extended to all creation and in which all creation subsists. In highly metaphorical language Paul speaks of all things having been created through Christ. This creative activity existed before all things existed. 'All things' is repeated in these six verses no fewer than six times. It is not that all things are a tumbled multitude of facts in an unrelated mass. No, all things are held together in a unity because of their subsistence in the persuasive love of God that is extended to all creation.

The error of the Colossians that Paul was addressing in his letter was their supposition that there were 'thrones, dominions, principalities and powers' which had a life of their own. It was the supposition that these authorities had a life quite apart from any activity of God in the world. The real world was a dualism, one part of which was evil and not subject to the influence of God. The other part participated in the influence of God's love. This error trapped the God and Christ of the Colossians exclusively in terms of the moral and spiritual life of humans. Paul, on the contrary, claims all for God. Elements of the whole can be estranged from the divine influence but none is without the possibility of at-one-ment.

The theologian Joseph Sittler gave an address entitled 'Called to Unity' to the third assembly of the World Council of Churches in 1961. He took the passage in Colossians about 'all things' as his theme because he wanted to speak against the dualism of the church and the world which piety always presumes. He spoke at a time when the ecological crisis was beginning to become evident to people outside the church. In a highly metaphorical and powerful statement he declared: 'It is now excruciatingly clear that Christ cannot be a light that lights every man coming into the world, if he is not also the light that falls upon the world into which every man comes. He enlightens this darkling world because the world was made through him'. I interpret this last sentence to mean that the same God who is present in the life of humans, including Jesus, is present also in the world in which humans live. 'Nature' and 'grace' are not contradictory categories. They are made to be contradictory when the doctrine of the creation is made a doctrine of the past. Because the church has committed that error, Sittler says, 'The address of Christian thought is most weak precisely where man's ache is most strong' (Sittler 1961). God is not before all creation but with all creation. This is the theme of Paul's statement to the Colossians. In a modern context it is the theme of process theology.

In this way of looking at things, salvation becomes an ecological word in the sense of the restoration of a right relation which has been corrupted. The relation is corrupted within human life and within the nature that we are destroying by what we call progress (see Chapter 3). The restoration of a right relationship, which is salvation, is also the meaning of atonement, the becoming one of that which has been sundered.

The Christian church has not consistently understood atonement in cosmic terms. On the contrary, it has been more usual to apply it exclusively to human salvation. On the basis of certain passages attributed to Paul, a theological proposition of the doctrine was elaborated by Anselm, Archbishop of Canterbury in the twelfth century. He had a legalistic approach in his theology. Justice requires that humans are punished for their sin. Yet God is merciful, so how can a merciful God punish people? According to Anselm, God found a way of escape by allowing Jesus to take upon himself all the sins of the world. The solution is the undeserved substitutional death of Jesus on the cross. This became known as the substitutionary doctrine of atonement.

Paul Tillich (1954) comments on this doctrine as follows: 'In spite of its theological weakness this remained the predominant doctrine of Western Christianity because of its psychological power' (p. 14). The psychological power that

Tillich refers to is that this system of symbols gives the individual the courage to accept himself in spite of his awareness that he is unacceptable. Tillich goes on to say that the proper relation between love and justice is not manifest in this legalistic form of the doctrine. There are no conflicts between the reconciling love of God and the justice of God. Persuasive love is extended to all, irrespective of the degree of estrangement of the individual. Where justice comes in is the experience of the self-destructive consequences of continued estrangement. Yet God participates in the suffering of our existential estrangement. God's suffering is not a substitute for our suffering. It is a sharing of it. So too God participates in the joy of the individual whose estrangement is converted to at-one-ment with God.

'Who are we?' asks Hans Kung (1991). 'The answer is: defective beings who are not what they might be and expectant, hoping, yearning beings who are continually excelling themselves ... what is the explanation of this strange pressure constantly to transcend ourselves?' (p. 61). At our deepest level we are responsive to the possibilities of ourselves not yet realised but ever pressing upon us as divine persuasive love. God lives, genuinely lives, in unison with our living. God gives to the world the life of the world and God takes into God's actuality the life of the world as it is lived in all its joys and sufferings. Could there be any more personal concept of God than that?

## GOD AS PERSONAL

The last question is deliberate. Discussions I have had on the concept of God nearly always lead to two questions. Is God personal? And how can you pray to and worship the sort of God you write about?

Is God personal? If I have to give a yes or no answer I would say, yes God is personal. But there are so many problems with the word personal that we cannot just leave it there. It all depends on what one means by person. The word is bound up with a substance way of thinking. That is to think of persons as separate entities in the way we think of chairs and tables. I have emphasised that persons are what they are by virtue of their internal relations. They are not like substances.

Person is not a biblical word. In relation to God it was first used by Tertullian in the third century. He was an anti-Gnostic church father who lived in Carthage where he was converted in AD 193. He introduced the doctrine of the trinity into ecclesiastical language to describe what he called the divine economy. He used the word economy in the sense in which we use the word ecology. Tertullian was anxious to find ways of expressing God's various activities in cosmic history. He used the Greek word *persona*. It means the mask of an actor through which a special character is portrayed. Is the incarnation of Christ a metamorphosis of God? No, replied Tertullian. It is the manifestation of the divine in a human life. Christ is one persona of God. The others he called God the father and God the holy spirit.

Unfortunately it was very easy for those who followed this formulation to convert the doctrine of the trinity into tritheism. That happened early on in the subsequent history of Christianity. The 'persons' of the trinity, in Christian thought, became analagous to the way people thought of human persons as independent entities, that is to say as substances. When Christian theology fell into this trap of substance thinking, all sorts of conundrums arose. If Jesus is a divine person, since no two substances can occupy the same space at the same time, then the human Jesus must be removed to let the divine Jesus in! If one thinks that we are somewhere God is not, then better say God is not a person. But if we believe that the relation of God to ourselves is love that gives and love that receives, then God is personal. Indeed the central issue of the Christian religion is response to the ultimate as personal.

Creeds, the canon of scripture (the books accepted as the official Bible) and the institutional structure of the church emerged only toward the end of the second century. How did Christians think before that?

McAfee Brown (1991) has made a somewhat fanciful, yet instructive, reconstruction of beliefs in that early church. With some variations of my own it goes something like this. The scene: an imaginary early discussion over coffee during the adult study hour of the First Church of Ephesus, AD 100. Topic: who is the God we worship?

First answer: We worship (attribute worth to) as creator, the one who was from the foundations of the universe. We see the same creativity of God all around us today in the life of plants and animals and in all things such as the waters of the ocean and the air we breathe.

Second answer: Amen to all that with the addition that it is that very same God who has drawn near to us and shared our lot in Jesus of Nazareth. Jesus reveals to us the possibilities of human nature when the divine life is released into human life. Jesus is the truth about life for us. He is not the truth about life because his teachings are true. His teachings are true because they express the truth which he himself lived. His teachings should not be used as infallible prescriptions for life and thought. What they do is point to the truth, to one whose life is the truth about life. Let us never forget that.

Third answer: Amen to both these claims with the addition that it is the same God — creator — also revealed in Jesus of Nazareth who has drawn near to our fathers and mothers, Abraham, Isaac, Jacob, Sarah and Rachel, and whose presence we ourselves feel here and now, day after day. We feel that especially when we gather to break bread and share wine. God's spirit makes God our contemporary.

Program chairperson: Anybody taking notes? Let's get it written down: one God (not three) in three manifestations. If that is helpful, so let it be. Yet when one considers the billions of individual entities in the universe from atoms to people there is a sense in which God is manifested in billions of ways. I would suggest that as the topic for the next seminar!

Can I pray to and worship the God who is presumed in this book? To worship means to ascribe worth to. I ascribe worth to whatever has intrinsic value. That includes all the qualities that make for richness of experience in human life and in the life of the world. I ascribe worth to the source of these values, which is God. Wieman (1946) made the distinction between created goods and creative good. Created goods are, for example, living things with all their feelings and values and all the communities and institutions they have created. Creative good is the Life of the universe, without which there could be no created goods. I call creative good by the name God.

Wieman (1929) considers there to be three preconditions which must be met before effective worship is possible. The first is that one must go into deep water. One must take life seriously. The common lot of men and women is to be destroyed by trivialities. Every one of the multitude of things that enter into our lives each day will sap away our strength unless they are assimilated into some integrated purpose for living. The second condition is sincerity. One must be honest with oneself about what one regards as of ultimate concern. No more sarcastic picture was ever drawn by Jesus than the portrait of a man who went up to the temple to pray and 'stood and prayed thus with himself' — a mean and self-centred act of worship. The third precondition of worship is seclusion from distracting activities. All three may be found in solitude. Or worship may be corporate.

As to prayer, it is too often thought of in terms of a telephone exchange with us at one end and God at the other. The activity at our end is to ask God to do something: break the drought, stop the holocaust, prevent the finger from pressing the nuclear button, annihilate the virus that causes AIDS. At the other end God decides whether or not to grant what is asked. This is a travesty of the meaning of prayer.

Prayer is not getting God to do what we want. It is not begging. It is not asking God to do anything. It is the endeavour to put ourselves in such a relationship with God that God can do in and for and through us what God wants. It is not that God changes things. God changes us to change things. We are changed by having revealed to us new possibilities of truth, beauty, goodness, peace and adventure that enable us to transcend the past quite profoundly. This is the main point of John Cobb's (1985) novelette, *Praying for Jennifer*. Jennifer, in the story, had been in a coma for three months, following a motor car crash. Her fellow students explored what praying could possibly mean in that tragic situation.

They did not need to ask God to do anything. Nor do we. God is already doing everything. God is ever active, never off duty. God's persuasive love is ever available to all, only blocked by us. It is always there, prior to any move on our part. To pray is to get ourselves to be receptive and then to do something we would not have otherwise done. When Paul wrote to Christians in Thessalonica, urging them 'to pray without ceasing', he surely was not suggesting that for every moment of every day they should be on their knees asking God to do things. The Christians in Thessalonica at the time were being severely persecuted. They were in deep need. What they needed was encouragement, courage, patience and hope. That is why Paul wrote to them. What should they do? They were to be on their guard. They were to be ever aware of an ever-present resource that could meet their deepest needs in their hour of trial and tribulation.

We don't know what the Christians in Thessalonica discovered as a result of Paul's injunction. We do know that Paul's spirit had survived shipwrecks, a stoning, beatings, long nights in goal and a near lynching. We do know what Hugh Latimer discovered in his hour of trial in the sixteenth century, tied to the stake in Oxford Square waiting for the logs to be lit. He turned to his companion in martyrdom: 'Be of good comfort, Master Ridley, and play the man; we shall this day light such a candle by God's grace in England as, I trust, shall never be put out'.

For these, and those who have followed since, to respond to the Spirit of the universe, which is God, is to give up the security of habitual, customary and socially approved actions and to live in terms of a radically new and open future. Every moment of our lives we are confronted with new possibilities that can lure us forwards to new purposes. If that were not so there would be little ground for hope.

# CONCLUSION

Life is separation and reunion. The human predicament is described by words such as estrangement and alienation. Yet life strives for what it could be and is not. The opposite of the state of estrangement is expressed in various words: at-one-ness, salvation, wholeness and in Whitehead's term 'Peace', which is a harmony of all harmonies. All life participates in a striving to unite with that which it lacks.

We are estranged in four ways: from self, from others, from nature and from God. The struggle with the feeling of estrangement from oneself may be experienced as an identity crisis. We are estranged from self when we choose to make ultimate in life something which is not of ultimate concern. This is idolatry in its basic meaning. Idolatry leads to pride which can be very destructive. Pride becomes transmuted to the will to power which eventually has to be opposed when it becomes oppressive of others. It is the genius of democracy to recognise the necessity of restraints on power.

Prejudice is a cause of estrangement of groups of people from society in general. Examples of such oppressed groups are the Jews, aboriginal peoples the world over, homosexuals and women. All are, or have been, estranged from the general community.

We are estranged from nature when we use nature primarily for our own purposes. Our domination of nature brings with it the illusion that we are separate from nature. We have a twofold responsibility to nature. One is to look after it because it looks after us. The other is to value living organisms because of their intrinsic value to themselves and to God.

Five principles can help us to rediscover a oneness with nature. First: all living organisms and all that have ever been stem from one, or at most a few, original forms of life. We have a common origin with the rest of creation. Second: modern biology shows there to be an extraordinary similarity between the biochemistry and physiology of all animals. The closer the evolutionary relationship, the closer the similarity. There is good biological evidence that animals have feelings of joy and unhappiness. They are like us. Third: by having pets we get to know the inner life of creatures other than ourselves. Fourth: a view of reality that is inclusive, rather than exclusive, that recognises all creatures as having both an objective aspect and as well a subjective 'within'. The concept of a 'within of things' and its related concept of 'internal relations' is fundamental to an overall view of reality that brings together both scientific understanding and the deepest probings of the human spirit. Fifth: an inclusive vision of reality leads to commitment to that which has value. It is respect for life. It is a commitment to ultimate concern, which is God.

Besides estrangement from self, from others and from nature, there is estrangement from 'the whole scheme of things'. The existential atheist denies there is any possibility of knowing any scheme of things, even if there is any. Alternatively we may discover that the universe is neither indifferent nor malevolent. It is on the side of life and its fulfilment, despite the tragedies and failures along the way. We can conceive this influence in the universe best as spirit or the persuasive lure of God upon the creation. God does not act by intervening as an external agent into the creation. God's action is best conceived in terms similar to our internal relations with one another. God is internally related to all that is. God is to the world as self is to the body. Christians find clues to this way of looking at the world in the life of Jesus. The restoration of a right relationship which has been corrupted is salvation or healing. It is the meaning of atonement.

The concept of God developed in this chapter is not academic and remote. There is real meaning to God as personal, provided we do not think of persons in terms of substance images. If we think of persons in relationships that are internal relationships, then the word person is appropriately applied to God. We can say with conviction — God is personal.

There is an intellectual aspect of atonement in seeking harmony in our conception of God and the cosmos. There is also an emotional aspect which is the experience of atonement of our inner life of feeling. Yet there is also the sense of incompleteness because we find ourselves in the midst of tragedy and with hopes not yet realised. An adequate religious faith should be intellectually humble, morally strenuous, with a sense of the tragic dimensions of life and a sense of human hopefulness.

# REFERENCES

Adams, Chris (1989 September 11) 'AIDS and changing realities' *Christianity and Crisis* pp. 257-9.

Anon, (1991) 'Measuring human development' *South Letter of the South Centre.* 11 18-9.

Barr, James (1975) *Fundamentalism.* London: SCM Press.

Barr, James (1984) *Escaping from Fundamentalism.* London: SCM Press.

Bartlett, Robert (1991) 'Witch hunting' *New York Review of Books* 38 (ii) pp. 37-8.

Bates, Erica & Lapsley, Helen (1982) 'Social implications of development in modern medical technology' in *Issues in Ethics* 1982 pp. 10-25 Melbourne: Centre for Human Bioethics Monash University.

Birch, Charles (1990) *On Purpose.* Kensington: New South Wales University Press.

Birch, Charles (1991) 'Process thought: Its value and meaning to me' *Process Studies* 19 219-29.

Birch, Charles & Cobb, John B. Jr. (1981) *The Liberation of Life: from the cell to the community* Cambridge University Press. Reprinted 1990 Denton Texas: Environmental Ethics Books.

Birch, Charles; Eakin, William & McDaniel, Jay B. (1990) *Liberating life: Contemporary approaches to ecological theology* Maryknoll, New York: Orbis Books.

Bishops' Statement (1992) 'Common Wealth and Common Good: A statement of wealth distribution in Australia' Melbourne: Collins Dove.

Blaustein, A. R. and Wake, D. B. (1990) 'Declining amphibian populations: A global phenomenon?' *Trends in Ecology and Evolution* 5 203-4.

Brody, Jane E. (1988, March 27) 'Mind over disease: Can happy thoughts help?' *New York Times Book Review* pp. 40-1.

Brown, Hanbury R. (1986) *The Wisdom of Science: Its relevance to culture and religion* Cambridge University Press.

Brown, Lester R. (1981) *Building a Sustainable Society* New York: Norton and Co.

Brown, Lester R. (1986) *State of the World: A Worldwatch Institute report on progress toward a sustainable society.* New York: Norton and Co.

Brown, Lester R. (1988) 'The changing world food prospect: The nineties and beyond' *Worldwatch Paper* 85, Washington, DC: Worldwatch Institute.

Brown, Lester R. (1990) *State of the World 1990.* New York: Norton and Co.

Brown, Lester R. (1991) *State of the World 1991.* New York: Norton and Co.

Buber, Martin (1958) *I and Thou* New York: Charles Scribners' Sons.

Campbell, Joseph (1988) *The Power of Myth* New York: Doubleday.

Chryssavgis, John (1991) 'Church and State in Byzantium' *Phronema* 6 27-37.

Churchland, Paul M. (1984) *Matter and Consciousness: a contemporary intro-duction to the philosophy of mind* Cambridge, MA: MIT Press.

Cobb, John B. Jr (1965) *A Christian Natural Theology* Philadelphia: West-minster Press.

Cobb, John B. Jr (1967) *The Structure of Christian Existence* Philadelphia: Westminster Press.

Cobb, John B. Jr. (1972) *Is it too Late? A theology of ecology* Beverly Hills, CA: Bruce.

Cobb, John B. Jr (1973) 'Ecology ethics and theology' in *Towards a Steady State Economy.*(ed. Herman E. Daly) pp. 307-20 San Francisco: W. H. Freeman.

Cobb, John B. Jr (1982) *Beyond Dialogue: toward a mutual transformation of Christianity and Buddhism* Philadelphia: Fortress Press.

Cobb, John B. Jr (1983) 'God and the scientific worldview' in *Talking with God* (eds. David Tracy & John B.Cobb Jr) pp. 39-56 New York: Seabury Press.

Cobb, John B. Jr (1985) *Praying for Jennifer: An exploration of intercessory prayer in story form'* Nashville,TE: The Upper Room.

Cobb, John B. Jr (1991a) *Matters of Life and Death* Louisville KT. Westmin-ster/John Knox Press.

Cobb, John B. Jr (1991b) *Can Christ Become Good News Again?* St Louis, MI: Chalice Press.

Cobb, John B. Jr & Griffin, David Ray (1976) *Process Theology: an introduc-tory exposition* Philadelphia: Westminster Press.

Coombs. H. C. (1990) *The Return of Scarcity* Cambridge University Press.

Costanza, Robert (ed.) (1991)*Ecological Economics: The science and manag-ment of Sustainability* New York: Columbia University Press.

Coulter, John (1990, July) 'Population policy' *Conservation News* p. 2.

Daly, Herman E. (1977) *Steady State Economics: the economics of biophysical equilibrium and moral growth* San Francisco: W. H. Freeman.

Daly, Herman E. (1991) 'Sustainable development is possible only if we forgo growth' *Development Forum* 19 (5) p. 15.

Daly, Herman E. & Cobb, John B. Jr (1989) *For the Common Good: Redi-recting the economy toward community, the environment and a sustain-able future.* Boston: Beacon Press.

Darwin, Charles (1887) 'Recollections of the development of mind and character' in *The Darwin Reader* (eds. Marston Bates & Philip S. Humphrey) pp. 3-33 London: Macmillan.

Davies, Paul (1989) *The Cosmic Blueprint* London: Unwin Paperbacks.

Davies, Paul (1992) *The Mind of God: Science and the search for ultimate meaning.* London: Simon & Schuster.

Davies, Paul & Gribbin, John (1991) *'The Matter Myth: Toward 21st century science.'* London: Viking.

Dean, William (1990) 'Empirical theology: a revisable tradition' *Process Studies* 19 85-102.

de Santa Ana (1991) 'Spirit of truth set us free' *The Ecumenical Review* 43,

364-71.

Devall, Bill & Sessions, George (1985) *Deep Ecology: Living as if nature mattered.* Salt Lake City UT: Gibbs M. Smith.

Diamond, Jared (1991) *The Rise and Fall of the Third Chimpanzee* London: Hutchinson.

Durning, Alan B. (1989) 'Poverty and the environment: reversing the downward spiral' *Worldwatch Paper* 92, Washington DC: Worldwatch Institute.

Eckersley, Robyn (1992) 'Ecosocialist dilemmas: The market rules OK?' *Political Studies* 40, 314–32.

Ehrlich, Paul R. (1984) 'Shared sensibilities' *Natural History* 93 (ii) pp. 93-4.

Ehrlich, Paul R. (1986) *The Machinery of Nature: The living world around us and how it works* New York: Simon and Schuster.

Ehrlich, Paul R. (1989) 'The limits to substitution: Meta-resource depletion and a new economic-ecological paradigm' *Ecological Economics* 1, 9-16.

Ehrlich, Paul R. (1990) 'Biodiversity and humanity: Science and public policy' Crafoord Lecture Stockholm (unpublished).

Ehrlich, Paul R. & Ehrlich, Anne H. (1981) *Extinction: The causes and consequences of the disappearance of species* New York: Random House.

Ehrlich, Paul R. & Ehrlich, Anne H. (1990). *The Population Explosion* New York: Simon and Schuster.

Ehrlich, Paul R.; Ehrlich, Anne H. & Holdren, John P. (1977) *Ecoscience: Population, resources, environment* San Francisco: W. H. Freeman.

Ehrlich, Paul R. & Sagan, Carl (1984) *The Cold and the Dark* New York: W. W Norton and Co.

Ekins, Paul (ed.) (1986) *The Living Economy: A new economics in the making* New York: Routledge Kegan Paul.

Erikson, Erik H. (1968) *Identity: Youth and crisis* New York: W.W. Norton.

Fosdick, Harry Emerson (1956) *A Great Time to be Alive* New York: Harper and Brothers.

Fosdick, Harry Emerson (1958) *Riverside Sermons* New York: Harper and Brothers.

Fox, Warwick (1990) *Toward a Transpersonal Ecology: Developing new frontiers for environmentalism* Boston: Shambala Publications.

Garton Ash, Timothy (1990) *The Magic Lantern: the revolution of '89 witnessed in Warsaw, Budapest, Berlin and Prague* New York: Random House.

Goodland, Robert; Daly, Herman E. & El Serafy, Salah (1991) *Environmentally Sustainable Economic Development: building on Brundtland* Environment Working paper 46 World Bank, Washington, DC.

Gosling, David (1992) *A New Earth* London: Council of Churches for Britain and Ireland.

Griffin, David Ray (ed.) (1988) *The Reenchantment of Science: Postmodern proposals* Albany NY: State University of New York Press.

Griffin, David Ray (1989) *God and Religion in the Postmodern World* Albany

NY: State University of New York Press.

Griffin, David Ray (1990) The restless universe: a postmodern vision' in *The Restless Earth. Nobel Conference XXIV* (ed. K.J.Carlson) pp. 59-111, San Francisco: Harper and Row.

Griffin, David Ray & Cobb, John B. Jr. (1991) 'A theological biography' in *Theology and the University* (eds. David Ray Griffin & Joseph C.Hough) pp. 225-42, Albany NY: State University of New York Press.

Hartshorne, Charles (1983) *Insights and Oversights of Great Thinkers: An Evaluation of Western Philosophy* Albany NY: State University of New York Press.

Hartshorne, Charles (1984) *Omnipotence and other Theological Mistakes* Ithaca NY: State University of New York Press.

Hawking, Stephen W. (1988) *A Brief History of Time* London: Bantam.

Havel, Vaclev (1991) 'Uncertain strength: An interview' *New York Review of Books* 38 (14), pp. 6-8.

Henderson-Sellers, Anne & Blong, Russell (1989) *The Greenhouse Effect: Living in a warmer Australia.* Kensington: New South Wales University Press.

Hetzel, Basil & McMichael, Tony (1987) *The L.S. Factor: Lifestyle and health* Ringwood: Penguin Books.

Holden, Constance (1981) 'Human-animal relationships under scrutiny' *Science* 214, 418-20.

House of Bishops (1991, December) *Issues in Human Sexuality: A statement by the House of Bishops of the general synod of the Church of England* London: Church House Publications.

Human Development Report (1991) *Development Forum* 19 (4), p. 14.

Jones, Caroline (1989) *The Search for Meaning* Crows Nest: Australian Broadcasting Corporation.

Jones, Caroline (1990) *The Search for Meaning: Book two* Crows Nest: Australian Broadcasting Corporation.

Keller, Steven; King, Sallie & Kraft, Steven (1991) 'Process philosophy and minimalism: Implications for public policy' *Environmental Ethics* 13, 23-47.

King, Alexander & Schneider, Bertrand(1991) *The First Global Revolution* New York: Simon and Schuster.

Kung, Hans (1991) 'God: the last taboo?' in *Theology and the University* (eds. David Ray Griffin & J.C.Hough) Albany NY: State University of New York Press.

La Piere, Richard T. (1965) *Social Change* New York: McGraw Hill.

Laszlo, E. (1990, April/June) 'Alternative approach for global environmental action discussed at the Bergen Conference in Norway' *One Country* pp. 12-6.

Leopold, Aldo (1949) *A Sand County Almanac* New York: Oxford University Press.

Leunig, Michael (1991) *The Prayer Tree.* North Blackburn: Collins Dove.

References

Levinson, Daniel J. (1978) *The Seasons of a Man's Life* New York: Alfred A.Knopf.

Lewis, C. S. (1973) *The Four Loves* London: Collins.

Lindermayer, Vivian (1991) 'Presbyterian bravery under fire' *Christianity and Crisis* 51 (8), p. 163.

Linn, Gerhard (1991) 'Clarity in ambiguity: The witness of the church in East Germany' *The Ecumenical Review* 43, 356-63.

Luft, Joseph (1984) 'The Johari window: a graphic model of awareness in group relations' in *Small group Communications. A reader* (4th edn) (eds. Robert S. Cathcart & Larry A. Samovar) pp. 29-57, Dubuque IO: W. C. Brown.

Lutzenberger, Jose (1991 Winter) 'Redefining progress *Earth Ethics* pp. 11-12.

McAfee Brown, Robert (1991) 'Thinking about God' *Christianity and Crisis* 51, 164-5.

McCusker B. (1983) *The Quest for Quarks* Cambridge University Press.

McDaniel, Jay B. (1989) *Of God and Pelicans: a theology of reverence for life* Louisville, KT: Westminster/John Knox Press.

Macek, Peter (1991) 'The role of the church in the Czechoslovakian revolution' *The Ecumenical Review* 43, 349-55.

McFague, Sallie (1987) *Models of God: Theology for an ecological, nuclear age* Philadelphia, Pa.: Fortress Press.

Marty, Martin E. & Appelby R. Scott (eds.) (1991) *Fundamentalism Observed* University of Chicago Press.

Mathews, Freya (1991) *The Ecological Self* London: Routledge.

Meadows, D. H; Meadows, D. L; Randers, J. & Behrens W. W. (1972) *Limits to Growth* New York: New American Library.

Meadows, D. H; Meadows, D. L. & Randers, J. (1992) *Beyond the Limits* London: Earthscan.

Mesarovic, M. & Pestel, E. (1974) *Mankind at the Turning Point: The second report to the Club of Rome* New York: E. P. Dutton and Co.

Murdoch, W. W. (1980) *The Poverty of Nations: The political economy of hunger and population* Baltimore: The Johns Hopkins University Press.

Murdoch, W. W. & Oaten, A. (1975) 'Population and food: Metaphors and the reality' *Bioscience* 25, 561-7.

Nagel, Thomas (1979) *Moral Questions* Cambridge University Press.

Newland, Kathleen (1982) 'Productivity: The new economic context' *Worldwatch Paper* 49, Washington DC: Worldwatch Institute.

Newsome, A. E. (1980) 'The ecomythology of the red kangaroo in central Australia *Mankind* 12 (4), 327-33.

Niebuhr, Reinhold (1941) *The Nature and Destiny of man: A Christian interpretation. Vol. 1. Human nature* New York: Charles Scribners' Sons.

Niebuhr, Reinhold (1944) *The Children of Light and the Children of Darkness* New York: Charles Scribners' Sons.

Oliphant, David (1991) 'Homosexualilty- A personal view' in *Male and fe-*

*male God created Them: explaining human sexuality* pp. 45-8, publication of the synod of the Anglican diocese of Canberra and Goulburn in Australia.

Ornstein, Robert E. & Ehrlich, Paul R. (1989) *New World and New Mind: Moving toward conscious evolution* New York: Doubleday.

Ovington, Derrick (1978) *Australian Endangered Species: Mammals, birds and reptiles* Stanmore, NSW: Cassell Australia.

Pauck, W. (1965) 'The source of Tillich's richness' *Union Seminary Quarterly Review* 21, 3-9.

Pagels, Elaine (1979) *The Gnostic Gospels* London: Penguin Books.

Passmore, John (1974) *Man's Reponsibility to Nature* London: Gerald Duckworth.

Pestel, Eduard (1989) *Beyond the Limits to Growth* New York: Universe Books.

Postel, S. (1987) 'Stabilising chemical cycles' in *State of the World 1987* (ed. Lester R. Brown) pp. 157-76, New York: W. W. Norton.

Preston, Ronald H. (1991) *Religion and the Ambiguities of Capitalism* London: SCM Press.

Pusey, Michael (1991) *Economic Rationalism in Canberra: A nation building state changes its mind* Cambridge University Press.

Regan, Tom & Singer, Peter (eds) (1976) *Animal Rights and Human Obligations* Englewood Cliffs, NJ: Prentice Hall.

Renner, Michael (1991) 'Jobs in a sustainable economy' *Worldwatch Paper* 104, Washington DC: Worldwatch Institute.

Robertson, James (1978a) *The Sane Alternative: Signposts to a self-fulfilling future* London: James Robertson.

Robertson, James (1978b July) 'Toward a post-industrial order' *Development Forum* p. 3.

Rolston, Holmes (1987) *Science and Religion: A critical survey* New York: Random House.

Roszak, Theodore (1971) 'Can Jack get out of his box?' *Anticipation* 9, pp. 5-9.

Ruether, Rosemary (1992, January) 'A world on fire with faith' *New York Times Book Review* pp. 10-11.

Sagan, Carl & Turco, Richard (1991) *A Path where No Man Thought: Nuclear winter and the end of the arms race* New York: Random/Century.

Sagan, Leonard A. (1987) *The Health of Nations: True causes of sickness and well-being* New York: Basic Books.

Sapolsky, Robert M. (1988,May/June) 'Lessons of the Serengeti: why some animals are more susceptible to stress' *The Sciences* pp. 38-42.

SCEP (1970) *Man's Impact on the Environment. Report of studies of critical environmental problems* Cambridge, MA: MIT Press.

Scott Peck, M. (1990) *The Road Less Travelled* London: Arrow Books.

Sheldrake, Rupert (1990) *The Rebirth of Nature: The greening of science and God* London: Random Century Group.

Shinn, Roger L. (1991 July 24-31) 'Christian faith and economic practice'

*The Christian Century* pp. 720-3.

Singer, Peter (1991) *Animal Liberation.* London: Jonathan Cape.

Singer, Peter (1992) 'Can we avoid assigning greater value to some human lives than to others?' in *Issues in Ethics* 1992, pp. 39-44, Melbourne: Centre for Human Bioethics. Monash University.

Sittler, Joseph A. (1961) 'Called to unity' *The Ecumenical Review* 14, 181-90.

Spong, John Shelby (1990) *Living in Sin? A bishop rethinks human sexuality* San Francisco: Harper and Row.

Spong. John Shelby (1991) *Rescuing the Bible from Fundamentalism: A bishop rethinks the meaning of scripture* San Francisco: Harper and Row.

Taylor, Paul W. (1986) *Respect for Nature: A theory of environmental ethics* Princeton, NJ: Princeton University Press.

Teilhard de Chardin (1965) *Hymn of the Universe* London: Collins.

Tennov, Dorothy (1979) *Love and Limerence : The experience of being in love* New York: Stein and Day.

Tillich, Paul (1954) *Love, Justice and Power* New York: Oxford University Press.

Tillich, Paul (1955) *The New Being* New York: Charles Scribners' Sons.

Tillich, Paul (1957) *Dynamics of Faith* New York: Harper and Brothers.

Tillich, Paul (1959) *Theology of Culture* New York: Oxford University Press.

Tillich, Paul (1961) *Christianity and the Encounter with World Religions* New York: Columbia University Press.

Tillich, Paul (1963) *The Eternal Now* London: SCM Press.

Tillich, Paul (1968) *A History of Christian Thought* New York: Simon and Schuster.

Tolba, Mostafa K. (1991) 'The state of the world environment 1991' *Our Planet* 3 (2) p. 10.

UNEP (1991) 'UNEP heads Aral Sea rescue mission' *Our Planet* 3 (1) p. 10.

Ved Mehta (1965 November 20) 'The new theologian' *New Yorker* pp. 65-144.

Van Ettinger, Jan (1989, February) 'Energy and environment in global perspective' Unpublished paper presented to the Club of Rome Annual meeting in Hanover.

von Wedemeyer-Weller, Maria (1967) 'The other letters from prison' *Union Seminary Quarterly Review* 23 (1) 23-9.

Wasdell, David (1986) *Response to Change* London: Private publication of the Unit for Research into Changing Institutions.

WCED (1987) *Our Common Future: Report of the world commission on environment and development* Oxford University Press.

White, Lynn (1978) 'The future of compassion' *The Ecumenical Review* 30 (2) pp. 99–109.

Whitehead, A. N. (1926) *Science and the Modern World* Cambridge University Press.

Whitehead, A. N. (1930) *Religion in the Making.* Cambridge University Press.

Whitehead, A. N. (1942) *Adventures of Ideas* Harmondsworth: Penguin Books.

Whitehead, A. N. (1978) *Process and Reality* (Corrected edition, eds David Ray Griffin & D. W. Sherbourne) New York: Free Press (original edition 1929).

Wieman, H. N. (1929) *Methods of Private Religious Living* New York: Macmillan Co.

Wieman, H. N. (1946) *The Source of Human Good* University of Chicago Press.

Williams, Daniel Day (1978) *The Spirit and the Forms of Love* New York: Harper and Row.

Williams, Graham (1992 February 2) 'Diocese's cold war against homosexuals' *Sydney Morning Herald.* pp. 1, 9.

Wilson, A. N. (1988) *Tolstoy* London: Hamish Hamilton.

Wilson, E. O. (1984) *Biophilia: the human bond to other species* Harvard University Press.

Wolf, E. C. (1985) 'Conserving biological diversity' in *State of the world 1985* (Lester R. Brown ed.) pp. 124-46 New York: W. W. Norton.

Wolf, E. C. (1987) 'On the brink of extinction: Conserving the diversity of life' *Worldwatch Paper* 78, Washington: Worldwatch Institute.

World Council of Churches (1974) 'Science and technology for human development: The ambiguous future and the Christian hope' *Anticipation* 19 (42 pp.).

Yannaras, C. (1932) *The Freedom of Morality* New York: St Vladimer Seminary Press.

Young, John (1991) *Sustaining the Earth: The past, present and future of the green revolution* Kensington: New South Wales University Press.

# INDEX